RUST BELT
UNION BLUES

RUST BELT
UNION BLUES

WHY WORKING-CLASS VOTERS
ARE TURNING AWAY FROM THE
DEMOCRATIC PARTY

LAINEY NEWMAN AND
THEDA SKOCPOL

Columbia University Press   *New York*

Columbia University Press
Publishers Since 1893
New York   Chichester, West Sussex
cup.columbia.edu

Printed and bound by CPI Group (UK) Ltd, Croydon, CR0 4YY
Library of Congress Cataloging-in-Publication Data
Names: Newman, Lainey, author. | Skocpol, Theda, author.
Title: Rust belt union blues : why working class voters are turning
away from the Democratic Party / Lainey Newman
and Theda Skocpol.
Description: [New York] : [Columbia University Press], [2023] |
Includes index.
Identifiers: LCCN 2023005692 | ISBN 9780231208826 (hardback) |
ISBN 9780231218795 (paperback) |ISBN 9780231557641 (ebook)
Subjects: LCSH: Labor unions—United States. |
Labor unions—Political activity—United States. |
Labor union members—Political activity—United States. |
Blue collar workers—United States.
Classification: LCC HD6508 .N47 2023 |
DDC 331.880973—dc23/eng/20230214
LC record available at https://lccn.loc.gov/2023005692

Cover design: Noah Arlow
Cover image: Lainey Newman and Theda Skocpol

GPSR Authorized Representative: Easy Access System Europe,
Mustamäe tee 50, 10621 Tallinn, Estonia, gpsr.requests@easproject.com

I think historically—this goes for our union as well—unions . . . played a more important role socially in the lives of their membership. . . . They had sporting leagues, large banquet halls. . . . In America we don't really have town squares, so there isn't a central meeting place for people to go, and I think the union hall, in some ways as a church or town hall would, . . . played a role in providing that forum for social engagement. And that has gone away, unfortunately.

—Current union organizer

CONTENTS

PREFACE

Rust Belt Union Blues is the outcome of an unusual academic endeavor. Most similarly-situated books are either sole-authored by established scholars or new PhDs, or emerge from research teams whose members have collaborated for years to produce many publications. In contrast, this book is the result of a unique partnership between a senior professor who has published dozens of books and articles over a long career and a recent Harvard College graduate who wrote her senior honors thesis about changing political views amongst unionists. For a year after that thesis was completed and won top honors, Lainey Newman worked with her former thesis advisor, Theda Skocpol, to gather more field observations and new organizational data and to then synthesize all those varied modes of analysis into this book.

When Lainey first read Theda's 2003 book *Diminished Democracy* in college, she felt it explained part of her own American experience. *Diminished Democracy* chronicles the gradual decline of membership-based voluntary involvements in the United States and the simultaneous gravitation toward top-down advocacy organizations with minimal opportunities for meaningful individual contribution. Lainey's late grandparents had been part of bridge clubs, the VFW, the League of Women Voters, and the Jewish community in Cleveland, Ohio. Older members on the other side of her family had been unionists and part of a tight-knit Latvian immigrant community. Lainey's immediate family, in contrast, represented an amalgamation of different identities; her mother is Indian and Latvian, and her father is Jewish American. This increasingly common characteristic amongst young Americans complicates traditional identity-based belongings. The decline of civic associations that create bridges and bonds among different groups of people in communities thus resonated with Lainey, who grew up far from extended family members located in Minnesota, Ohio, and New Jersey, and was not closely involved in a religious community in Pittsburgh. With that personal perspective, Lainey arrived during her junior year at Harvard at this project—an effort to understand community influences on people's social identities and political beliefs.

Having had family members who were proud members of the United Auto Workers in Minnesota and loyal, working-class Democrats in the mid- to late-twentieth century, Lainey knew she wanted to focus on unions and political realignment for her senior thesis. She had already worked on Skocpol research teams during her sophomore and junior years and was excited when Theda agreed to advise the senior thesis. Then the pandemic hit—and Lainey ended up at home in Pittsburgh, where she was able to continue with ethnographic research in the western Pennsylvania region. After the senior thesis wrapped up in May 2021, various faculty members in the Harvard Government Department encouraged Lainey to pursue publication of her senior thesis. Instead of going straight from Harvard College to the University of Pennsylvania Law School, Lainey deferred for a year to continue working on the research with Theda.

Although decades apart in age, the two authors of this book share a mutual fascination with untangling the social involvements that help make people who they are—including who they are as democratic citizens. Both of us believe that the networks and groups of which we are a part influence our identities, beliefs, loyalties, and values. When the makeup of the people and communities around individuals change—when friendships are forged in different contexts, with different underlying shared experiences—people's outlooks and choices, including political opinions, are likely to change as well.

Rust Belt Union Blues develops and applies this frame of reference to make sense of the sharp changes in industrial workers' political alignments over the past half century. Industrial and trades unions, which used to be part of dense networks of interpersonal and community-level ties, gained much of their capacity to shape members' political commitments from such embeddedness. Though strands of previous scholarship were certainly inspiring and helpful—including community ethnographies and studies of social capital as an underpinning of civic and political behavior—many of the findings in this book took shape from Lainey's interviews with workers and retirees. These interviews, as well as other forms of evidence collected, provided intimate insight into macro-level sociopolitical trends. Encouragement from Theda and others to pursue these findings beyond the submission of a senior thesis brought this book to fruition.

The results of the 2016 U.S. presidential election sparked much commentary about "why working-class Americans are failing to vote in their own best interests." We consider this question misplaced, because we view political choices as driven in large part by social identity: by how people see themselves within their communities and their perceptions of who is (and who is not) on their side. These self-identifications, in turn, are influenced by the information people accumulate as participants in broader social, informational, and occupational networks. The overriding argument we offer is that interpersonal and community influences for workers in the Rust Belt today, unionized and non-unionized alike, are very different from those of the mid-twentieth century, when local union groups occupied center stage in many towns and small cities. In contrast, grassroots union groups today, as well as many of those other groups with which they were closely intertwined, have dwindled or disappeared across much of the industrial Midwest. Even workers who are still employed in legacy industries and formally enrolled in unions live very different family and community lives—and the new groups they are involved with, if any, are often linked to organizations and institutions that convey right-wing political messages. These micro-level sociological changes have, in turn, had profound effects on both American politics and national identity.

Lainey Newman, Philadelphia, Pennsylvania
Theda Skocpol, Cambridge, Massachusetts
April 2023

ACKNOWLEDGMENTS

T his book has come together with the help and thoughtfulness of many people who we would like to acknowledge (and we ask the forgiveness of anyone we happen to overlook).

First and foremost, we owe a huge debt to our interviewees who graciously told us their stories and let us into their lives. Without those individuals' willingness to speak with us, there would be no narrative we could convey or conclusions we could draw within these pages. To protect people's anonymity, we rarely name our informants, but we hope each will understand our appreciation for the insights he or she shared—and find that we have accurately represented their experiences.

Second, we thank the wonderful professionals at Columbia University Press, including the editors, designers, and marketing people, and above all our editor, Eric Schwartz, and his assistant, Lowell Frye. We are very grateful for their belief in this project and for their support in making the book a reality. Thanks as well to the anonymous readers of the originally submitted prospectus and book manuscript for their helpful feedback.

A number of people generously devoted time and resources to helping us conduct research. Dr. Charlie McCollester was instrumental in introducing us to retirees and workers in western Pennsylvania. Thank you to Steffi Domike, who supplied us with materials on union history, and Bill Yund, who connected us with workers in the building trades. In addition, we thank Dr. Harrison Wick, who helped us access materials at the Indiana University of Pennsylvania's Special Collections. We are also grateful to staffers at the Penn State University Archives, the University of Pittsburgh Special Collections, and the Walter Reuther Library at Wayne State University for aiding our archival research in the midst of a global pandemic. Finally, thank you to the faculty, students, and staff within the Harvard Government Department who encouraged this project.

On a personal level, Lainey thanks her father, Larry Newman, for instilling in her a commitment to try to understand and help others, as well as for believing in her throughout this entire process and supporting her in countless ways, whether by driving her around to count bumper stickers in parking lots or discussing ideas with her in the living room late into the night. Lainey also thanks her mother, Silvija Singh, for everything she does and for being such a discerning reader of the news that whenever anything came out even tangentially related to this research, the article was emailed within the day. Lainey is profoundly thankful for her partner, Matt Kind, for keeping her steady and giving her the courage to take a year off to try to write a book, and for her sister, Lucy Newman, for being a sounding board and always inspiring her to be a better person. Lainey deeply appreciates her friend Ruth, who has been there through thick and thin, as well as Morgan, Allison, Jonah, Dan, Ari, and Tina, who have been incredibly supportive throughout the research process. Thanks also to Ellen and Burt Singerman, for being our extended family in Pittsburgh, and the Kind family, especially Tawni, for love and encouragement.

Theda's personal thanks go to Bill Skocpol, always the best supporter and critic and willing to put up with overwork, as well as to son Michael Skocpol and best friend and inspired U.S. historian, Ellen Fitzpatrick, each of whom offers good advice again and again. Working on this book brings back memories for Theda about growing up in Wyandotte, Michigan, then a thriving industrial city down river from Detroit. Beyond that, a lifetime of learning from other scholars, too many to name, goes into a book like this; Theda thanks them all and is especially grateful for all she learns by co-teaching a Harvard course on "American Society and Public Policy" with Mary Waters. Finally, over the past decade, Theda has gone into the field repeatedly to interview a range of Americans about their communities and experiences and political outlooks. The places she has visited include some in the Rust Belt, and from all of her visits there and elsewhere Theda has gained invaluable insights. She is deeply grateful to all the people across multiple states who, contacted out of the blue, have been willing to sit down and speak with her for this and other projects. Every weekday, too, Theda and Bill both learn a lot about social engagement and the roots of people's outlooks from fellow members of the 6 A.M. breakfast congeries at Andy's Diner in Cambridge, Massachusetts.

LIST OF FIGURES AND TABLES

RUST BELT
UNION BLUES

1

UNDERSTANDING SOCIAL
AND POLITICAL CHANGE IN
THE RUST BELT

"Back in my day, you couldn't find a single union guy who'd vote Republican," declared Herman, an eighty-year-old retired steelworker living in the town of Charleroi in western Pennsylvania. Not long ago, his home was the heart of America's manufacturing Rust Belt and a formidable redoubt for the United Steelworkers (USW) and other blue-collar unions. Herman's observations were echoed by fellow union retirees. "When I grew up, all steelworkers voted Democrat. That's just the way it was," said one of them. Another retiree laughed as he recalled the looming threat of getting "your fingers smashed in" if you drove a foreign-made truck to the mill from your nearby home—or if you were known to have voted for a Republican.

Across America's Rust Belt, the loyalties of many blue-collar workers are clearly different today—including the loyalties of those employed at the small number of still-unionized steel mills operating in western Pennsylvania. In the employee parking lots of still-operating union steel plants—such as Clairton Works, Irvin Works, and Edgar Thompson Works—cars and trucks proclaim loyalties nothing like those that retirees remember. Today, vehicles displaying pro-Trump bumper stickers or emblems touting gun rights and other conservative causes outnumber vehicles with pro-union or Democratic stickers by over ten to one. And if every one of today's workers who arrived in a foreign-made car—as many do, coming from a wide circumference in the Pennsylvania–Ohio–West Virginia tristate corner—got their fingers smashed in, not many would still be able to operate plant machinery.

Blue-collar workers we interviewed saw such changes clearly—and noted their political implications. "Now I can honestly tell you from firsthand experience," a recent retiree said, "the majority of steelworkers are not on the Democratic side anymore. That's a fact. And not only steelworkers, but other union people too." Over recent decades, shifts in worker loyalties in western Pennsylvania and more broadly across America's Rust Belt have paralleled Democrats' declining electoral fortunes. It is, of course, an exaggeration to say that not a *single* union worker in the mid-twentieth century would cast their ballot for a Republican. But the union retirees we had the chance to interview for this book did reflect on the import of changes in publicly declared loyalties across successive cohorts of blue-collar workers. Several pointed out that union workers' votes and party loyalties "back in their day" were part of two-way streets, grounded in heartfelt convictions about who was on their side. As one retiree explained, most blue-collar workers in the mid-twentieth century "figured there wasn't a Republican in the world who took care of the working guy." The declared loyalties of steelworkers and other workers indicated their views about the groups, leaders, and major political party that seemed committed to them. Worker support went to partners who workers felt were involved *with* them—day in, day out, month in, month out. Blue-collar unionists today rarely feel that the Democratic Party is committed to them in that way anymore.

This underscores the central point we will flesh out conceptually and empirically in this book—an argument that the "union man" of the mid-twentieth century was not a disaggregated bunch of (white male) lone wolves, but rather a dense social web of interconnected workers, family members, and neighbors that included grounded union and political organizations along with other community groups. In this social web, union members (mostly men, but some women, too) were committed to supporting one another and giving loyalty, votes, and time to their union and other supportive, community-rooted groups, often including the Democratic Party. Union members expressed loyalty and gave support because they expected these institutions to have their backs and act as partners to them and their families over the long term, in times of both fun and struggle. Voting Democrat was not just about particular issues for unionized workers; instead, it was in large part about socially embedded identities and mutualities—about *who they were.*

Over a half century, the phenomenon of automatic "union man" loyalty to the Democratic Party has disappeared, especially in regions with high proportions of white blue-collar workers. As we will show, this is not just a matter of union organizations declining or disappearing altogether—nor just a matter of white workers suddenly changing their personal attitudes about race, religion, and guns. Blue-collar workers have not necessarily shifted their cultural outlooks very much. What is more, many workers, including steelworkers and others in western Pennsylvania and nearby states, are still formally enrolled as union members. For these persisting and younger unionized industrial workers, however, union membership has lost much of the salience and positive valence it once had. At the same time, steadfast support for Democrats has all but disappeared and, for many, votes and publicly declared political loyalties have turned sharply to the right.

The big picture of change is clear enough. In the mid-twentieth century, union membership was a good predictor of blue-collar voting behavior, and as recently as twenty years ago, more highly unionized counties in Rust Belt states were more likely to deliver majorities for Democratic candidates in presidential years. In 1980, there was a strong 0.7 correlation between the percentage of union members and presidential votes for Democrats across Pennsylvania counties. By 2016, the correlation was less than 0.1. Voters' race and urban versus nonurban residence are now much better predictors of which party they will vote for. Not only do unions have much less of a presence in the Rust Belt, but, as historian and political analyst Lara Putnam sums up, the remaining "union ties . . . no longer translate into Democratic votes."[1]

THEORETICAL EXPLANATIONS FOR SHIFTING BLUE-COLLAR POLITICAL COMMITMENTS

Why are industrial workers in America today less likely to think that the Democratic Party is on their side? Scholars, activists, and analysts alike debate a range of factors that seem to lie behind realigned political loyalties of blue-collar workers in western Pennsylvania and other Rust Belt areas, including among workers still enrolled in unions. Previous major lines of explanation have focused on the declining formal organizational resources of international industrial unions or on presumed shifts in sociocultural attitudes among workers. Without dismissing such factors, we add new evidence and new ideas, focusing on industrial unions' reduced community-level underpinnings and changing community and organizational involvement in union members' lives. We hone in on the ground-level organizational and social contexts that surround blue-collar industrial workers—contexts that encourage people to express some potential identities and loyalties rather than others. The next two subsections situate our approach in juxtaposition to the currently predominant resource mobilization and attitudinal approaches.

International Union Capacities and Political Change

Most analysts who probe the cause of declining union support for the Democratic Party emphasize the political reverberations of the gross depletion of union organizational resources. They track the dwindling memberships, dues collections, and legal prerogatives that major international unions have at their disposal as they navigate employers' union busting, shifts in technology and international trade, and pressures from adverse regulatory and judicial decisions. In other words, these analysts focus on the formal organizational activities of mid-twentieth-century America's big international unions and the resources that supported them.

As this line of argument goes, working through national and regional offices, international union officials were previously better able to communicate steadily with their members, collect dues from them, and use money and people power to help Democrats win elections. Union resources could also be allocated to lobby legislators, governors, and presidents on major public policy issues vital to union operations. As political scientist David Macdonald sums up, labor unions have built political clout by "educating their members about the 'good things' that unions do for them and for the working/middle classes more generally" and by endorsing "Democratic candidates and liberal causes, signaling that the Democratic Party is an ally of organized labor."[2] This was how unions "foster[ed] identification" with the Democratic Party. Similarly, historian Timothy Minchin argues that resources and top-down communication from international unions in the 2008 presidential election effectively installed Barack Obama as president of the United States. Without the AFL-CIO's $250 million contribution to the Obama campaign and its efforts to "educate—and pressure—white [union] members" to vote Democrat, Minchin argues that Obama may not have won the presidency.[3]

From this perspective, it stands to reason that any contractions in dues-paying membership would undercut organizational capacity to conduct messaging, mobilize voters, and lobby—which would, in turn, adversely affect unions' ability to sway their members' political choices. Indeed, Macdonald's study argues convincingly that much of the recent erosion in white electoral support for Democrats is driven by declining union memberships. Empirical research bears out such expectations overall, including innovative recent studies such as "Informed Preferences? The Impact of Unions on Workers' Policy Views" by political scientists Sung Eun Kim and Yotam Margalit, which establishes that unions do communicate policy preferences to their members, with varying levels of effectiveness.[4] Other researchers, such as economist James Feigenbaum and political scientists Alexander Hertel-Fernandez and Vanessa Williamson, have probed in statistical detail the exact impact that union campaign dollars and campaign volunteers had on Democratic vote margins.[5] By comparing neighboring states with and without laws that weaken unions' ability to recruit members and collect and deploy union dues, this trio has shown that antiunion laws measurably contribute to lower Democratic vote shares versus Republican competitors.

We do not question the importance of deterioration in the organizational capacities of major industrial and mining unions, and we take careful account of the economic forces that have transformed industries and unions in western Pennsylvania. At the same time, we add new insights into the relationships between unions and parties by grounding our analysis in a deep understanding of social identities and community-based social ties. Tracking the ground-level changes in unions and their ties to other community groups takes us beyond aggregate economic trends into closer looks at the kinds of interactions that shape people's daily lives and outlooks on politics. The exact ways in which local union groups and activities are embedded in broader social webs matter because those links influence people's understandings of themselves and their social surroundings—and in turn give moral force and staying power to the choices unionized workers make as citizens.

Beyond Demography and Sociocultural Attitudes

The ground-level research we offer here helps to explain why voting for Democrats is no longer a taken-for-granted stance for many blue-collar workers—and it also illuminates the new conservative-inflected identities and ties that have flourished in the vacuums left by unions' receding community presence. This book does not provide a full analysis of the spread of conservative engagements among many sets of Americans. Instead, as it pertains to understanding the ties and loyalties seen now among many blue-collar union workers, especially white workers, our work adds crucial specificity to purely aggregate analyses of broad categories defined by race, gender, or family forms. We look more closely at where people live, the groups they join, and the people with whom they interact. Changes in such social involvements tell us as much or more about shifting political outlooks and loyalties as aggregate analyses do and simultaneously illuminate the specific mechanisms by which group identities and loyalties can shift over time. In overwhelmingly white Rust Belt areas like western Pennsylvania, male workers have not recently or suddenly started owning and using guns, nor have they recently or suddenly started harboring racist and sexist views. Attitudes tallied in snapshot polls may seem racist or sexist, but the overall demographics of many Rust Belt regions have not changed enormously, and there is little reason to believe that workers now are significantly more prejudiced than their predecessors were decades ago.

Of course, many ongoing transformations of U.S. society and politics since the middle of the twentieth century have contributed to changing Republican Party (GOP) and Democratic Party fortunes. The civil rights movement set in motion the realignment of regional and racial voting blocs, making the two parties both more competitive and more ideological from the 1970s onward.[6] Religious shifts and transformations of family, gender, and sexual norms spurred the rise of the politicized Christian right and its marriage to the GOP. Following the Immigration and Nationality Act of 1965, the arrival of new immigrant populations amid economic blows to U.S. manufacturing and unionized industries sparked ever-sharper controversies about immigrant rights and American national identity. All of these unfolding, large-scale trends have fueled party polarization as political elites have chosen to push correlative social divisions. Polarization has left Republicans and

Democrats in close competition nationwide, even as one party or the other has gained or lost ground in specific states or regions. These macro-level trends have informed the work of scholars who have used surveys and demographic analyses to explain the decline of the Democratic Party via demographic and attitudinal changes. Indeed, though some scholars point to union resource depletions as the key to changes in working-class politics, others point to macro social changes and stress evidence of conservative cultural values in current national opinion polls.[7]

We find answers in the changing meanings of union affiliation for workers who have become willing to ignore, or contravene, union messages they once accepted, and we stress the social accompaniments of waning union links to Rust Belt communities and regional activities. Previous scholarship has not fully grappled with these realities. Most authors presume that workers shift their political loyalties and votes when they are no longer unionized or, if they remain affiliated, when their unions lose resources and capacities to the point that even members see their unions as ineffective. For instance, in their working paper entitled "Union Membership Attitudes and Participation," management studies scholars Daniel Gallagher and George Strauss argue that union members perceive the union either as an agent for large-scale change or as a bureaucratic entity that looks out for their best interests.[8] But neither characterization captures what we have heard from our interviewees or what we see in related ethnographic data. Either speaking for themselves or noting changes in their co-unionists, many union members voice suspicion or even outright animosity about unions and their officials; many do not see the union as an organization that advocates on their behalf in any way. Why have such dismissive or hostile stances toward unions increased in prevalence?

Our analysis suggests that workers' changing views of unions and decreased willingness to take political cues from them are due in significant part to changes in degrees and kinds of social embeddedness. As unions seem less salient and more alien—even to those who are formally members—enrolled workers as well as their neighbors and community members are less amenable to supporting union-recommended policies or candidates. In line with ideas from political scientist Robert Putnam and sociologist Dan Clawson, we highlight ways in which waning interconnectedness among union workers contributes to shifts toward right-wing voting and advocacy.[9] Because workers are no longer as involved in union activities and groups as they used to be, their social identities are less connected to their unions and they thus pay less (if any) heed to political messages from union leadership. Often without explaining exactly how or why, scholars using cultural approaches posit that waning industrial areas have swung conservative in response to the increased "salience" of "social issues" about race, immigration, abortion, and guns. But a generalized cultural focus can obscure more specific, dynamic factors. How, when, where, and why have union members, many of whom have long held the same outlooks on guns, abortion, and even race, come to prioritize highly partisan and emotionally charged understandings of such questions—while increasingly ignoring or tuning out alternative emphases and arguments proclaimed by union leaders?

In this book, we cannot fully answer all the specific questions about the overarching rise of so-called social issues in Rust Belt America, but we will offer new insights and hypotheses about why so many of today's successors to proud "union men" and loyal working-class Democrats of the past have recently become self-declared conservatives and supporters of Donald Trump and his allies. We suggest that right-wing organizations and networks have moved into some of the space vacated by receding grassroots unionism.

To help account for shifting ties and loyalties, we also expand upon research by Matthew Lacombe in his book *Firepower*. Since the 1970s, Lacombe argues, the National Rifle Association (NRA) has used publications along with national, state, and local training programs to cultivate a shared group identity centered around gun ownership—an identity that in turn shapes members' stances on many other political issues and affiliations.[10] We use similar data and methods to track waning union impacts, documenting links between formal organizational features and locally embedded ties and identities. Looking across organizational spheres, we show that, even though membership in most older types of Rust Belt social associations have declined along with union locals over the past fifty years, one type—gun clubs—have kept going. In fact, gun clubs have proliferated and often expanded their offerings to become places for people to gather socially in many communities. We go beyond Lacombe's focus on the national role of the NRA to look more closely at the local implications of gun club membership and NRA affiliation. As we will show empirically, gun clubs in western Pennsylvania host bingo nights, holiday parties, and social activities, just as many unions used to. As such, workers today are more likely to interact with peers at gun clubs than at the union hall, providing a much different political backdrop to worker social networks.

RESEARCH AND ARGUMENTS TO COME

Having introduced our analytical perspective, we move on to explain why this book focuses especially on western Pennsylvania and then indicate the multiple strands of evidence we have collected and woven together to make sense of union and political changes in this storied Rust Belt region. In the final pages of this chapter, we preview the game plan for the rest of the book, the sequence by which we will lay out findings and arguments in the chapters to come.

A Focus on Western Pennsylvania

This book draws from the previous findings and ideas of many researchers, but our new evidence is mainly about one of America's most fabled twentieth-century industrial regions— the twenty-county area of western Pennsylvania stretching from Erie to Pittsburgh and Johnstown to Aliquippa, where steel manufacturing and associated industries were once king. The map in figure 1.1 shows the counties in the area we have studied. Appendix A provides details about the voting patterns in these

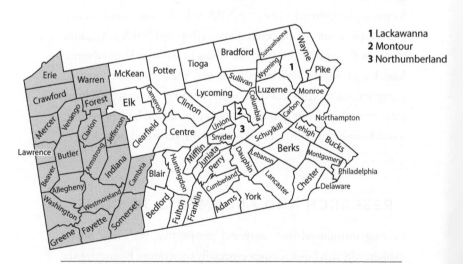

FIGURE 1.1 Map of 20-county research area in western Pennsylvania.

counties over time. This huge region serves as our diagnostic laboratory for trends that characterize many other eastern and midwestern Rust Belt regions populated primarily by whites, a place to trace in detail the impact of declining ground-level union presence for workers' social identities, community ties, and political loyalties.

In western Pennsylvania, unions have declined along various important dimensions. Shrinkage in the region's unionized share of the overall private-sector working population mirrors the nationwide contraction from 35 percent in 1955 to 6 percent by 2021.[11] Nevertheless, western Pennsylvania still has some unionized areas and plants—which is important for our project because it allows us to examine union changes, not just union disappearance. Even as we discuss the consequences of overall loss of union memberships and resources, we are able to track specifically how industrial unions in mills, mines, and plants used to be more deeply involved in workers' lives than they are today.

Democrats, not just unions, have also lost huge ground in the western Pennsylvania region, allowing us to dissect relationships between changing union ties and activities and declines in Democratic vote shares. Whereas Democrats used to be competitive in more than ten of these counties—even through the mid-1980s—Republican margins have skyrocketed since the early 2000s. In the past four presidential elections, Democrats have been competitive only in two of these twenty counties— Erie County, home to that city, and Allegheny County, home to Pittsburgh.

As for the unions themselves, we focus most closely on the United Steelworkers, but we also look at other industrial unions, including the United Electrical, Radio, and Machine Workers (UE); the United Mine Workers of America (UMWA); the United Auto Workers (UAW); and various unions in the building trades, including the International Brotherhood of Electrical Workers (IBEW) and the Heat and Frost Insulators and Allied Workers (which we refer to as the Insulators). In various places, we zero in on contrasts between USW, an industrial union, and IBEW, a building trades union. This juxtaposition is important for our contextual and organizational approach because there are telling differences in the institutional configurations of these two important international unions, differences that we show matter for their changing involvement with their worker members. Just as we argue that "union decline" and consequences for party politics are not only a single overarching story about national and regional formal organizational resources, we are also able to use comparisons between Steelworkers* and Electrical Workers to show consequential variations in the timing and nature of political shifts corresponding to the specific ways these unions relate to workers individually and in their workplaces and home communities. Not all unions have evolved in the same ways, and, in the future, remaining or new unions can develop alternative organizational tactics, possibly with different political consequences. Trends among the Electrical Workers and their union help us nail down some partial exceptions to the general rules we posit about the social underpinnings of union decline.

The building trades are very different from industrial unions, as we were told by many interviewees. "I think the industrial unions are sort of closer to the service unions in a sense," one retired IBEW member commented. "I don't know if they see that though, but I think we [in the building trades] would consider the industrial unions and the service unions more aligned than us and the

---

*Note that when we use the word Steelworker, with a capital "S," we are referring to a member of the United Steelworkers union. Without a capital "S," the word means someone whose occupation is that of a steelworker. As we discuss later in the book, some but not all Steelworkers are steelworkers.

industrial workers." The building trades, which organize workers by craft, are those unions that represent workers in commercial, industrial, and residential construction, including electrical workers, bricklayers, insulators, painters, plumbers, and others. In contrast, industrial unions organize workers across industry, often in a common workplace. Cornell University's Legal Information Institute (LII) defines industrial unionism as "a form of union organizing which organizes all of the workers in a particular industry into the same union without regard for the skill or trade of each worker."[12] For example, everyone employed at a certain steel mill, regardless of what job they do within the mill, would be a United Steelworker if the plant was represented by USW. In the chapters to come, we lay out the implications of the differences between the building trades and industrial unions more thoroughly.

As we spell out a more complete story than other observers have offered about the roots, modalities, and results of union decline in western Pennsylvania, we believe the basics of our account and explanatory hypotheses apply to other regions as well, so here and there we refer to other Rust Belt areas as appropriate. Everywhere we look, shifts in industrial and ex-industrial regions are about more than the decline of industry jobs or union organizational resources and the upshot for Democrats. The most basic story is about identity changes that have hit once locally embedded union clusters, like those nurtured by USW, harder than they have hit more loosely knit building trades like IBEW. In the once mighty USW redoubts of western Pennsylvania, the foundations have withered as much as the organizational heights. As union halls closed and membership numbers dwindled, other networks and community group influences, often propelling more conservative values and messages, have become more central to the daily lives of workers and residents. Shifts in political loyalties and votes have been part and parcel of these pervasive reworkings of the webs of everyday life.

Sources of Evidence

Many books or articles that tackle issues about unions and politics in the modern United States rely almost exclusively *either* on rich ethnographic observations of specific communities, industries, or regions or on large quantified data sets appropriate for statistical modeling. We draw on both kinds of previous research and, as appropriate, do each kind of work ourselves. Yet what sets our research apart is our reliance on combining findings from multiple kinds of data and adding several new kinds of sources to the mix—above all, insights gleaned from individual interviews, archival records, and data on various arrays of organizations such as union locals and Tea Party groups spread at given junctures across western Pennsylvania.

For our most important fresh evidence, we draw from more than fifty interviews, most conducted with current and former union members in western Pennsylvania. Some of these union interviewees are workers in still-operating industrial plants or various building trades, while others are union retirees who can comment on past as well as on current realities. Beyond those worker interviews, we also met with and interviewed other community stakeholders, including local civic, religious, and political party leaders. Interviews were conducted following academic rules about anonymity and, with a couple of exceptions, most were around an hour in length. We took an open-ended approach, guided by topics about the union, their fellow workers, and their own and others' affiliations (see appendix B for more details about interview questions). Because much of our research was conducted during the COVID-19 pandemic, most interviews were conducted via phone, but some did happen in person, often in union members' homes, where some were kind enough to offer us materials such as books, pamphlets, and union records. In many cases, we stayed in touch with interviewees by phone or email so we could go back with follow-up questions. Our first interviewees were usually contacts at various union headquarters, and beyond those we used a snowball approach to contact additional people that original interviewees told us might be willing to participate.

Further evidence comes from union-related archival material located in university collections or obtained from unions themselves. Beyond multiple in-person trips to various university archives, including at the Indiana University of Pennsylvania, the University of Pittsburgh, and Wayne State University, we worked with Pennsylvania State University librarians to obtain digital copies of union documents from the university's extensive holdings. Valuable archival materials that we obtained include union newsletters, meetings records, pamphlets, memos, and letters from both international and local union organizations. Some local and international unions allowed us to view and take photographs of publications and records that they had stored at their headquarters or at a local hall. Local and international union newsletters reveal much about union activities at various times. We are among the first scholars, we believe, to dig up and analyze chronological multidecade runs of such union outlets. Although available runs of newsletters are not always complete or across the same periods, by drawing from university, union, and online sources, we have been able to piece together national-level series from roughly the 1950s to today from USW, UMWA, and IBEW. In addition, we pieced together series of local union newsletters from USW Local 1211 in Aliquippa, Pennsylvania; UE Local 610 in Pittsburgh; IBEW Local 5 (also in Pittsburgh); and UAW Locals 600 and 306, both in Detroit, Michigan.

To learn from series of union publications about how group identity and unity was encouraged among members, we systematically coded decade-by-decade samples of stories, newsletter formats, and photographs from 1965 to 2015 for USW and IBEW. In this way, we gained systematic insight beyond interviews and membership trends about the ways in which unions cultivated and drew on community-based social identities. We draw additional evidence on such matters from convention proceedings, local union histories, and other primary document sources.

We also documented regional organizational arrays. Using directories from the Library of Congress, Ancestry.com, and Yellow Pages, we pieced together the location of local union offices across western Pennsylvania circa 1960. We also learned where physical union halls operated from a wonderful USW pamphlet called "Where Citizens Meet the Union," issued around 1960, with addresses and many pictures. We tracked changes between the 1960s and now for some of these union arrays. We have information on gun clubs and some kinds of megachurches in western Pennsylvania, along with specific information from previous research by Theda Skocpol on the location of right-wing Tea Party groups during the 2009–2011 period of mobilization against the Democratic Party and the Obama presidency. Much more could be done with organizational arrays than we manage in this book, but we aim to illustrate the usefulness of this rarely used kind of data.

Last but certainly not least, we used some ethnographic tools to provide color, context, and specificity to our research. We have traveled around western Pennsylvania to observe current realities and to compare them to pictures and memories of the past. Even during the pandemic, one of the authors, Lainey Newman, spent time traveling around the communities we discuss in this book—observing, talking to shopkeepers, taking photographs. Author Theda Skocpol also traveled and made observations in the region in 2017, 2019, and 2022.

The unique findings and arguments offered in this book depend very much on the efforts just outlined to find, analyze, and meld various kinds of evidence across a key region. Most previous scholarship about unions in U.S. politics either digs deep in one city or town, or takes a national bird's-eye view and depends on aggregate statistics about "union members" or "family members of union members" in general. Much can be learned from such studies, and we use their findings throughout. Nevertheless, we think great value can be added by the in-between level of analysis we do here, looking across a broad indicative region yet at the same time probing contexts, relationships, and organizational ties and tactics that are often missed in highly aggregated national studies reliant on polling and broad demographic categories.

Looking Ahead

The remainder of *Rust Belt Union Blues* proceeds by examining first *what used to be*, then *what changed over recent decades*, and finally *what the current and future political consequences may be*. Building throughout the volume, we develop our new lines of argument about why ground-level changes help account for political party fortunes.

Chapter 2 unpacks the mid-twentieth-century ideal of the "union man" and explains how it was grounded in a set of union ties and practices engrained in workers' everyday lives. This chapter principally uses interview data, archived local union newsletters, and survey data from USW to underscore our theory that the importance of local unions was not only about their collective bargaining power but also about their presence and actions as social and community institutions.

Chapter 3 examines *what happened* as unions lost clout and presence from the 1970s to the 2010s. We look at both the high-level economic and political changes that affected industrial towns in the Rust Belt and the intimate, local-level changes that had an impact on workers' daily lives. We show how many workers were forced to choose job security over union loyalty as manufacturing and industrial job supply declined. We then look at changes such as the diversification of industries represented by industrial unions to try to understand one of the causes of workers' identities becoming farther removed from their union membership. This section also considers family changes and the impact of increasing numbers of working women and wives on conceptions of the "union man."

We move on to explore the present and future in chapter 4, which examines the social identities and community ties of today's Rust Belt union members and highlights the ubiquity of local gun clubs as gathering places in many industrial and ex-industrial towns. This chapter also looks more closely at how two large unions—USW and IBEW—have handled these changes over time. We examine how, in the future, remaining or new unions can develop in alternative ways. Trends among the Electrical Workers and their union helps us nail down some partial exceptions to the general rules we posit about the social underpinnings of union decline.

Chapter 5 brings our analysis home by exploring the consequences of changing union presence for electoral politics. Using data from interviews with political chairs in western Pennsylvania, we discuss why many union workers have ultimately decided to forgo the political loyalties of their predecessors—or, in some cases, their older family members—to support more conservative causes and candidates. We look at why Democratic candidates relying on the union vote in western Pennsylvania and other areas of the Rust Belt have become less able to call on group identities and assumed loyalties and try instead to fall back on thin economic issue messages to sway industrial union workers in given elections.

In chapter 6, our concluding chapter, we provide comments about the implications of the research in this volume. We argue that, to counter conservative successes at offering alternative social ties and loyalties to workers, Democrats need to foster more robust and continuous group ties of all kinds, and persisting unions need to invest resources in local networks—not just in national staff members and lobbyists—and that this must happen not just during organizing, bargaining campaigns, or election seasons but continuously. Our conclusion also spells out practices and tactics that unions might adopt in the future to build stronger, politically consequential loyalties among remaining unionists as well as their families, neighbors, and communities.

Four appendices at the end of the volume provide additional details about our research tools and methodologies. Appendix A contains longitudinal data on voting patterns in western Pennsylvania. Appendix B includes sample interview questions. Appendix C details how we systematically analyzed photographs in international union newsletters. Finally, appendix D describes how we probed the relationship between members and their unions by looking at "local union mentions" in international union newsletters.

2

THE SOCIAL UNDERPINNINGS OF
THE "UNION MAN"

Being a *good union man* had "a lot to do with looking out for your fellow workers," said a retired member of Insulators Local 2, located in Aliquippa, Pennsylvania. "It's a phrase that's been around for a long time, but I'm not sure a lot of current members are paying attention." The union man is a well-known trope in American lore. Although no specific definition exists, the term brings to mind an image of a burly blue-collar family man whose days are spent working with his hands, lunch bucket in tow. His labor is what builds the modernized country—he makes the steel that supports city bridges, wires the telephone poles, and builds the nation's cars—and he's unswervingly loyal to his fellow union brothers. As Joe Glazer sings it in "Bricklayin' Union Man," "My voice is gruff, my hands are rough, the dust is on my shoes, I wear my union button, got no time, no time to sing the blues."[1] Many Americans can probably conjure an image of a union man of this era quite similar to what Glazer's lyrics describe.

But being a union man was about more than outward appearances. Much of what defined these archetypal workers of the mid-twentieth century was the sense of *meaning* that they derived from being part of a local union, a unionized workplace, and the labor movement as a whole, even if they didn't think about it as a movement. So integral was the union to the sense of self of many mid-twentieth-century workers that some gained peace of mind from envisaging the union continuing after their passing. As the country group Blue Highway sings, "And when my life is over / Don't mourn my passing long / Organize resistance / And keep the union strong!"[2] Meaning and purpose derived from union membership was expressed in many nonchoral ways as well. When longtime member Andy Johnson was honored for sixty years of membership in International Brotherhood of Electrical Workers (IBEW), the October 1980 Local 5 newsletter quoted him as saying that his "Local 5 membership ticket means more to [me] than any other possession."[3] Having started his career in the electrical industry during a time when workers had minimal legal labor protections, Johnson was part of the Herculean rise of organized labor. The newsletter recounts him explaining to younger IBEW members of the Pittsburgh-based local how lucky they were to be part of an industry protected by organized labor. Johnson was one of many members of his generation whose fidelity to his union was essential to his personhood.

Fidelity was not just an individual attitude or calculation. Unions of the mid-twentieth century were involved in almost every dimension of life for workers—at work, of course, but also in spiritual or religious groups; in political activities; and (perhaps most underestimated) in recreation, family engagement, and community events. Together in so many ways, members were devoted to union peers and aspired to meet their expectations. Although today's enrolled union members often feel at arm's length from their unions, mid-twentieth-century members experienced union presence intimately and in many realms of their lives.

How did union membership become so deeply ingrained in workers' sense of self? This chapter explores how union membership was woven into many facets of workers' social identities. Using evocative materials from union newsletters and interviews with members, we flesh out the ideal of the good union man and then consider the social underpinnings of this identity. We show that unions were essential to community relationships and family and group activities in many industrial regions. Their myriad social ties in turn encouraged union members to be active civic participants and laid a solid foundation for their political outlooks and choices as democratic citizens.

MEANINGS OF THE MIDCENTURY UNION MAN

In international and local union newsletters as well as in our retiree interviews, the expression "good union man" is echoed repeatedly both as a descriptor of laborers who gave their life's work to the union and as an exhortation for members to keep the union front and center in their daily lives. "We have all known Jim [Trivitt] many years and can only say he is one fine gentleman and a 100 percent union man," said a report to *The IBEW Journal* by the press secretary of Local 639 about a 1985 retirement party held for Jim at the local Elks lodge.[4] Similarly, a 1970 report from IBEW Local 605 in Jackson, Mississippi, praised two "hard-working, serious-minded union men" who "well deserve the honor bestowed upon them" of serving as delegates for the local, saying that these union men "will work hard and long to protect and promote the interests of our members."[5] Workers in many different unionized trades and industries had heard, of course, such relevant messaging many times before, in union publications and from fellow members. "Until next month, be a good union man," was how United Steelworkers (USW) member Nat "Peanuts" Latella ended his recurring "Strip Mill News" report on everything from Local 1211's recent election to the fortunes of its football league.[6] Likewise, some members concluded their reports to the Electrical Workers' magazine with declarations such as "Once a union man always a union man!" or "Be union, buy-rite, buy union, bye now!"

Other than the occasional reminder to attend union meetings or buy union-made products, there were few exact instructions on how to be a good union man—but that would have been unnecessary, our interviewees explained, because union members of yesteryear were well aware of unwritten peer and group expectations. As one Baton Rouge electrician explained in 1985, "If you think monthly dues and paychecks comprise the good union man, you are wrong."[7] Retirees today agree. As one told us, "It's disturbing to us old timers" that many younger members think that all union members have to do "is pay their dues and that's it." In contrast, members of yesteryear risked social ostracization if they failed to live up to their fellow workers' expectations. In the 1958 USW convention proceedings, delegate Stassfurth of Local 2287 explained, "The first thing I learned when I joined the labor union . . . was that the backbone of the organization is that you must be good to your fellow worker in the shop and in the union."[8] There were various ways to meet these unwritten expectations. As one electrician explained in a 1975 report on his local, "To this writer, there is one main ingredient to being a good union man—that is participating with and on behalf of the union—on and off the job."[9] Other members viewed being a good union man as more political, including some of our interviewees. A worker who wrote in the 1970s that a "well-informed Brother is a good union man," explained that his union has an "active registrar who keeps the local informed on political events on county, state, and national levels."[10]

Unions, of course, are not the only civic group that has sought to foster a shared group identity among members. For many civic groups, fostering a sense of shared identity is a top-down goal of group leadership. In his analysis of how formal organizations can foster active loyalty, Matthew Lacombe argues that the National Rifle Association (NRA) followed a four-step process of cultivation, politicization, dissemination, and mobilization that enabled this large national association to encourage a powerful shared identity among its members. Cultivation occurs when members begin to "see themselves as a distinct social group and feel emotionally tied to the group," politicization occurs when the group identity is perceived as "related to politics," dissemination occurs when the group promotes identity characteristics through publications or programming, and mobilization occurs when "individuals are motivated to take action when they believe that their identities are under threat."[11] In order for social identity cultivation based on group membership to be possible, some unifying characteristic must exist. For the NRA, that unifying characteristic is gun ownership, and for organized labor, it is enrollment in unions—which historically happened automatically for most organized industries and trades. But such formally shared characteristics are far from enough because the cultivation of a group identity requires emotional and social buy-in. High-level NRA leaders attempted—successfully, Lacombe argues—to create such buy-in by using newsletters and educational and service programs to indoctrinate participating gun owners in an "us versus them" mentality and instill in members a fear of the forces who purportedly aim to disarm them.

All organizations can be placed on a simplified spectrum of top-down to bottom-up group identity formation. Several factors, including the leadership structure of an organized group and the ways in which it engages with members, determine the extent to which group identity is formed by the members (bottom up) versus the leadership (top down). Top-down group identity is derived from top-level communications with members or individual information attainment. On the extreme end of top-down group identity might be an adherent to a talk radio show. She is part of a group of people who listen to the radio show, and the show may factor into her sense of self, but she has minimal if any ties to other members of the group. On the other side of the spectrum, group identity is formed via grassroots cultivation—these types of groups would likely be more loosely structured types of organizations, such a self-organized club that meets weekly to talk about politics at a local diner.

Of the larger types of institutional civic organizations, unions have historically relied heavily on bottom-up group identity. Union leaders have used deliberate action, of course, to build identity, but because unions serve the rank and file, the structural organization of federated unions make it nearly impossible for top leaders to use the same techniques as, for instance, managers can with subordinates or customers. Whereas Lacombe argues (and we agree) that NRA identity was cultivated mainly via top-down processes, unions built shared ideals and identities in more grounded and bottom-up ways, depending as they did on spread through member-to-member ties. In unions, the member-to-member spread of identity was most clearly encapsulated in the union man ideal, which members would invoke to encourage their fellow members to live their lives according to values derived from the union.

Through an analysis of hundreds of statements—from union records, university archives, and interviews—we have noticed several kinds of repeated messages that serve to define and reinforce beliefs about the good union man, including idealizations of relationships among workers, repeated historical remembrances stressing contrasts to pre-union times, and expressions of pride about arduous lines of work. For clarity and brevity, we refer to these three tenets of the "union man" as workers' *mutual commitment, historical awareness,* and *occupational pride,* all of which spread largely member to member. We briefly elaborate on each of these contributors in turn.

Mutual Commitment

To be good union men, as we have suggested, members had to be willing to put the good of the collective over their personal benefit, which included helping other union men—or, at times, community members—in need. A worker's sense of *mutual commitment* can be defined as this sense of loyalty that union members had for one another. In short, union members came to feel that they were engaged in ongoing give-and-take relationships with one another, in ways each person could depend upon at work and beyond.

Mutual commitment was perhaps most apparent when another worker was "down bad," as one of our interviewees put it. When a fellow unionist was sick, injured, unemployed, grieving, or for any reason unable to perform normal work or union duties, others would support him in whatever capacity they could. As one retired Steelworker recounted:

> For six months, I had a cement block on my leg. . . . It got to
> be a couple weeks before Christmas, and these guys I worked
> with came up and gave me $250 or something that they had col-
> lected. Everyone contributed, and when they gave me that money,

I could have cried. Even now I start tearing up. That's just the way it was back then. To work with a crew of guys like that, you'll never know, but everyone had everyone else's back. . . . I was sick one time, maybe the flu, and I went in, and one guy said go in the locker room and lie down. He said, "Don't worry, we'll handle it." They covered for me that shift; that's the way those guys were. But that's what we'd do; we'd do that for anyone. That's the kind of comradery that went on.

A similar story appears in a 1965 issue of the IBEW magazine, where the Local 1579 press secretary writes about a member who passed away: "When he got bad sick, the fellows on the job knew he was a union man and a member of 1579. The men on the job took up a collection and paid his union dues for six months."[12] Fundamentally, good union members were expected—and felt an obligation—to look out for one another and to reinforce the sense among members that, if you were one of us, we've *got your back*. Local unions formed a community in which members trusted each other and were willing to sacrifice for their own in-group—to be, as one retired unionist described of a member he deeply respected, "the type of guy that would give you the shirt off his back."

Beginning in the 1970s, hard times were frequent for many Rust Belt workers. Steelworkers in particular lost their jobs and some never were reemployed. Despite such widespread duress, many union members steadfastly tried to put their fellow workers—and the union—above themselves. As one op-ed writer for the *Pittsburgh Post-Gazette* recounts in 1992, his father—a Steelworker—remained loyal to his union brothers throughout it all. "Through strikes and layoffs, he was a union man," Tom Waselski writes. "And we were a union family."[13]

In order to help union members support one another during hard times, food drives and fundraisers at plants were organized.

Local unions assembled committees to support unemployed members and help them apply for welfare benefits so they could remain in their longtime homes. Many, although certainly not all, chose to stay in western Pennsylvania rather than seek a life elsewhere because it was their home and their community. As one person told us,

> I ran four copper wire machines at the Page plant [the former Page Steel and Wire plant in Monessen, PA], and right before the Page plant shut down, all that material went down to [a nonunion plant in] Bowling Green, Kentucky. They were having massive problems down there because they didn't know how to use the equipment. So, remember this, I'm collecting unemployment. The former plant manager calls me up and asks if I want to go down to Bowling Green and help them with the machines. You know what I told him? I basically told him to shove it. Here I was with six kids, scraping, and that's what I said. Honest to God, if I would've been out on the street begging, I wouldn't have done it.

As this Steelworker later explained, the "union provided the structure" for the sense of community among the workers. Without the union, "there would've been chaos between us all." His sense of membership in that broader community, which was centered on mutual commitment and shared sacrifice, made accepting a nonunion job in Kentucky intolerable.

Historical Awareness

To one retired member of IBEW, being a good union member meant "understanding that you are benefiting from a long history of people who have worked to make [progress] happen." The second component of being a good union man was grounded in this recognition; the *historical awareness* of what labor was like *without* unions engendered a deep sense of appreciation—and even a feeling of debt—among members for their predecessors. Loyalty to the in-group was strengthened by regularly reiterated first- or secondhand historical accounts about the nonunionized working conditions many Americans experienced in the late nineteenth and early twentieth centuries. Many midcentury unionists had either firsthand experience of this or had fathers, uncles, brothers, or coworkers who had toiled in dangerous nonunion mills or mines for pennies on the hour. One retiree explained it this way:

> When I started working when I was seventeen years old, the older guys told me about what would happen before the union. The boss would come in and choose who would get to work. All that these guys wanted to do was get a day's work in and feed their families. So, talking to those old heads, I never forgot anything, man. Those guys told me what the conditions were then and how things changed after the union came.

With such contrasts regularly brought to mind, many early unionists attributed their middle-class quality of life to the efforts and successes of the labor movement. Any chance that workers might return to situations where they could not bargain collectively or oppose managerial abuses inspired union members to invest more deeply in the union effort. A local union press secretary in IBEW wrote to *The Electrical Workers' Journal* in 1955 saying, "For as I read out the contract . . . I see too many benefits which even 10 years ago would have been called impossible of achievement. . . . In 1916 I worked seven days, 12 hours a day. . . . Those days . . . [are] what is often referred to as the good old days. . . . Why we softies would not survive six months of the 'good old days.'"[14] Hearing and reading stories in newsletters about the pre-union days, many workers in the mid-twentieth century felt deeply indebted to the older workers who laid the groundwork for workers' modern-day quality of life. "You owe your livelihood to that history," one retiree told us.

Even in later years, members expressed appreciation and indebtedness to the pioneers of the labor movement. One electrical worker from West Virginia wrote in 1970, "Our local was chartered in October 1939, and we give thanks to all of the hard-nosed union men who fought hard and untiringly to maintain a union spirit and effort in our town. They inspired others to follow in their footsteps."[15] In the IBEW Local 5 newsletter, a similar sentiment is expressed. "These men should never be forgotten," explained one newsletter contributor in 1980. "We, as union men and women, should record and remember always what our predecessors gained and entrusted to us."[16]

Remembering the past and honoring union builders was also essential to creating a strong "us versus them" paradigm among members, where "they" were the external forces aiming to bring unions and workers down. Such in-group versus out-group mentalities often lie at the heart of powerful social identities. Via repeated historical cues, union members learned that workers had to stick together to overcome enemies past and present and to counter both the company and the political forces aiming to suppress workers. The combination of members' awareness of the pre-union past and their mutual commitment to one another created a deep sense of in-group solidarity, which helped members feel socially supported by one another. Such workers felt that they were much more likely to be left at the will of the company or nonunion forces if they did not stand united.

Occupational Pride

If the first two constitutive processes united "union men" to one another and to their shared past, the third tied workers to the crafts, trades, or industries in which they worked, creating a sense of *occupational pride*. Rust Belt jobs for blue-collar unionists typically involved either building things or working in mills, mines, or plants. Because duties were physically demanding and often quite dangerous, workers recognized their inherent responsibility to look out for their fellow workers. As one retired Insulator said, "You got into some fairly hairy things on the job at times—toxic chemical plants and whatnot—you had to look out for the guy who was beside you, or a little later on, the lady next to you." Stories of one member saving another's life appear repeatedly in union publications from the mid-twentieth century. In 1964, IBEW began running a column called "IBEW Life Saving Awards," which discussed the awards given to union members who saved the lives of either other workers or community members. In January 1965, Arthur Culler and Elvin Kenoyer from IBEW Local 51 in Springfield, Illinois, were two of the members honored with the union's "most distinguished award" for performing mouth-to-mouth resuscitation after a fellow worker was electrocuted on the job. Similarly, the January 1965 article writes of William Thode of IBEW Local 109.[17] Thode was honored after he resuscitated a worker on top of a thirty-five-foot pole who went unconscious as a result of electrical shock. Because of the nature of the job that members were performing, being able to rely on one's fellow brothers was literally a matter of life or death.

This type of dangerous work also engendered a high degree of respect from the outside community. Similar almost in stature to military service, workers in mills and mines in particular

were respected because of the dangerous labor that they per-
formed. Twenty percent of male deaths in Pittsburgh in the
1880s were due to accidents in the steel mill.[18] Working in a steel
mill is still considered one of the most dangerous jobs today,
with the fatality rate around 30 per 100,000 workers.[19]

Despite job-related dangers, workers touted their own tough-
ness and resilience, asserting a tough-guy brand of masculinity.
Steelworkers and miners were proud to work in the mills and
mines; autoworkers were proud of building American-made
vehicles that transported the country; building tradesmen were
proud of their skill and extensive training in crafts such as electrical work, carpentry, and thermal insulation. Most of these
jobs were originally done by men who had homemaker wives
and traditional nuclear families for whom they were proud to
say they provided. Identity was formed around occupations that
many of these men, following family predecessors, had long
pursued, with other social commitments built around intergenerational work identities.[20] As one interviewee said, "When
I was a kid, all my dad's friends were steelworkers. They had a
lot of pride, and those stories [about the mill] rubbed off on us."
Another interviewee elaborated that there "was kind of a cama-
raderie in the trades. . . . If you sit down at the bar and find out
that the guy sitting next to you is in the trades, you talk about it,
you see what jobs he's been on, you relate to each other because
of that."

The intersection of workers' sense of *mutual commitment*
and *occupational pride* reinforced overarching *union* identity.
Union members were always highly aware of the possibility of
nonunion workers taking their jobs. Because the fear of being
replaced by nonunion "scabs" existed alongside occupational
pride, workers' feelings of occupational pride specifically meant
pride in *unionized work*.

Working together, *mutual commitment, historical awareness,* and *occupational pride* led workers to become socially, emotionally, and intellectually invested in their union. Many if not most members bought in. As a result, union affiliation was a powerful, deeply felt source of shared identity for many working Americans in the mid-twentieth century.

RACE, GENDER, AND FAMILY

The idealized identity we have fleshed out was implicitly—and many times explicitly—that of a white man, eventually married to a wife and the mother of his children. Of course, that does not mean that every worker in unionized and blue-collar ranks fit that mold, nor did this idealized identity exclude attention to the roles expected of wives and mothers in the community. Because the *changing* beliefs, identities, and citizen commitments of white male blue-collar workers have been so consequential for Democratic Party politics—and U.S. politics in general—this book focuses mainly on such workers and on the past meanings and recent shifts in ideals they have embodied and adopted. But taking this line of analysis seriously does not require overlooking the racial and gender realities of America's mid-twentieth century.

Black Union Brothers, Union Sisters, and the Struggle for Equality

Union sisters and Black union members made up small but consequential minority groups in most unions in the mid-twentieth century. In 1960, the majority of American unions had either no female membership or under 10 percent female membership.[21] Of all major unions, the United Auto Workers (UAW) had the most Black members during this time.

From 1960 to 1968, the percentage of nonwhite union autoworkers rose from 9 percent to 15 percent.[22] Black workers were more concentrated in some areas than others. For example, almost half of the autoworkers in Detroit were Black in the late 1960s. In other industries, Black members made up slightly lower proportions of the overall union population. Thus, in metal fabricating at large, 8 percent of workers were Black in 1968, and in electrical equipment manufacturing, 9 percent were Black.[23] Within USW, however, a larger percentage of members were Black than in the overarching metal fabricating industry. According to members of the Ad Hoc Committees for Black Steelworkers, about 20 to 25 percent of membership in the late 1960s was Black.[24] At the 1968 convention, the Ad Hoc Committee cited these facts to protest a dearth of Black representation on the USW executive board.[25]

Although midcentury industrial unions had their own significant issues related to race and representation, the building trades unions in the American Federation of Labor (AFL) were farther behind the times. The Congress of Industrial Organizations (CIO) was comparatively more progressive than the AFL. Although most Black workers were clustered in less privileged enclaves in CIO unions and the workplaces they dominated, CIO unions admitted Black members and treated them as titular equals. AFL building trades unions, however, rarely even *admitted* Black workers to their ranks until they were legally forced to do so in the 1960s. In "Affirmative Action from Below," historian Thomas J. Sugrue detailed the varied ways local unions preserved their white membership bases, including through requirements that new admittees be biologically related to current members.[26] Our interviewees agreed with Sugrue that family relation requirements were not uncommon in the building trades. In IBEW Local 5, one interviewee explained, "If you had family relations who were in good standing in the union, all you had to do was tell the union your last name, and they took you on." Preferences for familial recruits in building trades unions strengthened white majorities, perpetuating past imbalances into the next generations. Women in the building trades fared little better than Black workers because females were rarely admitted to skilled apprenticeship programs. In the view of many building trades leaders and members, females did not belong in the construction industry, where the work was gritty and labor physical.

The struggle for racial and gender equality in the building trades was ongoing throughout the 1960s. In Philadelphia, civil rights protestors surrounded the Democratic mayor's house in April 1963 to demand that the city stop awarding contracts to construction unions with no Black members. "African Americans sought construction jobs; white craftsmen sought to protect the security and fraternity of their trades," recounts Sugrue.[27] Shortly after the protests in Philadelphia, the Kennedy administration announced its opposition to discrimination on federal construction projects on June 4, 1963. On June 22, Kennedy signed an executive order that forbid such discrimination. This kick-started the struggles in the construction industry over how to deal with affirmative action policies. A year later, the recently merged AFL-CIO played a significant role in lobbying for the passage of the Civil Rights Act of 1964 and the Voting Rights Act of 1965.[28]

After the federations merged into the AFL-CIO in 1955, public stances by the major international unions shifted toward claiming support for racial equality. But in practice, discrimination against Black workers did not suddenly cease on the job or in local unions. As Herbert Hill wrote in 1996, "A record based upon thirty years of litigation initiated by black and other nonwhite workers under Title VII, the employment section of the Civil Rights Act of 1964, documents in great detail the discriminatory practices of many industrial unions in both northern and southern states."[29] USW was one of the unions found to have engaged in discriminatory practices. Black workers frequently reported that they were sidelined and bypassed by white coworkers for promotions or better job assignments. In the 1996 documentary *Struggles in Steel*, retired Black steelworkers discuss how they were often put on the dirtiest jobs in the steel mill. In due course, affirmative action policies, usually instituted at the behest of courts or top union management, tried to correct these problems, but they were not instituted quickly and they were not always fully successful.

Perhaps even more than in other organizations, policies on affirmative action rocked the boat in unions. In most unions, upward professional mobility was—and still largely is—determined almost entirely by seniority. When affirmative action policies came into effect in some unions, that changed. One retired Steelworker told us of the discomfort that some white members felt when their union was directed to use affirmative action policies to hire more Black workers. "When this judge came out with the consent decree, it meant that because Black people were discriminated in the past, they would get that job instead of someone with seniority. I don't have any prejudice, I work with Black people, I would go to war with these people, but [that policy] caused a lot of bitterness," he said. Similarly, an interviewee told us about trying to get a job at a coal mine but being rejected because the mine needed to hire a more diverse candidate.

> Whenever Page's was shut down, I needed a job. Now I go out to the mine, and I'm claustrophobic as hell, but I need a job. I got kids to feed. I went in and talked to the guy, and the guy told me

he would hire me tomorrow, but he said that he had to hire a Black woman before he hired me. I said, "Thank you very much," and left with a smile on my face. That's what he told me. Those were the rules, you had to hire certain amounts of people. . . . Those numbers and requirements kind of rubbed people the wrong way. Those Black guys were like brothers. [The policies] didn't have an effect on me one way or another, but a lot of guys resented it.

Doubtless, the breaking up of the "boys club" with the entry of women and people of different racial backgrounds in physically laborious industries and trades previously dominated by white men was difficult for everyone. Black workers and women rightly felt discriminated against. White male workers, whatever their personal feelings about it, had to acclimate to new workplace realities. One retired Insulator told us about the situation a Black tradesman faced when he was working on a job at a steel mill in Homestead, Pennsylvania. "Early on, when Blacks and women started coming in, when I was working at Homestead, there were some steamfitters there, and that was one of the first Black guys I saw on the job. These guys wouldn't talk to the guy or let him sit, so we invited him to have lunch with us," the retiree told us. He told us later in the conversation that "eventually, later on, [the Black worker] became a solid member of the steamfitters."

In many cases, after an initial transition period, cross-race union loyalty took the place of "us versus them" tensions. One retired IBEW member told us about how upsetting it was to witness Black brothers and sisters face racism and discrimination on the job.

The Black guys would always wear something that identified them as an electrician [on the job]. A t-shirt, a hat, something. At Labor Day parades, they would ask for any spare t-shirts because they would always wear them [to work]. Otherwise, [employers] would wonder what they were doing there—they would be suspicious. There was an instant distrust. It bothered most electricians because 95 percent of electricians backed up their Black brothers. Not everyone, but a pretty strong majority really didn't like to see that. It bothers you when you see someone you respect being treated like that.

For this white member and for many others, union loyalty came to predominate over racial differences. Seeing Black brothers treated badly on the job became discomforting to white members who felt allied with their co-unionists. Scholarship validates this idea. Political scientists Paul Frymer and Jacob Grumbach found in a 2021 analysis that racial animosity was significantly lower among white union members than in the general population of white Americans, in part because the union gives diverse populations a chance to interact in an equal setting.[30] Research and anecdotal interview data tell us that, even before the current era, unions were places where efforts were made to extend mutual solidarity across ethnic, religious, and racial lines, not perfectly, to be sure, but certainly more fully than in many other spheres of U.S. life at the time.

Despite their imperfect history, unions were also important agents of social mobility for Black communities in the mid-twentieth century. Mills, mines, and plants in various regions of the industrial Midwest provided good-paying jobs for Black workers, and, for a time, the jobs were plentiful. "One thing we didn't have to worry about was getting a job because there were plenty," one interviewee in *Struggles in Steel* explained [paraphrased].[31] But just as white working-class communities were devastated when the mills shut down, so too were Black communities. The jobs that were once available to almost all male high school graduates no longer existed. As Leon Haley of the

Urban League of Pittsburgh said, "The opportunities of the mills [were] very significant for the African American community. Not only the mills, but you can look at other cities. Look at Gary, Indiana, look at Detroit, look at Cleveland. [The] African American middle class really grew in those cities."[32] The growth of the Black middle class in these cities was unquestionably tied to their representation by labor unions.

In this vein, Black steelworkers were, by and large, appreciative of their unions. As in many working-class white families, steelwork was often passed down the family line in Black families. As one Black steelworker explained,

> Growing up in Pittsburgh, steelmaking was in my blood and lungs. After high school and the military, most guys went to work in the mill. . . . After the Navy I got a job at the Duquesne Steel Mill as a laborer. In 1967 the mills were part of everyday life. For Afro-Americans, the mills were part of a good life. Sure, the mills were hot and dirty, but they had the best paying jobs that a Black man could get.[33]

When asked to imagine what their lives would have looked like if not for the unions, Black interviewees were unambivalent about their positive feelings toward the union. "Even a bad union is better than no union because when you have a bad union you have an instrument that you can work with and it's in the people's control, it's in the workers' control," said one worker.[34] Another Black worker agreed, saying, "I wouldn't work for no company without a union. If it hadn't been for the union, I'd have been gone a long time ago." A Black female respondent agreed. "It would be impossible to work in the mill without a union. [Why?] Because you're not people down there," she said.[35] Almost all workers, regardless of race and gender (although likely accentuated by such factors), felt that the company viewed them as expendable. At the end of the day, it was the workers versus the company in many members' minds.

One of our interviewees powerfully described the intersection of race, gender, and economic mobility in her own life, both as a child and as an adult. "We grew up poor," she said, "we struggled." Things changed when her mom started working as a steelworker.

> When my mom started working in the mill, it literally lifted us out of poverty. I was probably about six when she went into the mill. To see those paychecks, it was like, wow. Not just that, but to see a woman do that—in the seventies, a woman actually working where there was physically engaging labor. When I was little, we would pick her, it was so exciting, you saw all these flames, [and] she was one woman out of thousands of men. She was like a superhero to me. It changed who I am as a person, woman, and as a Black woman. She was very active in her union.

Although nonwhite workers undoubtedly struggled to attain fair treatment even in unions that advocated for equality, many Black workers also deeply appreciated the union in their individual lives and in the larger sociopolitical context. Many of these workers proudly took on the idealized image of the union man, committed to their fellow union brothers across racial and gender lines.

Changing Faces

Over time, unions also endeavored to better represent diverse members within their ranks. Longitudinal trends in racial and gender diversification in unions are identifiable in union publications. In order to understand the evolution of representation of Black and female union members, we coded the apparent race and gender of all individuals pictured in six sets of USW and IBEW newsletters: the January and July issues in 1955, 1985, and 2015 (for more details about our methodology, please refer to appendix C). Photographs of unionists, leaders, and family members say a lot about who these newsletters represented and were intended to reach, and our simple findings parallel the realities in blue-collar communities and American society more generally. In 1955, out of 153 discernible individuals in the January and July issues of USW's "Steel Labor," eight individuals were Black, representing 5 percent of discernible individuals. In these same two magazines, nine white women were discernible, representing around 6 percent of individuals represented. There were more discernible individuals in the IBEW magazines from the same months in 1955, but even fewer members of color were represented. Of the 1,069 individuals pictured, only three individuals were Black (two Black men and one Black woman), accounting for only 0.3 percent of all represented individuals. The number of white women represented in the magazines is higher, but one important qualification must be made: most if not all of the women pictured were either wives or secretaries. In total, there were 139 discernible white women, making up 13 percent of those people represented in the photographs.

By 1985, both USW and IBEW featured more Black members and women in their magazines. In USW magazines, nonwhite members (Black and self-identified Mexican American) accounted for 11 percent of discernible individuals. White women accounted for just over 9 percent. Meanwhile, IBEW was relatively slow to represent nonwhite members. In 1985, still only 3.75 percent of discernible individuals in photographs were people of color. The percentage of white women depicted went down to 9 percent in 1985, but many of those pictured in the 1980s were not just wives, as they were in the 1950s, but fellow union members.

By 2015, the magazines were much more representative than in the twentieth century. Twenty-two percent of individuals represented in USW magazines were nonwhite, and 23 percent were women (both white women and women of color). IBEW had improved, too, for a trade in which still a significant majority of workers are white men. Thirteen percent of discernible individuals were people of color, and 13 percent of individuals were women (white or women of color) as well. These data show, in broad strokes, that union communications—perhaps especially in the AFL, as illustrated in IBEW newsletters—were indeed primarily intended for white male workers throughout most of the twentieth century.

Since the 1970s, most unions have made far-reaching efforts to support women and people of color. Traditional U.S. blue-collar unions can rightly be criticized for accommodating many racist and sexist hiring practices, but it is important to note as well that when nonwhite and women workers entered the unionized occupations and workplaces, most U.S. unions from World War II onward made more attempts than other institutions of their day to include them in the "brotherhoods," if only in order to counter employer efforts to weaken union solidarity and economic clout (see figure 2.1). After all, workers often *had* to rely on one another on the job. As one retired steelworker poignantly put it, "Black or white, when you were working next to each other and your lives depended on that guy to your right, it didn't matter: you were family."

Family Roles and Ladies Auxiliaries

Although nonwhite male unionists—including the roughly 20 percent of Steelworkers who were Black in the late 1960s—

FIGURE 2.1 USW pin. Theda Skocpol personal collection.

could perhaps most readily share the ideals and outlooks of the good union man, the fit was more difficult for women unionists in overwhelmingly male workplaces and unions, not just because of their gender but also because of responsibilities attributed to partners and mothers of union families. Union newsletters of the mid-twentieth century primarily depicted women fulfilling distinctly feminine roles in the community and largely ignored the small population of women who worked in heavy industry. When women were first integrated into industrial workplaces and trade unions, they were faced with hostility and harassment, as Black workers were. One top-level executive of an international industrial union who saw gender-based harassment firsthand as he was rising in the ranks of his union described it as "terrible." But, he said, treatment of women improved over time.

> We trained [women] how to fight back [when harassed], how to respond, how to not be afraid of that. Largely now, [men] don't try to do anything that they would've done in the past. Thirty years ago, it was not uncommon to walk into the lunch room and guys could go out of their way to just act like pigs. The union had to educate itself, we had to force the union to take the Playboy posters down. Now it would be very uncommon to find that type of thing.

In part, treatment was so hostile at the outset of gender integration because of the gendered expectations that permeated the prototypical union family. Many midcentury locals had ladies auxiliaries, ostensibly organized by wives to support their working husbands but also serving to reinforce women's ties to one another. Ladies auxiliaries often held their own meetings and sponsored social or charitable events such as dinners and dances, as writers from local areas often noted in the pages of the IBEW international magazine. A July 1965 report from IBEW Local 716 in Houston, Texas, recounted that the ladies auxiliary held a barbecue dinner in honor of its forty-first anniversary.[36] In July 1965, the ladies auxiliary of IBEW Local 861 in Lake Charles, Louisiana, sponsored a country store sale at the local union hall, and the ladies auxiliary of Local 111 in Oklahoma City bought new draperies for the offices in the union hall.[37] Even in the mid-1970s, there was still interest in starting ladies auxiliaries for local unions that did not already have one, as was explained by a report from Local 1837 in Portsmouth, New Hampshire.[38] Ladies auxiliary clubs even existed for union retiree organizations, where wives were already welcome to attend general meetings that were almost entirely social in nature.

Although ladies auxiliaries were the most obvious and official manifestations, there were other more informal ways in which unions reached out to women of the community. Of course, women and at times children were invited to much anticipated social events, such as holiday parties, summer picnics, and dinner dances. Many international union magazines also included specific columns for the women—such as IBEW magazine's "With the Ladies" column. A January 1955 editorial in that magazine section urged women to be grateful for what they have rather than lamenting over what they do not, saying, "Stop a minute and think. Suppose your husband was taken from you, or a child. Think for a moment how desolate you would feel."[39] USW's international magazine also had a column called "The Women's Corner: Patterns, Chatter, Recipes," which offered advice for women about shopping, recipes, appliances, and other things related to childrearing and homemaking.

In addition to the international newsletter's section for women, *local* union newsletters also often had specific sections devoted to women's topics. The "3:30 Caucus" was the women's section for UAW Local 306's newsletter, called "Voice of Local 306." The "3:30 Caucus" column reported on the personal lives of the women of the union, most of whom worked office jobs, as well as the wives of members of the union. In the May 17, 1967, issue of "Voice of Local 306," columnist Glenora Schumacher writes that "Hazel Reece, of Data Processing, won $100 at a raffle," which, Schumacher says, will help her pay for her upcoming wedding. Schumacher continues to report that about forty union girls attended the "lovely shower . . . for our recent radiant bride, Helen Popovich, at the home of Dee Beamish."[40] Whereas the women's sections of the international union magazines gave general information about homemaking, women's sections in local union newsletters often contributed personal news, including reports on engagements, weddings, babies, and other events related to the personal lives of women associated with the union.

Patterns of gendered responsibilities in unions did not persist in the face of changing societal gender roles and the growing ranks of female unionists. By 1970, USW had removed the "Women's Corner" name from the column and simply put recipes under the non-gender-specific heading "Kitchen Shelf." In 1984, IBEW ceased running the "With the Ladies" section altogether. As we will see in later chapters, shifts in family and gender roles did not occur in a vacuum—they were part of many societal changes that remade the world of the midcentury union man.

Formal efforts to include women *as unionists* sometimes replaced efforts to engage with women as wives and mothers. In the 1970s, USW introduced the Women of Steel program, which was designed to support women steelworkers and help them develop leadership skills that they could use to climb the union hierarchy. One woman who participates in the program today told us that the Women of Steel committees, which are supposed to exist at every USW local, were formed "to help [men] see that [women] weren't just there for the women's auxiliary clubs." A top-level leader at USW international explained the role of the Women of Steel committees saying, "They don't just run bake sales. . . . They're very politically active." Despite broad efforts from executive leadership, many interviewees testified that it was initially difficult to get participation in Women of Steel programs, perhaps for fear of male workers' reactions. Participation today, according to interviewees, is significantly stronger than it used to be.

Formal efforts to include women unionists aside, women always had more considerations on the job than their male colleagues. One retiree of IBEW explained that she was always incredibly careful about her appearance for fear of being treated differently based on men's judgement.

I remember thinking carefully about what to wear to my interview. And I never swore on the job. I felt that men would be more accepting if I looked like their wives or sisters or whatever. Other women did not [do the same], and they were fine. But I knew that at that time a lot of men thought women were either whores or virgins. I didn't want to be put in a situation where men were vulgar because, in a workplace, it's dangerous. I was old enough and mature enough to know that they didn't all have to like you. That's something women in every field should know.

This woman electrician also remembered that union sisters and Black brothers would often have special bonds with one another because they understood the difficulties that each faced on the job. But still, in many cases, women were forced to tolerate hostility and judgment, at least until such attitudes dissipated with time.

UNIONS IN THE COMMUNITY

Midcentury unionists were committed not only to one another—and to their families—but also to their communities at large. In an internal survey conducted by USW in 1955, members expressed overwhelming support for their union, but they did not stop there. Over 83 percent of respondents also agreed that both the union and its members should be involved in community groups and events.[41] From the 1980s on, international unions touted community engagement to counter media attacks by antiunion forces, but decades earlier, the magazines and newsletters of local and international UAW, IBEW, USW, United Mine Workers of America (UMWA), and United Electrical, Radio, and Machine Workers (UE) unions reported that members were regularly—and proudly—involved with their communities in meaningful and diverse ways. Being a union man did not stop when a worker left the gates of the steel mill or auto factory. In the mid-twentieth century, union ties and goals spread across almost all community institutions. Beyond collective bargaining and workplace services, unions reached into recreational leagues, family affairs, community events, places of worship, schools, and local politics. Across much of the Rust Belt and even other regions of the country, unions became cornerstone institutions in the fabric of community relations. Union locals were connected to ethnic and fraternal groups and other associations that figured in various aspects of social life for union members and their families, making them vital hubs and underlying social infrastructures in manufacturing towns and cities.

This reality is theoretically important because the salience and relevance of organizations and groups grow through multiple involvements in members' lives. A group attachment that is involved in only one domain of an individual's life is frequently perceived as less important than a group attachment that permeates multiple domains of that person's life. Unions, for instance, were relevant to workers when they went home, read the local labor newspaper, played in or watched the union's softball or bowling league, and helped their parents get access to Medicare. During the mid-twentieth century, most unions had such varied reaches. Even if not by name, the union presence was felt not just at the mill but in many daily nonworkplace settings.

In this section, we illustrate multiple forms of union reach from many sources, and we also focus closely on one large USW local union—Local 1211, in Aliquippa, Pennsylvania. The Aliquippa Works of the Jones and Laughlin Steel Corporation began operation in 1909 and became one of the largest mills in the country. To learn about union involvement in many dimensions of workers' lives from the 1960s to the 1980s, we have sampled issues of the "Aliquippa Steelworker: The Voice of Local 1211," the local union newsletter that circulated to some 14,500 potential readers in a city of about 26,000 in 1960.[42] In its pages, we see union and unionist involvement with recreational activities and social clubs, ties to churches and religious groups, and provision of regular information about government rules and programs as well as nonprofit services—each of which we will briefly describe. All these types of union involvement in turn laid the foundation for many members to become engaged and often politically involved democratic citizens.

Alongside Ethnic and Fraternal Groups

Socializing with fellow workers created the most basic kinds of ties beyond the workplace—and in this respect, it is important to understand that unions took shape in communities dense with ethnic clubs and fraternal organizations that included wage earners along with people from other occupations. To be sure, social clubs operated at plants, mills, or mines prior to the recognition of major international unions as collective bargaining entities, yet union locals, once established, continued and strengthened interactions with such groups. As Joshua Penrod writes in *Johnstown Industry*, while "industry eventually came to recognize organized labor, labor itself formed social clubs, another part of the fabric of society. For many in Johnstown [Pennsylvania], it was not uncommon to be a member of several different clubs, including ethnic and cultural clubs, and labor clubs."[43] Especially for industrial workers, labor social clubs were often tied to specific workplaces—as was, for example, the Conemaugh & Franklin Coke Plant Social Club in Johnstown.

Labor-related functions were also held at the community's ethnic or fraternal clubs. A December 1963 blurb in the "Aliquippa Steelworker" invites members of 1211 to the local Ukrainian club to plan a celebration for high school athletes. Announcements for local IBEW so-called "old-timer" nights, graduation banquets, or dinners frequently described events at the local American Legion Hall or fraternal lodges.

Midcentury blue-collar unions often had many overlapping members with fraternal groups built by ethnic groups like Slovaks, Hungarians, Germans, and Irish Catholics, and union membership also overlapped with those of large multiethnic fraternal orders for white men such as the Fraternal Order of Eagles and the Loyal Order of Moose. Both the Eagles and the Moose grew rapidly and established local lodges widely during the first two-thirds of the twentieth century, so they were invariably present in industrial towns and cities across western Pennsylvania and the rest of the Rust Belt. By the 1930s, these orders often supported values and causes similar to those advocated by growing unions. In particular, the Fraternal Order of Eagles championed the watchword virtues named in its motto of "Liberty, Truth, Justice, Equality."[44]

Many fraternal orders and other male brotherhood associations had taken root and grown in most cities and towns across the United States well before modern unions expanded and certainly before the advent of USW and other CIO giants.[45] The American Legion, for instance, formed after World War I and established posts nearly everywhere during the 1920s. Well before that, especially between the 1880s and 1920s, church-connected social benefit societies and pioneering fraternal orders founded their chapters and lodges across western Pennsylvania. With the exception of military veteran's groups that took a somewhat more inclusive stance, many such groups were racially or ethnically exclusive, even though they were structured in parallel ways—as brotherhoods and sisterhoods that met regularly (weekly, every other week, or once a month) to authorize sick or death benefits to dues-paying members and enact moral rituals trumpeting values touting patriotism, mutual support, honesty, and love of God. Ethnic associations in particular offered an array of programs, including language instruction to help immigrant workers from Slovakia, Bohemia, Hungary, Germany, and Scandinavia become full American citizens and patriots. Unlike union locals, ethnic and other fraternal groups claimed to operate secretly. They were not really very secretive in practice, however, because they were publicly known and highly visible—participating, for instance, in community fairs, parades, and holiday celebrations, when their members proudly proclaimed their identities and values on colorful ribbons. See figure 2.2 for a sampling of such ribbons worn by members of fraternal and ethnic associations in western Pennsylvania.

Figure 2.2a depicts what was a red, white, and blue badge from "Flood City Lodge No. 260" formed in 1894 as a chapter of the Ancient Order of United Workmen, an insurance order that included many workingmen in Pennsylvania and across all U.S. states. The magnificent badge pictured in figure 2.2b comes from a Hungarian workers sickness benefits society in Bishop, Pennsylvania (near Pittsburgh). Other badges are specifically identified by ethnic group, including the badge in figure 2.2c for "Bond of Love Lodge No. 2514," established in March 1884 as part of the nationwide African American Grand United Order of Odd Fellows; the ribbon in figure 2.2d for Mahonoy City Lodge 94 of the German Beneficial Union; and a Slovak-American church-connected fraternal badge from Johnstown, shown in figure 2.2e. The striking badge shown in figure 2.2f comes from the Columbia Lodge No. 8 of the Scandinavian

FIGURE 2.2 (a) Ancient Order of United Workmen—insurance fraternal group for white men, Johnstown, Pennsylvania. (b) Hungarian-American sick benefits association, Bishop, Pennsylvania. (c) Grand United Order of Odd Fellows—African American—Allegheny, Pennsylvania. (d) German Beneficial Union, Jenner, Pennsylvania. (e) Association of Slovak Greek Catholics, Johnstown, Pennsylvania. (f) Scandinavian Brotherhood of America, Titusville, Pennsylvania. Theda Skocpol personal collection.

(c)

BOND OF LOVE
LODGE
NO. 2514
G.U.O. OF O.F.
ALLEGHENY, PA.

(d)

GERMAN
BENEFICIAL UNION
DISTRICT 188
D. U. B.
JENNER, PA.

FIGURE 2.2 (*Continued*)

FIGURE 2.2 (*Continued*)

Brotherhood of America. Lodge No. 8 was established around 1900 in Titusville, Pennsylvania, an oil-producing boom area that attracted many Norwegian and Swedish immigrants in the later 1800s.

Midcentury industrial and allied unions wove themselves into community infrastructures already dotted with fraternal and ethnic groups, and these earlier U.S. associations also strongly influenced the structure and practices of unions themselves. The fraternal influence was clear for craft unions and railroad brotherhoods that were established before the 1930s; their members wore the same kinds of colorful ribbon badges and sometimes met in "lodges" with membership rules and rituals that closely resembled other fraternal orders. Members of other older unions—such as the American Flint Glass Workers Union—were also proud to portray the symbols of their occupations on ribbon badges that combined traditional brotherhood symbols with patriotic decorations (see figure 2.3).

Although attenuated, remnants of earlier fraternal forms persisted even for the CIO unions that emerged during the Great Depression and World War II. Many post-1930s union posters, pamphlets, and hat pins announcing dues payments featured the "In Union Strength" motto that many fraternal associations had long championed. Equally ubiquitous was the traditional fraternal brotherhood symbol of two shaking hands—as appeared, for example, on the cover of the USW pamphlet touting the achievements of the 1959 steel strike as a "triumph of unity and democracy."[46] Even industrial unions that did not use "lodge" nomenclature adopted choreographies for local meetings that resonated in many ways with long-standing fraternal practices. For example, a 1940s Workers Organizing Committee "Manual of Common Procedure for Local Unions" reads very much like a secularized version of fraternal meeting and ritual procedures, including instructions for ceremonial meeting openings, initiation of new members, and funeral ceremonies for deceased members.[47]

Like the local chapters of fraternal and ethnic groups, union locals held regular membership meetings, elected officers, and subsidized the travel expenses of representatives they sent to supralocal district and state meetings as well as to the international or national conventions where U.S. and Canadian unionists

FIGURE 2.3 (a) American Flint Glass Workers Union, Local 81, Toledo, Ohio. (b) Brotherhood of Railroad Trainmen, Ohio Valley Lodge No. 13, McMechen, West Virginia. Theda Skocpol personal collection.

assembled yearly or every other year. On their own or in joint events, union locals mounted more regularly the same sorts of events—dinners, anniversary celebrations, and rites of passage for entering and retiring members. In short, the social choreography of union locals rhymed with long-standing community routines that U.S. workers and their families already understood very well.

Union-Connected Associations

Once major unions like USW were up and running, they created new subunits and associational partners of their own. Sports leagues abounded, such as Local 1211's bowling league—where competitions were orchestrated among workmates in the Welded Tube team, the Wire Mill team, the Boiler Shop team, the Tin Mill number 1 and number 2 teams, and the Open Hearth team, along with others. Free golf field days were organized by Local 1211 for "any member of the local to display his skill or break up the daily routine of living."[48] In other local unions, softball or baseball leagues were organized for members (see figure 2.4). As one current steelworker told us about a league in a different USW local, "I'm a third-generation steelworker. . . . I remember my dad and grandfather going to the local's softball games and then the bar." Although he currently still works at the same mill as his father and grandfather, the union softball league no longer exists.

In addition to sports leagues, other recreational leagues were organized within the local union, including the Conservation, Fishing, and Hunting Club of USW Local 1211. Coin club meetings also convened at the local union hall, allowing union brothers and their neighbors to socialize as they examined and traded rare coins. The Local 1211 Community Service Committee encouraged members to donate both time and money to various

FIGURE 2.4 Pin from IBEW Local 90's softball team, New Haven, Connecticut. Theda Skocpol personal collection.

charitable causes, such as the March of Dimes organization and the Beaver County Cancer Society.

Sometimes unions provided resources to fund recreational and social clubs, but often the union itself simply created the underlying relationships while formally taking a behind-the-scenes role. No union officials roamed the room during coin-trading events to convince community members to support prolabor businesses, policies, or candidates. But union encouragement for this club and other recreational activities was important nonetheless, signaling that the local union was involved and invested in the lives of its members, their families, and their neighbors in the community at large. The involvement of union members, and perhaps union provision of space or other kinds of sponsorship to recreational groups or events, also sent enduring symbolic messages. Such contributions increased the salience of the local union and made it easy and appealing for members and others in the area to interact with the union in spaces or forums beyond unionized workplaces. Unions thus wove themselves— their people, their local leaders, their facilities, their names— into the very underpinnings of community social life.

Unions and Churches

Unions and religious organizations partnered for community events as well. Throughout the 1980s, District 2 of the UMWA, which covered most of central Pennsylvania, rallied support for miners by partnering with several different religious organizations to plan celebrations of labor. The annual celebration was held at St. Andrew's Catholic Church hall and, throughout the years, members of many local labor unions—Teamsters Local 110, Typographical Local 137, various building trades locals, Social Services Local 668, District 15 of the United Steelworkers, and others—attended the party.[49] Despite not getting much attention in the press, this recurring event showcased the solidarity between members of the religious community and members of the labor movement, wrote Reverend David J. Dodson, the president of the Greater Johnstown Clergy Association. The religious service during the 1980 celebration, which was a joint effort by members of various religious affiliations, thanked God for "His blessings upon the labor movement and for the ability to see in our labor and work a genuine means of creative participation in life," wrote Dodson in a letter to the *Johnstown Tribune Democrat*. "The entire labor celebration began as a brainchild of the Greater Johnstown Clergy Association," he added.[50]

Churches have, of course, been central to much of American community life, and midcentury union leaders often made an active effort to acknowledge and engage with the mostly

Christian faith commitments of their members. One of our interviewees, a retired mine inspector who worked in mining communities for more than fifty years, noted that unions and churches seemed to be the "two big organizations that tied those communities together." Workers were encouraged to participate in faith-based activities by their local union. "I would like to urge my fellow steelworkers their families and our readers attend [*sic*] the church of your faith and support its programs," wrote the chair of the Community Services Committee in the December 1965 "Aliquippa Steelworker." In its recurring column entitled "Religion in the News," the Local 1211 newsletter encouraged members to pray and reported on local church happenings. Union editors were also happy to feature religious leaders who advocated for unions. In an article entitled "About These 'Right-to-Work' Laws," the January 1955 IBEW international magazine explained that many "of our people are church goers" while citing the "harms inflicted on society and humanity by right-to-work laws" in statements from Rabbi Israel Goldstein of a congregation in New York City, Reverend Dr. Walter G. Mueller of the Methodist Church, and Reverend William J. Kelley, Oblate Father. Reverend Kelley was quoted saying that the antiunion laws are "immoral according to Catholic teachings."[51]

When the collapse of the steel industry began in the late 1970s, members of the religious community in western Pennsylvania were highly involved in helping and advocating for workers. The Tri-State Conference on Steel (TCS) and the Steel Valley Authority (SVA) emerged as grassroots efforts to save steel mills and industrial plants slated for closure. A 1982 flyer for a series of workshops run by TCS described its method for saving jobs in the region: "By gathering local unions, churches, local government officials and small business to seriously discuss the many critical issues which face the

Mon Valley, we believe a program and a strategy can be formed that will give us some reason to hope and ability to act."[52] Religious personnel were key members of these efforts, and many churches even officially endorsed proposals circulated by TCS and SVA for saving various plants. In attorney Staughton Lynd's defense of the proposal for the community to buy and operate U.S. Steel's Duquesne Works, nicknamed "Dorothy Six," he lists organizations that endorsed the proposal, which included politicians and local unions and also St. Stephen's Church, Hazelwood; Holy Trinity Church, Duquesne; Episcopal Dean George Werner; and the Capuchin-Franciscan Province of St. Augustine.[53] A 1985 article in the *Freemont News-Messenger* argued that it was not in fact surprising that so many religious organizations supported workers when industry collapsed. "In an area where religious faith runs deep, ancient churches stand as tribute to the immigrants who built them, and towns bear such slogans as 'City of Prayer,' perhaps it is no surprise that the current economic crisis in the Mon Valley has affected and is affected by matters of faith," the article states.[54]

The labor movement was founded on the principle of uplifting the common man, so many local unions were also deeply devoted to secular community service efforts. Blood drives were frequent in many locals, and unions even competed with one another to see which local could have the most participation. The "Community Service Committee Report" column in the "Aliquippa Steelworker" appears frequently in the newsletter, and members were often encouraged to donate to the United Funds of Beaver County, which supported the Aliquippa Hospital, Ambridge Veterans Advisory Center, public libraries, Boy and Girl Scout troops, the Mental Health Society, local YMCAs, and other organizations. In the "Local Lines" section of the IBEW international magazine, locals frequently wrote about members donating their labor, either to a grassroots effort like wiring the local high school football stadium or to organizations like Habitat for Humanity.

Social Service Hubs

Social services mattered for unionists, so the "Aliquippa Steelworker" regularly informed its readers about them. The June 1965 issue, for instance, included a page-long feature from the Beaver County Cancer Society on danger signs for disease and the preventive services available to workers. Later, in the 1980s, the union newsletter became a key resource for unemployed workers to learn about retraining opportunities or assistance programs. Writing in the February 1983 newsletter at a time when about 5,000 members of USW Local 1211 were laid off, steelworker Mike Nazarovitch explained that "one of our Union Brothers informed me of the great services available to the unemployed at the Community College of Beaver County Job Club Center."[55] After he "went to talk to the staff working there to get some information for our Union Brothers and Sisters," Nazorovitch detailed the kinds of help available to his fellow unionists in his column.

Local unions also often provided services directly to their own members. USW Local 1211 sponsored "Operation Oxygen," a "private blood bank for employees and their families on a 24-hour, seven day a week basis."[56] Alcoholism support groups also existed in many unions, and Local 1211 ran a recurring "Alcoholics Anonymous" column in the "Aliquippa Steelworker" to offer support and motivation for individuals with this malady. In the July 1962 column, the writer invites local union members struggling with alcoholism to Alcoholics Anonymous (AA) meetings at All Saints Episcopal Church on the same street as the local union hall. Some locals went even further and subsidized the fees for union members to seek drug or alcohol treatment—as did IBEW Local 332 in San Jose, California, which began offering the subsidization program to members in 1985.[57] During stints of unemployment and layoffs, union food pantries were set up. To support unemployed workers, the union solicited donations from employed members, local businesses, and community residents.

Of course, as discussed earlier in this chapter, unions were highly involved in family affairs through their engagement efforts with members' wives. But involvement with family did not stop there. Because midcentury unionism was expected to outlive members themselves, many locals worked to make a good impression on the next generation—and above all on members' sons. Many of Local 1211's membership meetings occurred at Aliquippa High School. Other locals, including UE Local 610, also met at nearby high schools. This was one way to expose high school students to industrial work and workers— worker-student interactions occurred even though students themselves did not attend formal meetings. Because Aliquippa was a relatively small and close-knit community, many workers were also highly attentive to high school sports played by their sons and school friends, and the "Aliquippa Steelworker" frequently reported on how the local high school was performing in regional or state contests. "Aliquippa is the cream of the crop," exclaimed Bernie Juth in the February 1963 issue. "I'm looking for the Quips to play Uniontown in the finals at the Civic Arena in March." The Aliquippa local was even involved in the lives of young children. In a December 1965 letter to the editor, for example, David Carr of the Blast Furnace Department asks union members to get involved in the Ambridge Area Soap

Box Derby, explaining that when "a program such as this is initiated, it is not started overnight. It is developed by men who work
within our towns—steelworkers, store clerks, barbers and the
like have taken the time to develop the boys of today who will
be the men of tomorrow." Carr ends his letter by noting that the
previous year, his nephew drove a derby car with a sign declaring
"Sponsored by Local 1211, Aliquippa, Pa."

Neighbors and Union Halls

The previous sections surveyed many kinds of local union programs and ties connecting workers to one another and to others in their local communities. Most of the connections we
discussed, ranging from social and recreational to religious and
charitable efforts, existed in many midcentury unions and were
illustrated by selections from a variety of union magazines and
newsletters beyond our many citations to the "Aliquippa Steelworker." But at this point, we should stress that some community ties were experienced more intensely by industrial workers
than by building tradespeople, or, for purposes of our analysis,
more intensely by USW members than IBEW members. An
added layer of solidarity came into play for Steelworkers because
most members of their local unions were congregated in relatively small residential areas and often worked under the same
roof as their neighbors for much of their careers.

In many of western Pennsylvania's industrial towns such
as Aliquippa, most steelworkers lived close to both their
workplace—a major mill or industrial facility—and very near
local union facilities. On top of the "us versus them" mentality
that major unions fostered, pitting unionized brothers against
company managers, geographical proximity facilitated additional

congeniality and mutual support among USW members. As one recently retired steelworker put it, "One thing I remember from being a kid when we moved [from Belle Vernon, Pennsylvania, to Monessen, Pennsylvania] was that everyone on the street was in the steel industry. Everyone's dad was a steelworker, it was really cool, and everyone was doing really well. We had a nice tight-knit community, the parents all knew each other, and everyone was happy." In addition to many official and de facto union engagements with workers and the community, the fact that many union members were neighbors reinforced the solidarity, shared identity, and social attitudes that made the ideals espoused by and for union men socially credible and civically powerful.

Workers living side by side as neighbors in the same community also made it possible for many USW locals to have buildings that concretely symbolized sociopolitical influence and epitomized the peak of union community presence. Since the 1800s, in U.S. communities from small to large, fraternal and veteran's associations as well as churches sustained their own downtown buildings where members and others could meet. In many industrial towns in the early twentieth century, "labor temples" were built and used by unions of various affiliations. In Pittsburgh, a building that had previously been occupied by the Shriners and known as the Syria Temple through the nineteenth century became the "Union Labor Temple" in 1910. Many different unions met in the Union Labor Temple, which the *Iron City Trades Journal* wrote was the "best equipped Labor Temple in the country and perhaps in the world."[58] Also in Pittsburgh, the Labor Lyceum was a Jewish socialist organization that hosted meetings for local unions that had majority immigrant Jewish members, such as the Garment Workers Local 65, the Stogie Workers Local 101, and the Jewish Bakery Workers.[59] In the late 1950s, some communities surrounding Pittsburgh, such as Charleroi and Warren, Pennsylvania, also had labor temples. Following the era of the labor temple was the era of industrial unions opening brick-and-mortar union halls specific to their union and their local. During this period, USW directly owned and ran many halls in western Pennsylvania and the broader industrial Midwest.

USW halls could be established by single locals or by teams of locals that pitched in. Once built or bought, they became convenient places where many union and nonunion events were held, including weddings and banquets as well as conferences, negotiation sessions, and governing meetings. The first USW union hall was bought by Local 1123 in Canton, Ohio, in 1940. By 1958 to 1960, the international leaders of USW were so proud of the proliferation of at least 228 USW union halls across the country and in Canada that they published two editions of a pamphlet entitled "Where Citizens Meet the Union," which touted the many functions of union halls—often located in town centers, just as prominent fraternal halls had long been—and included an array of pictures of these buildings ranging from humble to grand. The pamphlet also included a roster of names and addresses across many states. Figure 2.5 shows illustrations from this pamphlet. As it explained: "Although the smallest building cost only $3,000, local unions have invested as much as $650,000 and more in a home, such as the impressive, modern structure at Bethlehem, Pa. Steelworker properties range in size from the dimensions of a private home to that of a multi-storied department store, sprawling over most of a city block. While some are plain and utilitarian, most are modern and as well-equipped as tomorrow's skyscraper."[60]

United Steelworkers Local 1211 purchased its own hall in Aliquippa in 1943—a beautiful structure that had previously been a bank, which had failed during the Great Depression. According to a current National Park Service explanation, through "this building, the union built social, economic, and political clout

FIGURE 2.5 Western Pennsylvania United Steel Workers Halls, ca. 1960. (a) USW Local 2632 of District 13 in Johnstown, Pennsylvania. (b) USW Local 1082 of District 20 in Beaver Falls, Pennsylvania. (c) USW Local 1557 of District 12 in Clairton, Pennsylvania. (d) Philip Murray Hall, USW Local 1408 of District 15 in McKeesport, Pennsylvania. United Steelworkers of America, President's Office records (01961), Eberly Family Special Collections Library, Penn State University Libraries.

(d)

(c)

FIGURE 2.5 (*Continued*)

through the post-war peak of the steel industry."[61] Especially when halls were as large and centrally located as Aliquippa's was, they were "more than an ordinary pile of bricks, glass, steel and concrete. Each [was] also a symbol of the union's permanence . . . its stability . . . [offering] tangible evidence that the Steelworkers have put down their roots to stay, to be of service, and to take their rightful place as warm and friendly hosts in the growth and development of those they live with."[62]

Western Pennsylvania was one of the areas nationwide with the most USW halls. By the 1960s, there were at least thirty-seven

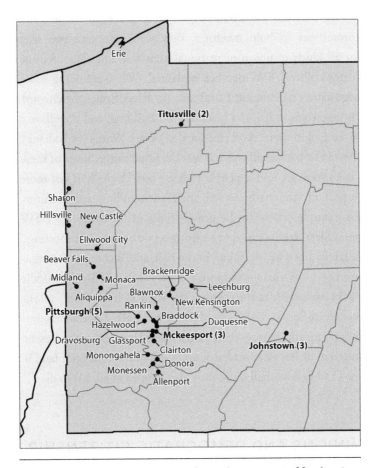

FIGURE 2.6 USW halls in western Pennsylvania ca. 1960. Numbers in parentheses represent the number of local union halls in that metropolitan area if there was more than one hall.

USW halls, including thirty-six listed in *Where the Union Meets the Community*, plus one more that we discovered in a city directory for Erie that was founded soon after the pamphlet was issued. The regional map in figure 2.6 shows where the industrial-era USW halls were located.

Not only did these buildings serve as places for leaders and committees to hold meetings, they were also rent-free sites for all kinds of union recreational activities and clubs. As one current older USW member explained, "We were doing some negotiating meetings at Local 1299 [in River Rouge, Michigan], and their union hall is a beautiful old building, and they have a social hall in there. And [the local at] Gary Works [in Indiana], they had a basketball court, it was the same thing. Some of these places were set up for people to hang out." Equally if not more important, the halls served their surrounding communities, for example, when (in the proud words of the 1960s-era USW pamphlet) "teen-agers or a scout troop want to hold a meeting," "a family has a big wedding" in the hall, and "a community organization . . . is anxious to sponsor a social affair."[63] By the middle of the twentieth century across the Rust Belt, in short, union-owned edifices served many of the same kinds of needs for community meeting spaces as had halls owned by the most successful fraternal orders once served. Community functions once held in the Odd Fellows hall could now also happen at a USW hall.

UNIONS AND DEMOCRATIC CITIZENSHIP

The social underpinnings of the mid-twentieth-century union man that we have detailed so far set the stage for democratic participation within and beyond unions and, for a time, support for the Democratic Party as well. To be a good union member meant, ideally, engaging in mutual solidarity at work, participating in community affairs, and being an active democratic citizen. One of our interviewees, whose mother was a Black steelworker in the 1970s, described being exposed to the democratic processes of labor activism while growing up: "We were involved in all the protests and parades and picnics, and we'd go to seminars. We got to witness a lot, there would be hundreds of people [at these events]—there was Black people, white people, women. There was more white people than anyone, but I never felt scared. We even went to Washington. It was amazing. I remember what that felt like." Unions were bridges to democratic citizenship for their members in large part because they helped weave or reinforce workplace and community ties but also because union leaders, peers, and communications conveyed vital information about democratic practices, U.S. government, and public policies. Such basics of U.S. democratic citizenship were conveyed prior to and more fundamentally than specific partisan commitments.

Schools of Democracy

Given that union locals with dues-paying members were connected to district, state, and national or international associations via voting delegates and elected leaders, unions embodied federated arrangements with similarities to the U.S. government itself—thus creating a two-way flow of information for many members, inspiring democratic voices within unions and encouraging unionists to participate in the broader U.S. democracy. Something as straightforward as a vividly written USW pamphlet explaining in detail "Here's How USWA Dues Work for You!" conveyed lessons relevant to taxation because it laid out in plain language why regular dues were necessary to pursue clear union goals and realize benefits that members wanted or needed.[64] At their best, meetings to reach decisions or elect leaders also conveyed messages about democracy. "To be a unionist is to participate in the democratic process in your union in the same way you are doing it for your government," said one retiree of the UE, who continued with the observation that this "means to not be afraid to criticize the union, run for office, and try to change things for the better—[it means that you] engage with the same seriousness in the union as you do with our democracy." Similarly, USW members who responded to an internal 1955 survey said that unions were important to American democracy and their sense of civic responsibility. Three-fifths of respondents agreed that "the Steelworkers Union gives [them] a feeling of being a more important and useful citizen" and a remarkable 81 percent endorsed the statement that "unions are one of the most important forces insuring [sic] democracy in our country."[65]

To these workers, unions were important forces because, by that juncture, they had helped workers build enough collective power to change the operations of powerful corporations and to persuade elected politicians to give at least a measure of legal support to union organizing from the 1930s through World War II and into the 1970s. Beyond their own experiences, most workers also got regular information from union communications that explained how government mattered to all aspects of their lives—by legalizing unions and regulating corporations and workplaces and by delivering services and benefits to them and their families.

Civic Engagement Through Union Publications

Union magazines and newsletters went beyond reporting on local events, community groups, and union contracts and business to convey a lot of information about the workings of government at all levels. Some information might seem of small consequence, as when the August 1966 issue of the "Aliquippa Steelworker" included a "Know the Law" section to tell members about the year's regulations on small game hunting: "The Pennsylvania Game Commission, in Harrisburg on June 11, 1966, established the following seasons and bag limits for resident game and furbearers for the 1966–1967 hunting license year which begins September 1," explained Matt Kostelic, the co-chair of the Local 1211 Conservation, Fishing, and Hunting Club.[66] Nevertheless, in this column, the local union gains credibility by informing members about what otherwise might be relatively opaque legal regulations governing a favorite pastime for families in western Pennsylvania. Many union men cared about this topic and used this information, and they did not have to look far to find it (see, e.g., figure 2.7).

More clearly relevant to major national and partisan affairs, the IBEW international magazine frequently ran multipage articles that simply sought to explain various functions of the federal government to members. The January 1955 article entitled, "This Is Your Government: The Department of Justice," explained what the Department of Justice does and how it is relevant to citizens.[67] The July 1955 issue did the same with the Treasury Department. Both local and international unions took on the responsibility of educating members about their government—something that may not happen in schools or through any other institutional channel. This coverage encouraged members to become more invested in their government, but it also meant that, when it came to interacting with the government, members often turned to their union for help and advice.

Examples of this phenomenon abound. Newsletters frequently ran informational sections about how to access benefits such as Social Security, unemployment compensation, or

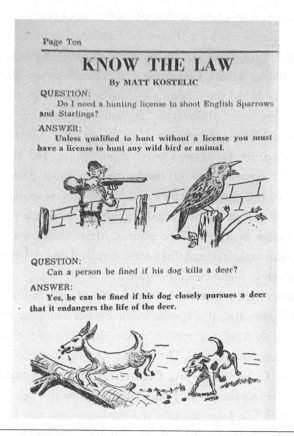

FIGURE 2.7 USW Local 1211 newsletter, "Aliquippa Steelworker,"
October 1962.

veteran's services. Local unions often took on the responsibility of advocating for workers who were having trouble with such benefits. In the November 1966 issue of the "Aliquippa Steelworker," the front page of the newsletter reassures workers and retirees attempting to access Medicare benefits that the union is working to make the process more transparent for them. In a previous newsletter, the union explained "how Medicare would operate and then explained how payments to the doctors are made." The November newsletter reports, "Since then however we have met with much confusion and misunderstanding in many areas of the Medicare program and our Local Union is making an effort to untangle this mess of confusion if we may so name it."[68] The executive board of the union pledged to do everything possible to help clarify the process for members, even saying the union would work with the congressional representative of the district to address the difficulties that members were facing.

In twenty-first-century America, people's preferred news outlets are a highly predictive indicator of their political affiliations. Several of our retired interviewees mentioned now ascendant conservative news outlets to explain the Republican bent of many white working-class union members. Echoing what social scientific studies show more systematically, one older informant observed that "right-wing talk radio tends to be on at travel times and sometimes you're driving 2 hours . . . the outrageous sensationalist stuff gets people's ear. I think that's had a big influence on people's vote." Not only is highly biased partisan broadcasting a relatively new phenomenon—because from 1949 to 1987, the Fairness Doctrine required all broadcast television and radio to present both sides of contentious political issues—Rust Belt workers also used to get more of their news-related information from union newsletters, labor newspapers, local newspapers, and, of course, word of mouth.

In areas in which there were workers enrolled in many different unions, local labor newspapers were often jointly funded by unions in the area (see figures 2.8 and 2.9). One interviewee, who went on to work for the UE as a political cartoonist, told us about growing up in a "very labor-centric culture" in Racine, Wisconsin. He became interested in drawing labor-related

FIGURE 2.8 USW Local 1211 newsletter, "Aliquippa Steelworker,"
August 1966.

FIGURE 2.9 USW Local 1211 newsletter, "Aliquippa Steelworker,"
August 1978.

political cartoons from reading the local labor paper as a child,
called the *Racine Labor Paper*, published weekly and later
biweekly from 1941 to 2001.[69] Eventually this paper shut down
like many other labor newspapers, when subscriptions dried
up as plants closed and union membership declined. During
their years of publication, however, labor papers were important
sources of information not only for workers but also for their
families and the community.

In addition to local labor papers and the monthly magazines
that international unions sent to all members, many locals also

had their own newsletters, like the "Aliquippa Steelworker" newsletter serving members and families of USW Local 1211. These were closed-circuit information-providing enterprises from which members and families received selected information about their workplace, community, region, and country. Whereas international union magazines addressed general topics in order to appeal to a broader readership, local union newsletters were community-specific. Because they reached and wrote about peers, local union newsletters were ideal vehicles for the sorts of influence that scholars, such as political scientist Betsy Sinclair, argue that social networks can have on members.[70] Along with delivering contextualized information, such communications subtly encouraged readers to conform to union expectations. Opening such a newsletter, readers immediately encountered clear depictions of how union men and their families were expected to conduct themselves. "No Local 5 member should be seen driving a foreign car," is a bolded catchphrase in almost every IBEW Local 5 newsletter from the late 1970s. "Buy a Ford product and save a job," is a frequent blurb in the UAW Local 600 newsletter. Also frequent were "Don't Buy" lists—sometimes featuring cartoons such as the one in figure 2.10 from the November 1966 "Aliquippa Steelworker."

In the context of locally grounded union ties, such communications meant that worker support for candidates and policies considered "pro-labor" was hardly determined solely by individuals' isolated choices. Social expectations were apparent, and discussions were ongoing among equals. As one eighty-year-old retired steelworker said, "You could not go to the steel mill or mine and find a guy who would vote for a Republican. It was just a given. They figure that there was not a Republican in the world who took care of a working guy." Most workers held such

FIGURE 2.10 USW Local 1211 newsletter, "Aliquippa Steelworker,"
November 1966.

views because they had seen Democrats and Republicans take
positions on laws and social benefits they cared about—and they
knew that happened in part from union publications. Most people in their horizontal social networks read, heard, and believed
similar things. When individual workers voted for Democrats,
that did not happen because some top leader at a Washington,
DC, international headquarters told them to do so. In many
unionized industries and regions, such as western Pennsylvania
steel country, workers voted for Democrats because of constantly
reinforced involvements that informed who they were—because
of their social identities as union men or union family members and their regional identities as good neighbors in union-
influenced communities.

Even at the height of labor union influence, many union members expressed reservations about formal union involvements in politics. In a 1955 internal USW survey, most of the rank-and-file respondents felt that the union should *not* get involved in political campaigning. More than 70 percent agreed that the union "can't do much to help the members by getting mixed up in political activities." Twenty-seven percent of members did feel that the union could help *inform* their votes by giving them information about the records of political candidates. But when it came to directions aimed at influencing candidacies or the votes of members, the union hierarchy, even then, was met with resistance. "I do not believe in such things as political donations, sending delegates to inaugurations (political) and other such foolish expenditures," says one respondent in the open-ended portion of the survey. "I am a firm believer in unions, but the unions as run today, both local and nationa [*sic*] dabble to [*sic*] much in politics," comments another respondent. "I think the union is spending to [*sic*] much time and money supporting political candidates," states a third.[71]

Although we can take such survey comments with a grain of salt, they do suggest that union organizational resources and supralocal endorsements were not the reason most union members and their families voted for Democrats. Union members and families voted as they did as part of ongoing commitments to their fellow workers and their communities. Union political clout flowed through relations among workers and between them and their family members and community peers. Because of the union, "everyone knew the rules" of the industry, as one retiree told us, and workers did not need to compete with one another for a day's work. Local unions bolstered community relations by being highly involved and connected to community organizations and events. The political nature of unions was important to members insofar as unions worked through such channels and used communications to give members information about candidates' records and the impact of actual or potential government policies. Nevertheless, rank-and-file members never wanted to feel that the union was dictating vote choices to them.

Social-Political Union Influence

Most of us would like to believe that our identities and political beliefs are based solely on our values and opinions. Midcentury unionists in USW and beyond were like most Americans in this regard, certainly in their resistance to top-down direction about their citizen choices, including voting choices. Still, people are not isolated decision makers; our ongoing social networks and communities play a significant role in how we develop identities and are drawn into social and political commitments. Sociologist Ziad Munson's landmark study on individuals in the prolife movement found that a plurality of members originally became involved in the movement not because of an intrinsic passion for it but because they attended prolife events with friends.[72] Some of our interviewees discussed the same phenomenon but with regard to the union. One current Steelworker told us about how she got involved in union political activities:

> I got hired in the area that just so happened to be where the union grievance chair worked also. She was very interesting and enticing to work with . . . she literally tricked me into my first union meeting. She said, "What are you doing after work?" and I said, "Nothing," and then she took me to the union meeting. Once you're in it and friends with people, it's an addiction, you start

volunteering, I've been on everything imaginable. From there, I got involved in the political aspect, going to Washington and lobbying. I'm still involved in Rapid Response [a USW political education program].

This Steelworker wasn't the only one who got politically involved with the union through friends. One young Steelworker to whom we spoke joined the leadership of his local because another worker with whom he was friends asked him for help. Experiencing an appealing sense of community, he stuck with it. A report from an IBEW local in Frankfort, Indiana, sent to the international magazine in 1975 explained the importance of hosting social engagements. Tony Rainaldi, the organizer of a union bowling tournament, explained, "You'd be surprised what this means to our people. I've seen many members become involved in their union through its sports activities."[73] Friend-to-friend, member-to-member links like this pay off for both unions and the Democratic Party.

This chapter has laid out arguments we will carry further in chapters to come. As we've described, union men were united by shared commitments to one other, their history, and their industry or trade. For many midcentury union members, multistrand involvements through families and communities as well as workplaces sustained a union identity that was much more than a formality or an economic convenience. That shared identity laid the basis for powerful, emotionally grounded social identities and political loyalties. Union roots mattered as much as, or more than, union bureaucracies.

Of course, major unions like the United Steelworkers and many others reached peaks of membership and cultural and political clout only shortly before they suffered reverses starting in the 1970s. The decline of Big Labor, as we are about to see, entailed not only upheavals in regional industries and dwindling resources for organized labor. Communities and local ties were also affected, which in turn affected the social loyalties, self-esteem, and political beliefs of many union members who lived through that decline or started working in its aftermath.

3

THE ECONOMIC BREAKDOWN
OF BIG LABOR FROM
WITHOUT AND WITHIN

On Labor Day, September 1, 1958, President Walter
Reuther of the United Auto Workers (UAW)
declared that American unions had achieved the self-
actualization of the working man—something no other economic
system had experienced before. Organized labor, he proclaimed,
had managed to allow American workers to become the first to
be afforded material and economic success along with the ability to advocate for themselves and control their work environment, at least to some degree. "Thus we are at a place," Reuther
declared, "where we can begin to devote more time and greater
resources to facilitate man's growth as a social, cultural and spiritual being and bring to fulfillment man's higher aspirations."[1]

In the apex of the era in which Big Labor was respected as a
major national force, Reuther's speech was broadcast at prime
time across the nation.[2] Reuther surely reflected—and gave voice
to—the feelings of many unionized workers at the time: solidarity, strength, and the desire to look toward the future, aiming
to build on what organized labor had already gained. During
the middle of the twentieth century, union workers had either
experienced firsthand or heard secondhand about the abomi-
nable working conditions prior to mass organizing efforts and

labor reform. Reuther's Labor Day speech played on the contrast between those times and the 1950s. When workers were just trying to feed their families, they could not really concern themselves with fulfilling "man's higher aspirations" or facilitating his "social, cultural and spiritual being." But by the late 1950s, with the advancements in quality of work and life that unions had achieved, many workers could aspire to more lofty goals for themselves and for America as a whole.

For some time after the 1950s, U.S. unionized labor appeared in many ways to have made major gains and be poised to do more. This heyday of organized labor has been well documented by labor historians and social scientists. In the mid-twentieth century, "over a third of the non-agricultural workforce belonged to a labor union . . . and millions more Americans resided in households reliant on a union wage."[3] Around 1960, approximately 186 unions were organized into more than 78,000 union locals across the country, with a total of over 18 million members.[4] The biggest unions at this time, in descending order, were the International Brotherhood of Teamsters (IBT), the United Steel Workers (USW), the UAW, the International Association of Machinists (IAM), the United Brotherhood of Carpenters (UBC), the International Brotherhood of Electrical Workers (IBEW), and the United Mine Workers of America (UMWA) (see table 3.1).[5] Together these seven unions accounted for roughly 15 percent of American male jobs in 1960, but a far higher percentage in the industrial heartland, where about 40 percent of *citizens*—counting both men and women—were members of unions.[6] The relative strength of union presence around 1960 stands in sharp contrast to what was to come. Four decades later, in 2000, the biggest seven unions of the mid-twentieth century would no longer be the largest nationwide, and their members would account for less than 4 percent of the U.S. labor force.[7]

TABLE 3.1 MEMBERSHIP TRENDS IN MAJOR U.S. INDUSTRIAL UNIONS

Union	Membership 1960	Membership 2000
International Brotherhood of Teamsters (IBT)	1,484,433	1,402,000
United Steel Workers (USW)	1,152,000	612,157
United Automobile Workers (UAW)	1,136,140	700,000
International Association of Machinists (IAM)	898,139	670,000
United Brotherhood of Carpenters (UBC)	800,000	531,000
International Brotherhood of Electrical Workers (IBEW)	771,000	720,000
United Mine Workers of America (UMWA)	600,000	100,000

Sources: Andrew Wallender, "Teamsters Membership Drops While SEIU Numbers Rise in 2019," *Bloomberg Law*, April 23, 2020, https://news.bloomberglaw.com /daily-labor-report/teamsters-membership-drops-while-seiu-numbers-rise -in-2019; UnionFacts.com.

Although it could not be known at the time, the bold picture Reuther painted in 1958 was destined to prove closer to a high point for union clout in the United States than an opening for future advances. Economic and technological winds would soon shift in both the U.S. and global economies, with impacts starting to be felt by workers in the 1970s. By the 1980s and beyond, U.S. government choices and laws would add insult to economic injuries, further undermining the gains and future potential of organized labor. Within two decades of Reuther's speech, many of the once mighty international unions named in table 3.1 were already experiencing major declines in membership and closings or consolidations of shrinking locals, and most of the international unions not already experiencing contraction would follow downward paths by 2000.

Changes continued past the turn of the twenty-first century as all the major industrial unions and many other U.S. blue-collar unions lost more and more members. The numbers of industrial union locals declined significantly during the first decades after 2000. By 2010, union density—the proportion of employees unionized relative to the overall working population—was greater in the U.S. public sector among salaried workers such as teachers than it was among blue-collar industrial workers and traditional tradespeople who had once been at the vanguard of union strength. This shift was especially apparent across the Rust Belt, in regions such as western Pennsylvania where heavy industry had been king. By 2019, the largest U.S. union had become the National Education Association (NEA); followed by the Service Employees International Union (SEIU); the American Federation of State, County, and Municipal Employees (AFSCME); IBT; and the United Food and Commercial Workers International Union (UFCW).[8]

To explore this massive set of economic and organizational shifts further, we start by drawing on work by scholars of U.S. political economy to flesh out the mid-century clout of blue-collar organized labor and the ways economic and political shifts have undermined union clout from the 1970s to today. Then we pivot from a big picture analysis to look more closely at the reactions and unraveling that simultaneously unfolded in communities where unions and unionists were once a keystone presence. This shift in perspective makes sense because crucial local and individual-level changes accompanied the weakening of the formal powers of organized Big Labor. We will also show that industrial changes and union decline did not happen without grassroots pushback. In western Pennsylvania, strong community-level roots for unions enabled powerful efforts to resist and adapt to threatening changes. But ultimately, most such grassroots efforts proved unsuccessful—and as they faltered, people's support for union ideals declined, even among workers who remained employed in unionized enterprises. Surviving blue-collar unions thereafter became less central to workers' social lives and political outlooks.

BIG LABOR'S BRIEF ASCENDANCY

The long-term rise and fall of U.S. industrial prowess is a crucial backdrop to union fortunes in this country. A look back in time tells us that nineteenth-century American unionization happened, when it did at all, chiefly in craft trades such as shoemaking and carpentry. Attempts at mass union organizing did not advance significantly until well into the Industrial Revolution, and neither craft nor industrial organizing proceeded quickly or made linear progress given adverse legal conditions and fierce business opposition. Expanding mass production and factory work, however, eventually offered more openings for unions. Many workers were physically centralized under a single roof at large factories or mills, where work was dangerous and hours were long.

After the Wagner Act was passed by Congress and signed by President Franklin Delano Roosevelt in 1935, unionization of industrial workers skyrocketed. The act "required businesses to bargain in good faith with any union supported by the majority of their employees," giving unions vital legal protection as organizing units.[9] Growth in union density during the late 1930s and 1940s was fueled by more friendly laws on unionization and by the increase of material production that was necessary for the war effort. Unions in manufacturing industries especially grew during these years. The UAW, for example, had 195,000 members in 1937. By 1944, it had well over one million.[10]

Industrial manufacturing unions, as we have seen, became the largest in the country. Of the seven largest U.S. unions as of 1960 (see table 3.1) only one, IBT, was not concentrated in construction or industrial manufacturing. In their mid-twentieth-century heyday, America's mightiest international unions wielded great economic and political influence—including USW with its national headquarters in Pittsburgh and twenty-nine regional districts covering the United States and Canada around 1960. Western Pennsylvania was at the center of union influence in that period. Around 1960, our research area of twenty western Pennsylvania counties was home to over 100 USW locals across six of the international union's districts—the thirteenth, fifteenth, sixteenth, nineteenth, twentieth, and twenty-first.[*]

With dues-paying members employed across the Rust Belt, the formal power of unions was undergirded by two major tools: the ability to bargain collectively on behalf of workers and the threat of striking if employers balked. Through collective bargaining coupled with explicit or implicit threats to go on strike, unions were able to negotiate with even the most powerful corporate employers for better wages. Negotiations happened every few years, and unions could advance new sets of demands; they could also refrain from accepting a contract until management accommodated many of them. Because significant shares of workers were unionized in key industries by the end of World War II, unions had the ability to turn off the switch for major

---

[*]The number of local unions, it should be noted, is distinct from the number of local union *halls*. As noted in the previous chapter, there were an estimated 37 USW union halls in western Pennsylvania in 1960, but there were many more union locals that would use various community spaces or other locals' halls to meet.

sectors of the American economy. Such possibilities were particularly daunting during wartime, when domestic production of materials was important not only to the market economy but also to national security. The World War II–era National Defense Mediation Board is a microcosm of what sociologist Jake Rosenfeld refers to as the mid-twentieth-century "tripartite": the conjunction of a powerful labor sector represented by unions, an engaged regulatory state, and a relatively consolidated group of large-scale private-sector employers consisting of companies such as U.S. Steel and General Motors.[11] Because workers at most of these large-scale employers were unionized, cooperation between companies and unions was vital to the war effort. The tripartite arrangement set the stage for years of government-business-labor relations: begrudging cooperation, at the minimum, was essential.

Collective bargaining is the primary—or according to some, the only—formal responsibility with which unions are tasked. And indeed, collective bargaining makes a big difference. Researchers who have studied the estimated 35 percent increase in American male income inequality since the late 1970s attribute much of it to union decline and the accompanying erosion of bargaining capacities.[12] Stagnant wages and benefits have hurt the remaining unionized workers and others in their regions and industries as well. Nevertheless, collective bargaining is only one form of labor's influence. Beyond functioning as a set of organizations pushing for improved economic and workplace standards in specific employment contracts, unions amassed political influence both electorally and as advocates of public policies that reinforced their own prerogatives and frequently sought to help workers and citizens in general.

Although party-union ties never became as formalized in the United States as they did in many European countries with dedicated social democratic and labor parties, American organized labor did become what political scientist Daniel Schlozman calls an "anchoring movement" for Democrats in many of the non-Southern states and certainly across the Rust Belt.[13] Because such a sizable percentage of the mid-twentieth-century American workforce was unionized, politicians had to be wary of the union vote. As of 1952, about 60 percent of union members identified as Democrats, and most of the rest labeled themselves as independents who in practice leaned Democratic.[14] Thus, Democratic Party candidates tended to court—and listen to—unions that enrolled so many voters open to their party's messages.

Union members not only leaned toward Democrats; they also voted at higher rates than nonunion members. Even in the mid-1950s, when electoral turnout was at a modern high, union membership increased the chances that an individual would go to the polls. In 1958, a midterm election year, for example, self-reported national turnout among nonunionized individuals was 56 percent, compared to 69 percent for union members.[15] This same election year gave Democrats a 64 to 34 majority in the Senate as well as control of the House.

Republicans knew that union loyalty encouraged Democratic support because they, like members of the public, could hardly overlook the advocacy of local and international unions every election cycle. Local union newsletters urged members to support their candidates in national and state elections, in some cases, urging members to do so explicitly by saying in big, bold print to "Make it emphatic! Vote Straight 'D' This November." Hoping to peel off at least a handful of sympathetic voters, many Republicans used public praise and sometimes legislative action to reach out to union members. Although GOP platforms were not outwardly supportive of organized labor, many Republicans had cooperative relationships with organized labor during the mid-twentieth century. In 1952, for example, Dwight Eisenhower declared that "only a handful of unreconstructed reactionaries harbor the ugly thought of breaking unions," signaling to union members that, although he was a Republican, he would not think of going against organized labor.[16] In 1970, President Richard Nixon invited labor leaders and their spouses to the White House for an extravagant dinner and that same year signed the Occupational Safety and Health Act, which is still today counted as a defining legislative victory for the labor movement.[17] Republican president Gerald Ford then signed legislation to protect the pensions of laid-off workers.[18]

The fact that Republican policymakers repeatedly acknowledged union priorities was testament to labor's collective political strength grounded in worker loyalties. Had union voters been less loyal to each other, to their organizations, and in general to Democrats who were seen as allied with unions, Republicans would not have bothered to appease labor leaders or praise union members. Without such union power, midcentury Democrats may have been tempted to appease business leaders, dance around union issues, or try to win votes in other ways, as they often do today.

Union density peaked in 1954, with 35 percent of workers across the country belonging to a labor union—with even higher shares in the Rust Belt.[19] High membership rates meant that unions had the resources and numbers to threaten or conduct strikes in support of collective bargaining and also to mount electoral and lobbying campaigns. Unions could not only defend and further their own interests but they could also build sufficient clout to advocate on behalf of broader egalitarian goals. By the 1960s, the United States had achieved the highest overall living standards of any nation throughout history.[20] This progress occurred in many domains and for many reasons, but among the driving forces were most certainly the efforts of major blue-collar labor unions in advocating for increased standards of work and life for their members.

As African American and other equal rights movements gathered steam in American society and politics in the 1960s and 1970s, industrial union leaders were, little by little, going beyond advocating for members and workers regardless of race, ethnicity, and gender to offer broader support for regulatory and affirmative action measures. The process was slow. Scholars such as Dennis C. Dickerson, author of *Out of the Crucible: Black Steelworkers in Western Pennsylvania, 1875–1880*, have documented that, faced with reluctance among rank-and-file white workers, many leaders in USW and other internationals needed considerable prodding to support full Black occupational and civil rights.[21] Some leaders in big industrial unions, especially Congress of Industrial Organizations (CIO) figures such as Walter Reuther, were progressive on racial equity issues all along. Nevertheless, as Big Labor reached its apogee, many international union leaders were only starting to move beyond modest gestures (such as appointing Black unionists to advisory positions). Then, when countervailing forces kicked in to weaken industrial international unions, union leaders and activists not only faced setbacks in their ongoing efforts to enhance worker well-being across the board but they also lost potential to add crucial new heft to civil rights coalitions.

MARKET SHIFTS AND POLITICAL TURNAROUNDS

In retrospect, we can see clearly that the predictions in Reuther's 1958 speech did not come to pass as he and other union leaders hoped. Not long after blue-collar Big Labor gained sufficient national clout to flex its muscles in core market sectors and public policymaking, union fortunes took a downturn. Economic and technological forces were certainly at work as America's shift from an industrial to a service economy weakened many unions. Unions involved with core mass production industries were hurt the most, especially those with locals that were tied to industrial plants. Yet economic and technological changes were not automatic or simply impersonally foreordained. By the 1980s, powerful elite forces redirected politics and government in ways that sped up and worsened the decline of unions.

Many explanations have been offered for American industrial decline. For steel and adjacent sectors, analysts argue that U.S. corporations did not update aging mill technology and thus lost their innovative edge and failed to keep up with foreign competition.[22] International shifts also had an impact on steel production and demand, including the Organization of the Petroleum Exporting Countries (OPEC) embargo of the 1970s.[23] Similar to the steel industry, the American auto industry began to face increasingly serious foreign competitors, such as Honda and Toyota, beginning in the 1970s. When Congress imposed a limitation on the number of imported cars in 1981, Japanese companies built facilities in the United States to circumvent restrictions. Although these facilities provided some American jobs, they were almost always nonunion jobs, which functioned to drive down industry working standards. As of 2021, no foreign automaker had plants in the United States represented by UAW or any other union.[24]

In other sectors of the economy, industrial decline was spurred by the offshoring of American jobs, changing environmental and trade regulations, and the advancement of energy technology. In the late 1970s, President Deng Xiaoping of China opened the Chinese economy and labor market to foreign companies. The lack of labor regulations meant that employing a Chinese manufacturing workforce and shipping goods back to the United States was often less expensive than producing goods domestically.[25] Increased environmental regulations in the United States, beginning in the 1970s, further incentivized the offshoring of manufacturing industries. The 1980s and 1990s brought in a new era of international trade fostered by various trade agreements, including the Canada-U.S. Free Trade Agreement of 1988 and NAFTA, the North American Free Trade Agreement of 1994. These and other agreements made between the United States and foreign states increased the ease with which U.S. companies could employ foreign labor and import goods manufactured in other countries. In the energy industry, fracking significantly affected the cost-benefit analysis of coal mining, and where mining has remained, fewer workers were needed due to advancements in technology.[26] The combination of regulatory, economic, environmental, and international changes contributed to the overall decrease of U.S. manufacturing beginning in the 1970s and lasting through today.

Although some may argue that such changes were inevitable, they are not the whole story because U.S. political leaders often made fateful policy moves that also undercut industrial manufacturing. Political choices at critical junctures can make a difference, as we saw in 2009 when President Barack Obama decided to use $80 billion of taxpayer money to bail out the automobile industry.[27] In contrast, during the late 1970s and early 1980s, no such actions were taken to help the floundering steel industry, despite pleas for help from various stakeholders. President Jimmy Carter rejected a $10 billion modernization plan for the steel industry, believing, as many policymakers did at the time, that the waning of the U.S. steel industry was simply inevitable.[28] Carter also declined to provide financial support for a group of community members who wanted to take over the Youngstown steel mill via eminent domain.[29] Because of what was *not* done, politics as well as shifting technological and market forces deepened the crisis of U.S. heavy industry.

Affirmative policy also mattered. Quite a few leading Democratic and Republican politicians, along with pundits and scholars, advocated for a hastening of the inevitable "modernization" process of the U.S. economy from industry to service as the basis for American jobs and revenue.[30] Before long, members of the GOP and corporate leaders shifted from passive observers to active participants in the decline of both domestic industry and organized labor. In August 1981, conservative Republican president Ronald Reagan delivered an ultimatum to a group of over 12,000 striking air traffic controllers. Go back to work or you are fired, he told them. Never before had a U.S. government leader given workers this type of ultimatum. Under the National Labor Relations Act of 1935, private-sector workers are guaranteed the right to strike, but rights and rules for public-sector employees are less clear cut. The Professional Air Traffic Controllers Organization (PATCO) was overseen by the federal authorities because its workers were employed by the Federal Aviation Authority (FAA). Thus, the top executive to whom the PATCO members reported was the president himself—who gave workers forty-eight hours to decide whether to abandon their strike. Despite knowing that they would lose their jobs, the vast majority of air traffic controllers held the line: they refused to go back to work by the 11:00 A.M. deadline that Reagan had set.[31] Part of what led to such defiant solidarity was likely collective resentment. PATCO had endorsed Reagan in the 1980 election after he promised to support FAA employees in their quest for better working conditions. Many air traffic controllers were understandably angry when Reagan renounced his apparent commitment to them.

PATCO workers did not prevail, however, and their 1981 strike proved costly—and not just for them. In addition to some 11,000 air traffic controllers being fired and barred from working in their industry for years (until President Bill Clinton lifted the ban in 1993), organized labor as a whole suffered in the years that followed. The breaking of the PATCO strike marked a downward trajectory of organized labor's power because President Reagan's actions signaled a hardening elite consensus that, in disputes between management and unions, management could and should hold out and even *break* the union. As the Reagan administration restructured labor regulations to allow for more loopholes that recalcitrant managements could exploit, companies adopted more aggressive tactics—sometimes even provoking strikes and then hiring replacement workers.[32] Strikes became less common, and thus even the threat of striking carried less weight in collective bargaining. During 1955 there were 363 work stoppages involving over 1,000 workers; three decades later, in 1985, there were only fifty-four stoppages.[33] After 1981—at least until 2022 in the aftermath of the COVID-19 pandemic—work stoppages declined to a rate of no more than one hundred per year. In 2022, there were twenty-three work stoppages.[34] In turn, union leverage in collective bargaining waned in the absence of credible possibilities to mount strikes.

When union market power faltered, political forces shifted against unions too. Before Reagan, many Republicans had reluctantly worked with or at least tolerated unions, but mainstream GOP and corporate stances shifted after 1981 when corporations, conservative interest groups, and Republican policymakers sought not only to undermine union legal and market leverage but also adopted many new political tactics to weaken worker union ties and loyalties.

In key respects, of course, the Reagan era simply crystallized and made nationally explicit the antiunion elite efforts that, since the Wagner Act, had been gaining organizational ground for some time. In the 1950s, business leaders organized a group to crush unionization efforts. Edwin Dillard, the executive of a Southern paper manufacturing company, led confidential meetings, which culminated in 1954 in the organization of the National Right to Work Committee.[35] This committee was inspired by the passage of the Taft-Hartley Act of 1947, which had asserted that "employees had the right to refrain from participating in unions,"[36] effectively prohibiting workplaces from hiring only union workers.

The Taft-Hartley Act also included a provision that allowed, if not encouraged, states to pass their own right-to-work laws, which allow workers represented by unions to refrain from paying union dues. The National Right to Work Committee then pursued the enactment of right-to-work laws across the country. Beyond weakening unions' resource deployment abilities— principally their collective bargaining power—right-to-work legislation was intended to break down social and political solidarity among workers. With right-to-work legislation, workers could become titular "members" of the union, but they did not have real skin in the game. Everyone was still protected by the union, but not everyone paid dues. This was an important issue because for many midcentury members, paying union dues was about more than simply spending some personal income to further economic gains from collective bargaining. Many union members proudly wore pins like the ones from USW and IBEW displayed in figure 3.1 to show their support for something bigger than an income boost to coworkers, neighbors, and friends.

Antiunion forces historically were—and still are—highly intertwined with plutocrats in elite conservative circles intent

FIGURE 3.1 (a) USW (then USA) "Dues Paid by Check-Off" pins ca. 1953–60. (b) IBEW dues pin ca. 1962. Theda Skocpol personal collection.

on maintaining power among the few. In the beginning, the leaders of the National Right to Work Committee had success in Southern states where the history of labor was marked by the generations-long struggle of Black people—formerly enslaved and then ruthlessly discriminated against—to gain any rights whatsoever. Southern states were more amenable to right-to-work legislation that restricted the ability of the underclass labor force to advocate for itself. Over time, however, what were once considered radically conservative efforts to undercut workers' rights to organize for collective gains became more widespread.

The National Right to Work Committee's right-to-work campaign turned out to be just one example of elite conservative lobbying efforts that would take center stage in Republican policy agendas. The committee's first big win was in the state of Kansas, where, in 1958, right-to-work legislation was passed via constitutional amendment. Financial support for the legislation was provided by Fred Koch, the Wichita-based oil baron and father of today's infamous conservative donors Fred (Jr.) and Charles Koch.[37] Less than a month after the right-to-work amendment was passed into law in Kansas, Koch, along with other prominent conservatives, founded the John Birch Society.[38] To this day, the John Birch Society promotes deeply conservative ideas that were "once on the fringe" but are now "increasingly commonplace."[39] In its early years, there was significant overlap between the John Birch Society and the National Right to Work Committee. At times, the groups were even led by the same individuals.[40] Since the senior Fred Koch initially became involved in the right-to-work campaign in 1950s Kansas, Koch money has augmented other right-wing funding to spread right-to-work legislation across the country. When the next generation of Kochs took over in the 1980s, other monied organizations on the political right made breaking unions a key policy priority.

At first, progress—as defined by the conservative interests seeking to break labor unions—was gradual. Between 1980 and 2010, only Oklahoma and Idaho became right-to-work states, but this three-decade span nevertheless proved foundational for conservative elite efforts to dismantle union power in core labor strongholds. Founded in 1973, the American Legislative Exchange Council grew in scale and deepened in conservatism from the mid-1990s onward. The State Policy Network was founded in 1992, and Americans for Prosperity was founded by the Koch brothers in 2004 as a successor to the brothers' original organization called Citizens for a Sound Economy. These organizations developed close ties with state legislators and donors in the early twenty-first century, which became highly apparent in national politics in the 2010s. From the peak of the Tea Party movement to the precipice of the Trump era, six historically union blue states in America's industrial heartland—Michigan, Wisconsin, Missouri, Indiana, Kentucky, and West Virginia— became right-to-work states in swift succession.

UNITY DISSOLVES FROM WITHIN

"Unions are about making a living in your community," one retired union electrician aptly told us. "But people today are less connected that way. People are less connected to their community— by ethnicity, religion, and even geography." When, in 2015, Edwin D. Hill announced his retirement from serving as president of IBEW, he reflected on community relations among unionists in the twenty-first century versus the mid-twentieth century. He commented:

> When I was a young man coming up through the ranks in Pennsylvania, every town had two or three union halls. Weddings, community meetings and other affairs would be held there. Union meetings were a place one went for camaraderie, not just to discuss the problems of the day. Along with the union halls were clubs of all types. Today, too many union halls are closed down.

The remaining ones often turn out only a few members for meetings. And clubs are dwindling. But the need to be our brother's and sister's keeper is still there.[41]

Hill's somber analysis of how union communities had changed by 2015 could not be further from Walter Reuther's comments on the power of collective unity among union families in the mid-twentieth century. Yet Hill offers an equally valuable perspective on the nature of midcentury industrial union influence.

As we have argued, union power rested not only on the resource capacities of the giant industrial international unions but also on the community-based ties and loyalties of rank-and-file union members, their families, and their neighbors. It follows that a large part of what happened as labor ascendency turned into labor decline occurred within communities and regions, such as the western Pennsylvania region of big steel and associated industries and unions. Thus, we turn now to the unfolding stories in this region, beginning with a close look at collaborative community efforts spearheaded mainly by union leaders that attempted to save the industry and firms with which worker livelihoods and union solidarities were intertwined.

Given the strong community and regional moorings of USW in particular, we would not expect those workers to go quietly—and they did not. Across much of western Pennsylvania, unions marshalled entire communities to fight back, but in the end, efforts to save mills, plants, and mines were largely unsuccessful. As the late twentieth century progressed, unions struggled to regain lost ground. Companies viciously opposed unionization efforts, and some unionized plants moved or built new facilities in places inhospitable to labor organization. Industrial union organizations facing blue-collar membership declines expanded representation into other sectors of the economy. A new generation of workers, made anxious by manufacturing decline and unsure about the power of refurbished conglomerate unions to protect their jobs, began to place a higher value on individual job security and gains rather than communal union loyalty.

From Community Commitment to Collective Loss

"Adversity produces energy," declared a 1985 *Rolling Stone* article about the difficulties faced by unemployed steelworkers in southwestern Pennsylvania.[42] Indeed, fighting adversity can crystallize existing underlying potential for cohesion within organizations and the community at large. At the beginning of the period of industrial collapse in southwestern Pennsylvania, local union leadership stepped up to realize those potentials. Mike Stout, the former grievance man of USW Local 1397 in Homestead, Pennsylvania, wrote that in the final years of Local 1397's existence, the "union hall was a beehive of activity."[43] "With more layoffs looming," he continues, Local 1397 "continued its fight to make the union more effective . . . by initiating a number of new programs for the membership. . . . Sports programs and activities were revved up; bowling and basketball leagues were established, and the golf league was expanded to five teams. Alcoholic Anonymous meetings were held every week at the Local 1397 union hall. . . . In these years, union members were united by the hope of warding off a common threat: the demise of industry."

In the 1970s and 1980s, communities in Ohio and western Pennsylvania came together in a way not seen before. Local unions and labor activists spearheaded grassroots efforts to save the industrial jobs in the region by directing organizational efforts and filing legal claims of eminent domain to attempt to obtain worker ownership of closing plants. Throughout the multiple campaigns to save jobs, there was an outpouring of support for steelworkers and involvement from surrounding communities.

For reasons unrelated to the amount of community support, union pushback against industrial losses failed—and that failure sent a disheartening message to union communities nation-wide: when push comes to shove, it's not the union that controls your fate—it is the corporation. The failure of the campaigns understandably stoked anxiety among union members about the fundamental security of their jobs and livelihoods. Before the collapse, workers united for the betterment of their lives, fami-lies, and communities. During and after the collapse, the narra-tive became simply about jobs, and workers became much more preoccupied with preserving their own jobs than with advocat-ing for collective causes via the union. In the years that followed the collapse—and for the workers who remained—union loyalty took a backseat to a focus on the jobs themselves.

In western Pennsylvania, community members came together to oppose the closure of steel mills by forming two grassroots organizations to push for alternatives to plant shutdowns: the Tri-State Conference on Steel (TCS) and the Steel Valley Author-ity (SVA). A 1982 flyer for a series of workshops run by TCS described its method for saving jobs in the region: "By gathering local unions, churches, local government officials and small busi-ness to seriously discuss the many critical issues which face the Mon Valley, we believe a program and a strategy can be formed that will give us some reason to hope and ability to act."[44] The TCS grew out of the effort in Youngstown, Ohio, to save the Youngstown mill, which was ultimately unsuccessful. In 1983, the TCS focused its efforts on organizing the SVA, which was modeled after the Tennessee Valley Authority. Instead of being an agency of the federal government like the Tennessee Valley Authority, however, the SVA was designed to be a "locally controlled, government supported community corporation."[45] The overarching goal of SVA was to acquire, through eminent domain, one or more of the mills that were being shut down in the region.

In order to accomplish worker ownership over one or more southwestern Pennsylvania mills, TCS organizers saw community involvement as essential. Union leaders became leaders of TCS and SVA and used the social engagement tools in their arsenal to solicit support for the community takeover plans. Organizers hosted bingo nights, cabarets, and benefit concerts to garner support for saving the mills and plants during the 1980s. The grievance men, stewards, and presidents of local unions that were being threatened by the shutdowns took leadership roles in organizing the TCS and SVA. As one interviewee, a retired member of United Electrical, Radio, and Machine Workers (UE) told us, "I organized the communities north of the Mon [River], and the grievance man at 1397 [the USW local affiliated with Homestead Steel Works] organized the communities south of the Mon." Engagement efforts during these campaigns involved tying the survival of plants and local unions to other community institutions, such as churches, schools, city or borough councils, and businesses within the community.

The efforts of TCS and SVA hinged on getting various boroughs to help with plans to use eminent domain to take over the steel mills. The organizers of the efforts were therefore keenly aware of the importance of engaging and persuading community members that such plans were both possible and the only optimistic path forward. A newsletter recapping the activities of TCS in 1982 states, "Throughout the winter of 1982, we presented our slide show, Save the Mon Valley, Keep Steel in Pittsburgh, to different church groups, and other community organizations. Spring 1982: We assisted local union unemployed committees in setting up local food banks. May 1982: We held a conference at Steel Valley High School to explore programs to save the mills. . . . August 1982: We had a picnic for our members at South Park."[46] The newsletter continues discussing TCS events and activities throughout the year, emphasizing the importance of community engagement. These different activities—food banks, conferences, picnics—brought in the members of the local unions as key stakeholders in TCS and SVA organizing efforts and also brought union members closer to their communities.

Efforts to get the community on board were largely successful. Mike Stout, the former grievance man for USW 1397, said in an interview in 1986 that residents of the communities would come to meetings hosted by TCS doubtful of the organization's plans and leave "convinced that it might be the only solution." He continued, "I think that the town meetings—whether it was in Duquesne with 800 people, or McKeesport with 300, or Munhall with 250, or Homestead with 150, or whatever—were, in fact, probably some of the best, most positive things that the Tri-State coalition did."[47] Staughton Lynd, an attorney for TCS, wrote that "the breadth and depth of community support [that] was engendered around 'Dorothy' (the Duquesne plant)" was generally only produced "for football teams and incumbent Presidents of the United States."[48] Reflecting on TCS over thirty years later in his interview with us, one of the movement's leaders described the organizational effort of TCS as "quite the job." Because many of the communities around western Pennsylvania were so dependent on U.S. Steel or other industrial corporations for both jobs and community resources, it was difficult to convince residents and local officials that the best, and perhaps only, path forward was a community-owned corporation. But ultimately, as community members began to get a sense of what life was like without *any* large-scale mill or plant in their hometown, many residents and organizations got on board with the campaigns.

All these efforts were organized to save the jobs and livelihoods of western Pennsylvania unionized workers who were desperately struggling at this time. By 1983, 65,000 of the 90,000 basic steelworkers in the four-county area around Pittsburgh had already been laid off.[49] Despite initial excitement about the campaigns, shutdown after shutdown discouraged even those most loyal to the cause. As the campaigns wore on and more and more jobs were lost, belief in the "reason for hope" outlined in the 1982 TCS pamphlet dwindled. Community interconnectivity receded as workers and residents alike felt defeated.

The problem for the campaigns to save the mills was not legality or a lack of community support. In fact, it looked as though some of the campaigns might have been successful, "until we were redlined by Wall Street," a former steelworker told us. According to interviewees who had participated in the movement, the collective efforts failed because of moneyed interests; corporations were threatened by the idea of community-owned steel plants and sought to block the movement from succeeding. Workers, both those who were unemployed and the remaining who were employed, were overpowered. As one former TCS organizer said to us about this period:

> It was very discouraging because you rile up a whole community over saving a particular mill—after '79, when they shut down 13 mills at once, they began a method of shutting down a mill every couple months. They didn't want to give us a chance to build a large enough movement to make a difference. We organized and then we'd lose most of our activists. We had four or five major campaigns, but we couldn't unite the campaigns, because as it was dragged on or defeated, we had to shift.

As campaign after campaign to save the plants failed, people grew discouraged and community ties that were developed receded. It occurred to people that companies could pick up and leave when they wanted to, that even massive efforts by union members and residents could not preserve the jobs in the area. What persisted after this period of intense organizing were mostly social service institutions running food banks, unemployment centers, and the like in the former mill towns of western Pennsylvania.

Over time, community members also tired of giving to food banks and charities to support unemployed steelworkers and others. A *Pittsburgh Post-Gazette* article from February 1984 remarked that sources for food banks were "drying up" because "people who give are getting burnt out with it."[50] As unemployment continued through the 1980s, support waned for social initiatives such as food banks and community initiatives such as TCS campaigns. As a former UE member told us, "The Tri-State died out because . . . we kept losing, and because of the fact that so many people left [the region]."

The decline of the steel industry affected almost all other sectors of domestic manufacturing. By the mid-1980s, layoffs of auto workers by the tens of thousands were relatively frequent, and these layoffs affected hundreds of thousands of families in Michigan and other states of the Rust Belt.[51] Industrial collapse and mass layoffs showed that the company—not the union—controlled the fate of workers. The feeling of "you've got my back and I've got yours" from the union's heyday paled in comparison to what the company had: the ability to give and take a person and family's livelihood. More than anything, the decline of steel and other types of manufacturing across the Rust Belt resulted in a huge sense of *loss*: loss of resources, pride, and perhaps most important, community. As one retired steelworker said, "In the early seventies, the communities were good, the neighborhoods were nice. Let's face it, [now] the buildings are dilapidated, the houses are shot, there's drugs and crime. That's what happens when there's no community and people aren't working. We've really suffered quite a bit."

New Obstacles to Union Solidarity

Decades ago in western Pennsylvania, our retired interviewees told us that if they were laid off from one job, they could simply go across the street or down the road to a different mill, plant, or factory to get a new good-paying union job. Good jobs in the industrial Midwest were plentiful, and they were close to where people already lived. But toward the end of the century, manufacturing companies stopped building new factories in these regions. If there were any new facilities created in the United States at all, they were often built in antiunion states in the American South rather than in more densely unionized states such as Michigan or Pennsylvania. States like Virginia and North Carolina saw increases in manufacturing jobs, by up to 62 percent in some counties, from 1954 to 2002.[52] Meanwhile, states in the Rust Belt experienced manufacturing job losses at similar rates. In the 1980s and 1990s, Toyota built plants in Kentucky and Indiana in response to limits on imported cars. Since 2007, nine Southern states have produced more of America's gross domestic product than the nine states tradition-ally considered to be the Rust Belt, a drastic change from the mid-twentieth century.[53]

As a result of the economic and political changes of the latter half of the twentieth century, international unions experienced geographic and organizational side effects that hindered the extent to which community could be sustained or reconstructed based on local union membership. Even in places where unionized workplaces remained, the mill centers, mining surrounds, and other types of industrially focused communities common in the mid-twentieth century disappeared with the jobs that left the region. Such towns slowly became ghost towns, in the words of some of our interviewees, with main streets defined mostly by boarded-up storefronts. As a result, rather than most workers residing in town near the worksite, members of the same local union were spread out across many suburbs or exurbs. With fewer union jobs overall, funds from membership dues dwindled, leaving many surviving union locals unable to devote significant resources to social activities that were not essential for sheer organizational survival.

Manufacturing decline in the North, of course, decreased the number of union members in the region. But beyond the decline in numbers, worker dispersion made it harder for local union leaders to persuade rank-and-file members to be active or to attend union-sponsored activities and events. Older union members recall when blocks of neighborhoods were comprised of members of the same union. As one retired steelworker from southwestern Pennsylvania explained, the "majority of workers who worked in the mill back then lived in the surrounding communities . . . and that's not the case anymore. If you went to any steel mill in western Pennsylvania, I'd guess that 98 percent of the workers don't live in those communities anymore." A current USW member affirmed this retiree's point, noting that a lot of his coworkers commute far distances: "I work with guys who live in Ohio and West Virginia who commute to Irvin Works [a steel mill in southwestern Pennsylvania]. . . . If it's a good job, you're gonna make the drive." This phenomenon happened not only in western Pennsylvania in the latter part of the twentieth century but all across the country. In 1952, almost 50 percent of union workers lived in urban areas, compared to 30 percent in the suburbs. By 1998, these figures had flipped, with over 50 percent of union workers residing in the suburbs and less than 30 percent in the city.[54] Community dispersion can have profound effects on the sense of closeness among workers. Speaking of the typical union worker of the mid-twentieth century, political scientists Herbert Asher, Eric Heberlig, Randall Ripley, and Karen Snyder note:

> Among his neighbors were fellow union members, many of whom were coworkers in the same factory. They attended the same churches, their children attended the same schools, their stay-at-home wives exchanged recipes and baby-sitting favors, and they socialized together at neighborhood diners and bars. And their local union hall was a short distance from both their home and place of work. It was the site of frequent meetings, wedding receptions, weekend dances, and summertime potlucks. Factory, family, union, and neighbors were intertwined.[55]

By the late twentieth century, such local ties were gone. Coworkers commuting from West Virginia, Ohio, and Pennsylvania are unlikely to run into each other at parent-teacher meetings.

According to recent leaders of local unions in western Pennsylvania, members who are spread far and wide are less keen on going out of their way to attend union meetings or other noncompulsory union activities. To accommodate commuting members, some unions have tried to hold meetings right after work. As one recent USW local president stated, "We used to have meetings at 7:30 at night, but [members weren't coming], so we started having them right after work at 4:15. We tried cooking food, we tried to get pizzas, give tickets away or jackets—it still doesn't entice the people to come." This former local president estimated that friendship groups for workers in his union are now "70 percent [made up of people from their] home communities and 10 percent coworkers, maybe. That's pushing it," he added. That matters, because a chance to socialize with friends beyond work was likely a major incentive for members to attend union meetings in labor's heyday. After the official business of the meeting concluded, members would hang around the union hall with one another, sometimes with food or refreshments provided by the union. Now, because many workers' families live miles away and their social circles are comprised of people from their home communities, people either drive off right after work or leave quickly at the end of meetings. Leaders in turn find it that much harder to sustain or deepen engagement with the union among members who are minimally connected to one another.

Social engagement was a main priority for local unions for a long time. In a January 1985 write-in to IBEW's international magazine, IBEW Local 2145 provided a picture of members socializing with one another after the union meeting. Socializing "is just as important as the business at hand during the meeting," the caption of the photograph states.[56] Similarly, in 1980, when asked if UMW Local 6461 could use some of its funds for banquets and picnics, District 2 president Valerio Scarton responded via letter that using funding in such a way is acceptable "if the picnic and/or banquet is approved by the membership solely for the membership to promote one of the primary purposes of the Union, unity through social interaction."[57] Labor leaders of the mid-twentieth century were cognizant of the fact that social unity was a key means of achieving economic and political unity.

Union efforts to strengthen social unity were one of the first things to go, however, when unions began to struggle. In 1980,

District 2 of the UMW started an annual labor celebration that brought together numerous local unions, members of the religious community, and various honorees for a banquet and ceremony. Attendance at these labor celebrations peaked in 1983, when the *Johnstown Tribune-Democrat* reported that approximately six hundred people attended the event.[58] But by 1991, a series of handwritten notes that appear to have been from a meeting of the planning committee of the event—primarily comprised of labor members and members of the clergy—imply that it was no longer worthwhile to organize the labor celebration because "each year [there is] less and less participation."[59] One of the bullet points from the notes from the meeting for the 1991 labor celebration reads, "Locals don't have funds to participate."[60] Members and laid-off workers were requesting that the money used to fund the banquet instead be directed toward political advocacy efforts in Washington for unemployed workers. As more pressure was put on the union to fight to protect jobs, less emphasis was placed on socialization and community-building efforts.

During and especially after industrial collapse, members and former members of the unions were no longer able to socialize easily with one another. In the words of one interviewee, "The friends and all the socializing, for the most part, it was done." Even casual forms of socialization among members, which occurred in large part as a product of workers living within the same neighborhood, had mostly dissipated by the late twentieth and early twenty-first century. Some retirees still get together, though. "I still go hunting with the people I worked with," one steelworker retiree told us. "We still hang out. We go to the casino; the older guys still get together. One thing I always say, you never lose a friendship over a union job."

In the span of thirty years, labor went from endeavoring to "bring to fulfillment man's higher aspirations" to, according to one current UE member to whom we spoke, "just trying to survive . . . [not even] working on the bigger project of building a labor movement." The transfer of company facilities out of the region, the geographical dispersion of remaining employees, and reduced funding for social activities together kept unions in the Rust Belt from sustaining or recreating the sense of member community that had flourished at the height of Big Labor power and influence in the mid-twentieth century. Big Labor power was not just a matter of resourceful national bureaucracies and the sheer number of dues-paying members; it was rooted in local interactions and fellow good feeling. With thinner local roots and interactions now, the loyalties, goals, and ties of the unionized workers who remain have shifted—toward prioritizing job security over union loyalty and toward new outlooks and group involvements, if any, especially among younger recruits who never experienced the old union ways.

The Diversification of Occupational Representation

Another building block of union solidarity among industrial workers is also worth noting—the sense of shared experience in any given industry and type of job that we earlier called *occupational pride*. Steelworkers developed common bonds with other steelworkers, as did miners and autoworkers. Because unionists were always wary of nonunion workers taking their jobs, we noted earlier that the common bond among workers in the same industry became a product of one's industry *and* one's union membership, thereby bringing such workers closer to their unions as well as to one another. But this situation changed when industrial unions, now facing massive drops in the number of enrollees and dues, started negotiating mergers or looking for new economic sectors to organize—including in entirely unrelated industries and types of jobs. This could leave blue-collar unionists feeling less connected. As one interviewee put it, "The Steelworkers started [going into other industries] when the steel industry went down, they wanted to represent anyone they could so their union would survive."

Indeed, many mergers and jurisdictional expansions occurred in the aftermath of industrial decline. In 1985, the international executive board of the UMWA voted to approve the recommendation to incorporate other industries.[61] USW began ramping up mergers with smaller unions that represented different industries around the same time. USW merged with the United Stone and Allied Products Workers of America in 1971; in 1985, the Upholsterers International Union; in 1995, the United Rubber Workers. Since then, many other unions have merged with USW, but USW has also started simply organizing workers outside those industries—such as teachers, librarians, and nurses—as nominal "Steelworkers." UE now represents not only metal or electrical machine workers but also some teachers, grocery workers, and others. UMWA represents correctional officers, employees in Navajo Nation, and others. UAW has also expanded, representing, for instance, graduate students at Harvard University and museum workers in New York City. The building trades unions have largely resisted integrating with other industries or crafts, which we will discuss in chapter 4. Unions representing electrical workers, bricklayers, insulators, and other trades have kept organizing limited to their respective industry.

Some union members understand and accept that the expansion of their unions to unrelated fields is necessary to maintain influence as older industrial sectors shrink, but others feel that representing a more diverse group of employees skews the union's priorities. Now that "anyone can be a Steelworker—a librarian can be a Steelworker," as one interviewee commented, the union is less representative of its original members. In essence, the diversification of workers represented by industrial unions has likely contributed to members' detachment from their union, which is no longer a straightforward expression of *occupational pride*. Some traditional members feel less of a sense of social and political investment in the union. "The workers from the original UE and USW felt betrayed," one retiree told us in response to a question about how the diversification of industries affected older union members. Another said that workers felt the union was moving on and forgetting about them.

JOB SECURITY COMES FIRST NOW

In his song entitled "When the Heyday Was Here," the former grievance man of Local 1397 in Homestead, Pennsylvania, Mike Stout, writes, "You talk about gangs, we really had one. . . . When one of us was messed with, the others were right by their side."[62] Over the years, however, the sense of worker loyalty described by songwriter Stout declined. Beginning in the late 1970s, when layoffs and shutdowns began increasing in frequency, most workers wanted to protect their own job more than anything else. In the wake of the industrial collapse and the failed attempts of collective action to preserve jobs, economic and social individualism proliferated among members of industrial unions. As one former USW worker said to us, the plant closures, occurring one after another throughout the 1980s, "pitted workers against one another." In another interviewee's words, "survival instincts came out." In other words, the union was no longer unified— it was every man for himself. In a 1985 *Rolling Stone* article, two former steelworkers from southwestern Pennsylvania reminisced about their time in the mill. One commented on how much he missed it, saying, "We became so close in the mill, so many friends depending on you." His friend responded, "Not toward the end. Toward the end it was like fist-fight city."[63] The threat of layoffs caused workers to try to maximize their individual productivity in an attempt to preserve their own jobs, realizing that there were not enough jobs to go around. Workers became competitive with one another, which, of course, had an adverse impact on workers' sense of *mutual commitment* to one another.

The legacy of employment anxiety left by the industrial collapse remains. Today, industrial union members do not feel the sense of collective obligation to their union brothers and sisters that was common in the older generation. Instead, in an America in which there are fewer and fewer industrial manufacturing jobs, workers feel desperate to safeguard their own jobs by whatever means possible. As one recent USW retiree put it, "People now just want to protect their job. They'll do anything to do it, they'll rat you out in a heartbeat. It's not like the older days. [Workers today] align themselves more with the company than the union. There's [*sic*] still older workers who try to teach the young guys what it's about, but you're running out of the older guys now." As this Steelworker says, the desperation to protect one's job often resulted in workers aligning themselves more closely with the company than with the union—an act that would have been egregious to union members in the past. But because workers' first priority was simply to *keep* their jobs, the boldness of union members in the face of the company has decreased. For example, members are no longer as willing to vote to strike because of the fear of jobs being lost to nonunion members. Knowing the outsized amount of power the employer wields, workers endeavor to stay on the company's good side.

The principal goal for laid-off workers after industrial collapse was to find employment. For younger and middle-aged workers in the 1980s, this often meant moving away from the area—the most literal way to depart the union community. An interviewee and former member of the UE told us, "People had to leave, get new jobs, move away. With the massive loss of manufacturing jobs, people had to do what they had to do economically. My wife and I were part of that. Once my job was eliminated, there was minimal economic opportunity here. So we moved to California." For workers who remained, it did not matter so much whether they were employed at union or nonunion facilities. A 1991 *Pittsburgh Press* article discussed a laid-off USW member later rehired at Elliott Company, a Jeannette, Pennsylvania, mill represented by USW, who described feeling "neither excited nor dismayed" about becoming a USW member again.[64] From his perspective, it did not matter whether the plant was unionized—it was a job, and it paid. The attitude expressed by this worker was reflected by many of our interviewees as well. As a former district president of the UMWA commented to us, "Our guys say, 'What good is a union when I don't have a job?' And I say, 'You know what, you're right.'" As a result of the fear of being laid off, job security was prioritized over the union, and this evolved over time into a disregard for the union as the provider of "good" jobs.

In some places, companies took up the mantle of building community when unions declined. Sociologist Shannon Bell makes this point about mining communities: "Unions used to occupy a central space in the lives of not just miners, but their families," she writes. "When that was gone, there was a hole in the community's identity. Coal companies grabbed that space."[65] Coal companies, through the Friends of Coal campaign in Appalachia, sponsored events such as the Friends of Coal football game between West Virginia University and Marshall University. Soon, the narrative about community in industrial towns went from something that was built by workers to something predicated on company presence, furthering a shift of worker loyalties from the union to the company.

Industrial manufacturing in the United States has never gotten near to what it was in the mid-twentieth century, so it is understandable that many workers still feel uneasy about holding onto their jobs. With the ever-present risk of shutdowns and layoffs, many remaining union members choose company loyalty over union loyalty. As another retired USW member commented, "Workers today have gone 360 degrees backward: they don't fight the company. They're on the side of the company. They want to protect the jobs that they have, but they don't realize that the company is cutting their throats."

Generational differences have exacerbated the waning of union loyalties. Younger members may still agree with certain union economic priorities, but many of them no longer see the union as the *best means* by which workers can protect themselves and advocate for improvements in working conditions and job security.

Our interviews and observations suggest more broadly that generations of union members have different conceptions of the role and purpose of the union. Baby boomers reached their critical period of socialization during the peak of America's steel and manufacturing industries in the twentieth century. Members of that generation have a deep appreciation for the union and express a sense of nostalgia about the golden era of industry. One baby boomer retiree wistfully recalled the closeness of the Steelworkers' community in his hometown: "One thing I remember being a kid, everyone on the street was in the steel industry. . . . It was a beautiful community at that time. . . . When my dad worked, he had a lot of pride. He had good friends and great stories. They told great stories. You could just see when you were a kid that closeness amongst the steelworkers." For baby boomers, the combination of growing up in this period of industrial glory and then watching it collapse in the 1980s cemented a sense of nostalgia for all that was lost, including the closeness formerly fostered by the union.

In contrast, members of the millennial generation grew up after the golden age of industrial unionism. Millennials reached their generational critical period from the 1990s to the early 2000s, an era defined within the manufacturing sector by increased globalization and automation. Although unions fought these changes, they were often unsuccessful in protecting American workers from the progression toward modernization. One of the major recent successes of USW, in fact, was the Trump administration's imposition of import tariffs on steel and aluminum products from China and other countries—a policy that USW had supported for decades. For millennials, the success of the union has been tied less to the organized labor movement and more to the survival of the company and the cooperation of government with industry.

Difference in generational understandings of the importance of the union has also led to some animosity. Some older members expressed hostility toward younger workers because of their decision to ally themselves more closely with the company than with the union. In the words of one retired USW member: "They don't want to get involved [with the union] because of the company or whatever. . . . The younger generation, they're in it for what they can get out of it. It's not like the older generations who stuck together outside of work too. Older guys you went out to the bar, you had something to eat after work. Now you're not associated with the people you work with outside of work." This interviewee is describing the loss of the collectivist spirit that defined the union for baby boomers. Multiple older workers described younger members as being more focused on themselves than their fellow workers, thereby breeding resentment between the young and the old. One older worker even repeatedly referred to younger workers as "Generation Me." For older members, the union represents the struggle that industrial workers have had to endure for generations. Younger workers are less apt to sense the depth of impact of the union. Workers' connection to the past via *historical awareness* becomes looser as time goes on; instead of union loyalty being part of one's identity, the union is often "just a job" to younger workers.

In sum, our discussions in this chapter reinforce the bottom line that, by the early 2000s, in western Pennsylvania and other Rust Belt regions, the economic, political, and community moorings of the "union man" had greatly weakened—and in many places, had been eliminated entirely. The scene was set for alternative identities, outlooks, and social involvements.

4

UNION MEMBERSHIP TRANSFORMED

"I don't think the union is as popular as it once was with the membership," said one older but still employed steelworker from western Pennsylvania. "People don't understand that this is a good job *because* of the union." In the previous chapters, we discussed what unions meant to workers of the mid-twentieth century and how loyalties started to shift as political and economic changes affected union power and worker unity. Now we turn to workers today: how have families and communities changed, especially for blue-collar workers still enrolled in unions in western Pennsylvania and across the Rust Belt?

We start by looking at changes in families and the implications for working-class men in particular. Then we probe the changing landscape of community associations and networks that have attracted engagement as union presence recedes. Finally, we consider key differences between factory-based industrial unions like United Steelworkers (USW) and more craft-focused construction unions such as International Brotherhood of Electrical Workers (IBEW). Not all unions have been affected in the same ways by the momentous economic and social changes we describe in this book—it is possible that modernized versions of older, craft-focused unions may find it easier to keep in touch with their members in today's changed world.

Of course, unionization in the United States—and in western Pennsylvania—has shifted overall toward public-sector and health services unions, whose memberships include higher shares of women and minorities. But we keep our focus on industrial and building trades unions that have historically been—and still largely are—comprised mostly of white men. Along with other blue-collar workers, members of these unions now live in profoundly changed social worlds, where work and family life intersect in new ways and where ties to union halls, ethnic clubs, and churches have given way to longer and lonelier commutes to work plus involvements in gun clubs and conservative churches. In chapter 5, we will explore the implications for U.S. politics and the Democratic Party of the changes for workers and unions that we describe in this chapter.

CHANGING FAMILY REALITIES

In the typical union member's family of the mid-twentieth century, the wife stayed at home and cooked, took care of the children, did housework, and navigated many family involvements in the community. When we think about the average middle-class white family of the 1950s, this *Leave It to Beaver* picture often comes to mind. But many might be surprised to know that a nuclear family division of labor between a male breadwinner doing work for wages and a wife doing unsalaried work in the home and volunteer community activities was *especially* characteristic for midcentury *unionized* Americans. In 1952, "housewife" was the occupation of more than 70 percent of the female respondents from union households. In contrast, fewer than 40 percent of female respondents in nonunion households categorized themselves that way.[1]

Abrupt family changes soon ensued, however. Over just a few decades, the male-breadwinner union family of the mid-twentieth century gave way to dual or single working-parent models. For unionized workers, this change was so fully accomplished by the end of the twentieth century that their family forms converged with those of nonunionized workers, closing what used to be a substantial gap between the two groups.[2] New combinations of family and wage-earning responsibilities for parents, spouses, and partners have persisted. Today, two-partner, child-raising union families usually have both adults working for wages or salaries while dealing together with all the other challenges of household and community life.

It is clear that the supposedly traditional breadwinner family construct was not really a long-standing phenomenon, yet this family form was made possible for millions of ordinary Americans by the higher salaries and better benefits that unions helped to win during and after World War II. Well-paying union jobs were plentiful and stable enough in the mid-twentieth century to allow one worker to provide for his family over the life course. "When I was getting out of high school," one retired interviewee recalled, "you could go to college or get a job working in the mine or steel mill. At the time, that was a lifetime job. Your dad would get you a job in the mine or mill. That was the way it was, man—your old man would get you a job there because they were good-paying jobs. It was a retirement job." Employment in the steel or coal industries was passed through male lineages in innumerable families throughout Pennsylvania, Ohio, West Virginia, and other areas of the Rust Belt. Although there were some women in the industrial workforce at this time, the vast majority of workers were men. In the coal industry, for example, a publication from 1980 by the President's Commission on Coal estimated that 97 percent of coal miners nationwide were men.[3]

During and after the collapse of Rust Belt industries in the 1970s and 1980s, former employees had few opportunities for employment within their trade. In a mid-1980s survey of dislocated workers conducted by the Steel Valley Authority (SVA), many workers reported finding jobs with wages that could not support the needs of their families. As one survey respondent stated, "The mills are gone, big paychecks are gone, now it's a struggle just to make a meager living and paying [sic] my bills."[4] Another stated, "There are jobs, but the money is small. . . . All of these jobs that are offered to people, you have to work at two of these to try and make a go of it." A third said that his "entire lifestyle changed" and that he was "very discouraged working for minimum wage"because of the lack of benefits. In many families, economic frustration drove women to work. Of the over 4,000 SVA dislocated worker survey respondents, 55 percent reported that their spouse was employed either full- or part-time, a stark contrast to the 70 percent or more of union members' wives in 1952 whose occupation was housewife.[5]

Almost half of workers reported experiencing family problems as a result of their employment dislocation.[6] One reporter for the *Beaver County Times* found in 1986 that some wives in Aliquippa "wanted to stay home with their young children" but were "forced to go to work at low wages" as a result of their husbands' unemployment.[7] Men were not pleased that their wives had to go to work in order to keep the family afloat. The frustration among dislocated workers permeated family dynamics and traditional gender roles regarding child-rearing as well. Many men felt that, because their wives had to work, children were no longer being raised properly. As one retired interviewee said to us, "So, you know what would happen [when men lost their jobs in the mills], now here's the mom, she didn't have to work before, but now he's out scraping around. So, now the mom would go out and [work] some minimum-wage job. So what happened with that was [that] mom's not home and dad's not home, so the kids would suffer—they wouldn't get a proper upbringing." Getting a "proper upbringing" for this respondent, espousing a view held by many in the steel or coal industry, reflected traditionally gendered roles of bread-winning and child-rearing.

Many male workers felt their own dignity suffered along with their children's upbringing when their wives went to work to bring in additional income for the family. As one dislocated worker explained in response to the SVA survey, "I was a flexible, dependable, hardworking man for WABCO [Westinghouse Air Brake Company, represented by United Electrical, Radio, and Machine Workers (UE)] for twelve and a half years. . . . Now . . . I have been stripped of my dignity through my family helping me, through these types of things."[8] Another worker commented, "Any help in restoring dignity and fairness in the [new] workplace would be greatly appreciated."[9] Workers who had formerly felt celebrated and appreciated began to feel replaceable, either by their own wives working to pay for the family's needs or by competing workers in overseas plants. More generally, such workers could feel overlooked by their communities, whose source of prosperity had formerly been attributed to their unionized, good-paying jobs. As social researchers have found again and again, losing a job entails much more than the loss of work—it threatens established roles and identities in families and communities.[10]

Experiencing a sense of failure as the family provider left some men also feeling emasculated. A *Time* magazine article from 1980 entitled "The Idle Army of Unemployed" discusses the stark life differences after industrial workers had been laid off. Giving the example of a thirty-one-year-old man named Wilson Painter Jr., who formerly worked as an apprentice machinist for U.S. Steel in southwestern Pennsylvania, the article comments that Painter now "spends his empty hours playing with his two children, helping his wife Kathy around the house, or ritualistically unpacking and cleaning the precision calipers, gauges and scales that lie neatly slotted in his tool chest."[11] Still, Painter felt strongly that he had to figure out a way to provide for his family, commenting to *Time*, "A man's got to keep his hands in tune, his mind alert. You can't let them slowly kill you and let your family go naked. Not this man."[12]

Due to both economic shifts and new social norms, the percentage of married women in the workforce significantly increased throughout the 1970s and 1980s.[13] In 1978, Congress passed the Pregnancy Discrimination Act and also formally recognized workplace sexual harassment. As barriers for women workers lowered, so did wages for male non-college-degree workers, making industrial wages even for the unionized not as generous as they once were. Young men could no longer rely on good-paying "retirement jobs," which a worker could expect to keep until he decided to leave the workforce. Men also had more people with whom they had to compete to attain good-paying jobs. Today, 70 percent of women who have children under the age of eighteen participate in the workforce, and almost 60 percent of all women over the age of sixteen work (compared to almost 70 percent for men).[14] Over just a few decades, the once highly gendered nature of the union family changed drastically. Union membership bases today include many more working women—as well as growing ranks of nonwhite women and men—and long-accepted relationships in marriages and homes regarding work have transformed.

It was a lot of change for people to process. As many wives became essential wage earners, homemaking responsibilities were often divided in new ways between hard-pressed adults.

In generations past, married male workers could stay out late after work to fraternize with union brothers at a local union hall or ethnic club. Today, most attend to child-rearing responsibilities or simply choose to go home to spend time with their families. In our interviews, many stressed that today's union members are much more involved in child-rearing. One female retiree of IBEW observed "a huge difference between young guys and old guys. Old guys didn't really do things with their kids or talk about their families, the young guys, all they talk about is their families. Their wives work, and [the men] go pick up their kids and stuff. Now the guys compare what they feed their kids for dinner. Someone a couple decades ago wouldn't believe that!" This interviewee saw the priorities and responsibilities of men in the home change from the beginning of her career in 1979 to when she retired from the trade in the mid-2000s. Several younger workers also cited "more emphasis on the family" today as one reason for a decrease in union participation. As one late-thirties Steelworker explained, "People are more prioritizing family life [now] so it's hard to get participation in union things." Another interviewee told us, "We used to have union meetings on Friday nights, but these younger guys are busy with their families on Friday nights." The reordering of gender responsibilities in and outside the home functions to pull against significant engagement in union affairs, at least those union activities that once presumed gender-divided family roles.

Layoffs in traditionally male-dominated heavy industries piled new stresses atop the ongoing shifts in gender responsibilities. In response to layoffs in coal country, women have often undertaken the economic responsibility to keep the family afloat. A 2019 *New York Times* article about Letcher County, Kentucky, reported a huge shift in the number of women working after the coal mines shut down.[15] Ten years ago, less than two-fifths of

Letcher County's labor force was female; today, more than half is. A comparable increase in women working has occurred in other areas where male-dominated industries are now in decline. As the district director of USW in Kentucky put it, "The mines have shut down and the women have gone to work. It's not complicated at all."[16]

Attention to major transformations in families and gender roles since the 1970s underscores that, for many blue-collar men, the very meaning of manhood has undergone emotionally and socially demanding shifts. In the mid-twentieth century, many Americans associated masculine identity with heavy industry. Union men working in such industries were proud to provide for their families but generally did not participate equally in child-rearing responsibilities. Many union men took pride in having a middle-class lifestyle that allowed their wives to stay at home. The housewife was a symbol of not only economic success but also masculinity. As one interviewee put it (in remarks we paraphrase), these men were living the blue-collar American dream, and everyone knew it.

DISAPPEARING UNION HALLS AND CIVIC GROUPS

Mid-twentieth century associational life was vibrant in industrial towns and the neighborhoods of mill cities. The 1956 business directory for Monongahela, Pennsylvania, listed forty-five civic groups under the heading "Associations," including the Lithuanian Literary Association, the Loyal Order of Moose No. 125, three Masonic Lodges, the Polish American Club, the Veterans Club of Charleroi, and five USW locals. Forty-seven religious institutions are listed under the heading "Churches and Synagogues." Separate from "Associations," a whopping eighty-six organizations were also listed under "Clubs," including six Slovak organizations, four Eagles clubs, and three veteran's organizations (not including the Veterans Club of Charleroi listed previously).[17] The town of Monongahela itself had a population of 8,388 in 1960.[18] Because this directory covered a couple of other towns as well with similar populations, the overall population relevant to the directory was probably somewhere around 75,000.

The proliferation of membership associations reached its peak in mid-twentieth-century America, with blue-collar workers participating in many federated yet locally rooted associations.[19] The number of groups that people could join was remarkable, and we know from announcements of events in newspapers and newsletters that there were constant rounds of meetings and celebratory occasions, sometimes cosponsored by unions and other groups, often held in space lent by community associations. Union groups were full partners in these midcentury webs of community connections and social occasions—and in dozens of communities across western Pennsylvania, prominently visible union halls were places where many labor and community groups could gather.

In sharp contrast to the dozens of associations listed in the 1956 Monongahela directory, today's online Monongahela business directory lists just ten associations and clubs, some overlapping, including the Boy Scouts of America, the Monongahela Valley Country Club, and the Victory Hill Gun Club. Once-prominent ethnic and fraternal groups are either gone or no longer considered important enough to list, and Local 210 of USW and its hall are both gone as well. Monongahela's changes are typical for Rust Belt industrial towns that once featured homes and social organizations around one or two major plants or mills.

Community associations in such places suffered immensely during the decline of U.S. heavy manufacturing. Many long-standing social and religious organizations simply closed, leaving those remaining workers and families less connected to one another. If new forms of association moved into the vacuum, they were more geographically dispersed organizations and networks, especially those centered in gun clubs and megachurches.

For a period of time after the collapse of industry in western Pennsylvania, the importance of union halls connected to other community groups was apparent. Not only were many local union halls gathering spaces for protests and organizing meetings, they also served as food pantries and as information hubs connecting unemployed workers with government welfare services. Many local unions set up unemployment committees to support laid-off workers in accessing government resources such as food stamps or were involved in community food pantries. "Government cheese [was being] given out at the union hall," one retired steelworker recalled.

During the early layoffs phase, many workers and family members valued and turned to the local union hall as a safe haven. A 1985 article about the layoffs in southwestern Pennsylvania's steel industry profiled Art Leibowitz, a forty-one-year-old former steelworker at the Homestead Mill, who contemplated suicide but "just couldn't pull the trigger." Former coworkers found him "depressed and incoherent" in his local union hall.[20] The union hall was a place of refuge not only in extreme situations such as Leibowitz's case but also simply as a place to see former coworkers and find solace in a shared sense of loss. Interactions among members—both laid-off and still working—thus continued for some time after the steel collapse, nourished both by the lingering sense of community and the services that unions brokered.

Over months and years, however, social interconnectedness faded. After the collapse of the steel industry in western Pennsylvania, former steelworkers—who had bonded through shared experiences at the mill but were now each attempting to stay economically afloat in their own way—had fewer and fewer reasons to stay in touch with one another. As more industrial workers were laid off and many plants shut down, union locals either merged or shut down, and most of the union halls that once dotted western Pennsylvania permanently closed their doors. The costs of maintaining often large union halls that included banquet and recreational rooms caught up with many local unions, so the only answer was to consolidate meeting places. "Back when I took office [in the 1980s]," one United Mine Workers of America (UMWA) local president explained, "there were a lot of [union halls], but they were just too expensive. . . . [Around 2000] our local hall heating cost was $7,000 to $8,000 a year, and that's a lot of money. So as soon as the mine was no longer running, we . . . sold it and got a nice chunk of cash, so whenever something comes up, we have cash to do things. We now meet at our International district office in Uniontown." As membership declined during layoffs throughout the 1980s, local unions with or without their own halls made difficult decisions to amalgamate. Money thus saved could be redirected toward political efforts to save jobs. Yet a side effect of both local amalgamations and the closure of so many halls was that such changes centralized the union organizational and fiscal presence, pulling it away from neighborhood locales. As one retired steelworker said, "When you had a source of money, that money got spread throughout [the town]. When it dried up, everything went with it."

Manufacturing internationals like USW were especially affected by this centralization and withdrawal process. Steelworker locals, social groups, and halls were originally tied closely to specific steel or manufacturing megaplex mills, one or at most a few of which dominated entire industrial towns and city areas—around Pittsburgh, McKeesport, Monongahela, Aliquippa, and Johnstown. Our tallies suggest that in the 1960s, there were at least 119 local USW unions in the twenty-county region of western Pennsylvania (and more likely as many as 143 if we included unnumbered directory entries and district offices). These are likely conservative estimates because systematic lists of local unions at that time are not readily available. Out of these many dozens of local USW locals back then, sixty-eight had actual union halls (not counting rented spaces), as displayed in the map presented in figure 2.6 in chapter 2. Those USW union halls open in the 1960s included thirty-three halls owned by single local unions, plus another four halls run by an additional thirty-five local unions that were part of teams running joint halls.

By the twenty-first century, *only sixteen USW locals remained in operation* out of the original 143 local USW unions we identified in western Pennsylvania in the 1960s. Most of the 1960s locals that have disappeared or merged were organizations of steelworkers, and most of the additional USW-affiliated locals that have newly emerged since the 1970s represent at least major shares of employees in industries other than steel or manufacturing.[21] As for union-owned halls, only eight of the original thirty-seven USW locals with *halls* in the 1960s still operate local union halls today. Union-owned halls seem to no longer be an investment many locals are willing to make—both long-standing and recently formed local unions now tend to rent office space instead of buying or building their own halls.

During the same decades that local union roots withered, fraternal lodges and ethnic clubs also disappeared. By the 1960s and 1970s, many U.S. fraternal orders faced sharp membership declines for a variety reasons, including changing views about associations that historically admitted whites only and stressed separate spheres of activity for men and women.[22] Many ethnic associations stayed in operation longer than fraternal lodges— until the steel industry collapse. After originally helping new immigrants assimilate and learn English from the late 1800s through the mid-twentieth century, they became primarily social clubs where workers stopped after work to share drinks and conversation. One retired interviewee described this evolution during his time working in the mill:

> In the early days, there were different social groups based on nationality. So you might belong to a Lithuanian club or a Russian club. . . . But [in the 1970s], you could go to any of the clubs. Hell, I probably belonged to three different clubs at one time. You'd go to different clubs and meet different people and see different people. The guys from work, they would say . . . "I'm going to the Slovak club." Naturally after [the collapse], a lot of those clubs shut down, but that's the way it was back then.

Nevertheless, following the demise of so many western Pennsylvania mills, even ethnic social clubs that survived through the mid-twentieth century ended up closing as their former regulars moved out of the area, stopped socializing, or died. In once vibrant towns and cities, the ethnic clubs that remain are frequented primarily by older retirees.

SOCIAL TIES AND LOYALTIES TODAY

The decline of union identity and community in western Pennsylvania has left current workers seeking alternative social outlets. If we ask what has replaced loyalty to their union for most Rust Belt workers, including those still formally enrolled in unions, the basic answer is that many of them, like Americans in general, simply are not very socially or civically interconnected.[23] They may not be "bowling alone," to use the title of Robert Putnam's book, but they likely are either driving alone or watching television or playing video games at home alone. As discussed earlier, for many workers, current social patterns are in large part rooted in new family roles. Even in this era of declining community involvement, however, people still naturally seek out social belonging and social activities. Working people to whom we spoke reported two kinds of organizational ties—to gun clubs and religious groups—as more prevalent than others in industrial and ex-industrial towns.

To get a sense of workers' new loyalties, we visited the parking lots of three still-functioning U.S. steel plants in southwestern Pennsylvania. Edgar Thomson Steel Works, Irvin Steel Works, and Clairton Steel Works are all union shops, meaning that all workers are represented by USW. Lainey Newman visited each of the parking lots twice, from 2 P.M. to 4 P.M. on a Monday and then a Wednesday in early 2021. On the second visit, she tallied the total number of cars as well as the number of car bumper or window stickers that fit into categories defined after the first visit. As displayed in figure 4.1, the most common types of stickers were, in descending order, hunting or gun-related stickers; stickers that express support for the GOP or Donald Trump (who was president at the time); motorcycle-related stickers; union stickers; pro-police stickers; Christian stickers; and then Democrat stickers, making up only 1.4 percent of the stickers we saw that invoked civic or political commitments. Not tallied here were a handful of other stickers unrelated to political or civic interests, such as those regarding alcoholic beverages, professional sports teams, or pets.

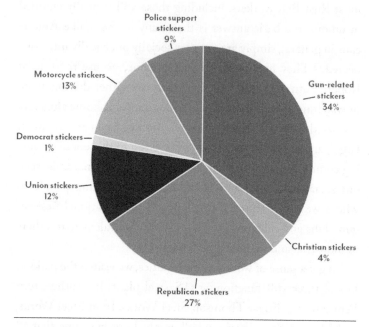

FIGURE 4.1 Percentage of bumper or window stickers by type.

Gun-related stickers were frequently visible on workers' cars in these parking lots. Many proclaimed gun rights or made political statements about gun ownership, although some simply expressed an interest in hunting or signaled membership in the National Rifle Association (NRA). Some stickers expressed combined interests—such as one that read "Pro-God, Pro-Life, Pro-Guns" (which we tallied as both gun-related and religion-related). Others mocked gun control, such as one that read, "Gun control means hitting your target."

Most Republican stickers on these workers' cars were specifically pro-Trump. To show support for the police, some vehicles had Thin Blue Line flag stickers and others had "Punisher

FIGURE 4.2 (a) Gun-related stickers. (b) NRA stickers.
(c) Trump stickers and QAnon sticker in the middle photograph at
the bottom. (d) Pro-police Thin Blue Line flag stickers.
Author photographs of USW employee parking lots.

skull" stickers featuring the Thin Blue Line flag. The Punisher skull symbol originated in the Marvel Universe to represent a vigilante who fought crime without adhering to the laws of the government. Various pro-police and right-wing groups have adopted the combined Punisher skull–Thin Blue Line logo, especially in response to protests about police brutality in the summer of 2020. Police units in several states have even adopted the Punisher skull logo on their official uniforms or cars.[24] Groups espousing the far-right QAnon conspiracy theory have also adopted the Punisher skull as a symbol.[25]

The stickers so prevalent in 2021 employee parking lots are a reasonable indicator of allegiances that industrial union workers in western Pennsylvania are eager to proclaim today—and they signal very different engagements and loyalties than in the mid-century era of the union man. This experiment is not an opinion poll that gets at the full variety of individual views, but we do see in these parking lots that many are proud to announce stances aligned with the Republican Party and the far right— marking a 180-degree turn from the time just decades ago when it was "unthinkable" for union workers in this region to declare Republican preferences publicly. Indeed, the shifts right may go further than sheer partisanship because numerous stickers touting the police, the Confederacy, QAnon, and Donald Trump show that outlooks are implicitly or explicitly imbued with prowhite ethnonationalism and attraction to authoritarianism. Many of the bumper stickers in turn hint at social involvement such as participation in online far-right social media sites and attendance at gun clubs—and perhaps militia groups—and Christian nationalist churches or religious networks. Gun clubs and megachurches are worth a closer look as associational sites where much of interactive community life now happens in Rust Belt America.

Gun Clubs

In our interviews, gun clubs were mentioned more than any other category of group when we asked about associations present in today's industrial and ex-industrial communities. Not only were gun stickers the most common on the back of Steelworker cars and trucks but actual groups of gun enthusiasts are also common in this region. Within a 100-mile radius of the city of Pittsburgh, excluding those areas that fall outside the state of Pennsylvania, there are over 250 NRA-affiliated gun clubs, hunting leagues, and rifle ranges according to a database we constructed of gun-related organizations in the region. Such clubs are thriving—so much so that a large number have website notices that they have reached the upper limit of their membership capacity. Many of these clubs have been around for a long time—in a region where hunting has always been an important recreational activity—but others have been newly founded since the 1980s, including very recently. Many have also expanded their facilities in recent years, acquiring more land or renovating buildings and shooting ranges.

Because Pennsylvania is the eleventh-most heavily armed state in the country and because western areas are rich in wildlife, the ubiquity of the gun clubs is in some ways unsurprising.[26] But we should not think of these clubs simply as backdrops to hunting by individuals or small groups because there are many indications that they have grown in importance as social sites tied to politicized identities. Most of the gun clubs within the region are affiliated with the NRA and have websites featuring a plethora of social activities—new versions of the constant rounds of occasions we used to see for local union halls, ethnic clubs, and fraternal lodges. The clubhouses of gun groups often serve as community gathering places, and they typically encourage adherents to attend monthly membership meetings. Many clubs have holiday parties, such as Christmas or Halloween parties, or regularly scheduled ladies nights, Bingo nights, or card-playing events. Some clubs explicitly stress that their gun-related programs attempt to foster community among members. For example, one pistol club located in New Castle, Pennsylvania, explains on its website that Thursday evening, when the indoor range is open for all members, "is a great time to meet other members and hone those handgun shooting skills."[27] Volunteering for club maintenance is also encouraged, such as participating in "work parties" of members to clean up the facilities or build equipment for the ranges. Clubs also keep in touch with scattered members— almost all have active Facebook pages with regular updates about events and activities, and some have regular or semiregular digital or paper newsletters. Just as unions once did, some gun clubs also have associated golf leagues or baseball teams.

According to our interviewees, many of the people with whom they work at the surviving steel mills are part of sports or hunting clubs. As one current steelworker said, "Of course we go [to gun clubs]. I live on a farm, so I'm a big hunter and fisher." A former Steelworker commented that when he worked at the mill, he was the only member of his seventeen-person work crew who was not a hunter. "Hunting was their thing," he said. Others similarly affirmed that many workers own guns, hunt, and partake in activities at local gun clubs.

It has not been hard for gun clubs affiliated with the NRA or other federated progun groups to move into social spaces vacated by receding unions. Quite a few blue-collar union newsletters all along had recurring sections about hunting or safe gun use because local and supralocal labor leaders were well aware that many of their members participated in gun sports. Indeed, some local unions even held recurring events at local gun clubs, such as IBEW Local 177 in Jacksonville, Florida, which reported in July 1975 that they were holding a skeet shoot at the Jacksonville Gun Club "for all members and their wives or girlfriends."[28] The report added, "Light refreshments are planned." USW's international publication ran a recurring section called the "Rod and Gun," which included reports about individual members' hunting and fishing triumphs (see figure 4.3). When it eventually became clear that guns and unions were pulling on opposing political heartstrings for many workers, however, discussion of hunting and gun use in union newsletters declined. Of course, that did not prevent unionists from getting such information elsewhere—from gun clubs and their communications or Facebook pages.

For some gun clubs, individual membership in the NRA is a prerequisite to being a member of the club itself. On its Facebook page and website, the East Monongahela Sportsmen's Club (EMSC) touts itself as a "100 percent NRA-enrolled, members-only club that promotes recreational shooting and fishing."[29] As a Facebook post from April 2019 puts it, "All of our members know, you must be an NRA member to be a member of EMSC. We ran a mandatory check thru the NRA and a few came back as nonmembers. If this pertains to you, please become current with the NRA before our renewal period." The EMSC hosts and participates in popular community events, just as many other gun clubs do. It hosts a youth fishing tournament and sponsors a local high school baseball team, as well as having regular member meetings and work parties to clean up the club's facilities and take care of the shooting ranges. The EMSC clubhouse hosts gatherings with food and refreshments—for example, after one trap shoot in September 2020, members enjoyed barbecue porkchops and chicken together at the clubhouse, according to their Facebook page. The backdrop to this community building and socialization,

January, 1975

STEEL LA

ROD AND GUN

By FRED GOETZ, Steel Labor Outdoor Editor

According to recent flow of photos from hunt-loving members of the United Steelworkers of America, it's been a good season and a variety of big game over far-flung acres has been harvested. Here's an over-the-shoulder look at past action with a promise of more to come:

Crane Operator Raymond J. Socher of Blawnox, Pa., a member of Local 1579, travelled far west and considerably north in quest of a big game trophy and found it in the northern sec-

Brian Rodoski holds 8-point mounted deer which dad bagged near Jamestown, N.Y. Right: Art Betker in nearby Buffalo went to Quebec to get this black bear.

tion of the province of British Columbia. He's p i c t u r e d below with his prize, a giant bull moose, bagged this past September.

speckled trout. (We're indebted to District Director Mitchel F. Mazuca for pic.)

Mrs. W. M. Reed, wife of Webster M. Reed, of Friedens, Pa., who is a retired member of Johnstown Local 1288, kneels beside black bear which Steelworker Reed downed on a 12-day hunt this past September in Ontario's Gogama Forest. It was an adult male and tipped the scales down to 300 pounds.

* * *

What'll it be? A fly or spinner. USWA m e m b e r s, members of the family and, of course, retired members can earn e i t h e r one: A Bolo spinner or Teeny Nymph. All that's required is a clear snapshot of a fishing or hunting s c e n e—and a few words as to what the snapshot is about. Send it to: Fred Goetz, Dept. SW, 2833 S.E. 33rd Place, Portland, Ore. 97202. Please mention your local number and specify spinner or fly.

FIGURE 4.3 A page from a United Steelworkers international newsletter featuring its "Rod and Gun" section, January 1975.

however, is a requirement to enroll in America's overtly conservative gun rights federation, the NRA. But even when people participate in clubs that do not have stringent rules about NRA enrollment, they may experience either implicit or explicit peer pressures from fierce supporters of the Second Amendment or advocates of other political positions favored by the NRA.

In response to the increasing sway that the NRA had over union members, the Union Sportsmen's Alliance (USA) was founded in 2007. With the backing of the AFL-CIO, this group was created for unionists and family members who enjoy outdoor activities such as shooting, hunting, and fishing, but unlike the NRA, the USA bills itself as nonpartisan and "does not take positions on or endorse political agendas, parties or candidates."[30] Nonpartisan positioning may not provide much moral force to wall members off from right-leaning gun networks, but some current union members do support the USA. As a 2015 letter to the editor of the IBEW newsletter from a St. Louis member put it, any "union member who believes in their union and is a hunter or gun enthusiast and wants to join with others should join the Union Sportsmen's Alliance and not the NRA. The USA is a great organization that I strongly support as a 45-year member of IBEW," he added.[31]

From Parishes to Megachurches

Many of our interviewees pointed to religious organizations, in addition to gun clubs, as local community institutions with which they and many of their union coworkers interact. Religious adherence is, of course, a long-standing tradition in the Rust Belt. The welcome sign to the town of Monessen, about twenty-five miles south of the city of Pittsburgh and located on the Monongahela River, reads "The Churches of Monessen Welcome You." Clairton, another mill town in western Pennsylvania, has long been nicknamed the "City of Prayer." Churches were a major presence in the industrial towns of western Pennsylvania during the industrial heyday, and they still are today. The types of churches attracting large or growing congregations, however, often differ from those that used to be scattered throughout industrial towns. After the collapse of industry in the 1980s, smaller ethnic churches struggled to survive. Many closed or joined with other churches. As the *Uniontown Herald-Standard* reported in 2002, "From 1988 to 1995, the Pittsburgh diocese closed 19 ethnic parishes; at the same time, 19 territorial parishes—those serving people within established boundaries—closed because of costs and a declining number of congregants."[32] The same phenomenon occurred elsewhere in the Rust Belt. Since the 1980s, nondenominational or standalone megachurches have proliferated, both in suburban areas and in smaller, more rural communities.

There are thirty-four megachurches across Pennsylvania, including six located within the 100-mile radius of the city of Pittsburgh.[33] The Hartford Institute for Religion Research defines "megachurch" as a "Christian congregation with a sustained average weekly attendance of 2000 persons or more in its worship services."[34] In the institute's tallies, a plurality (about 40 percent) of megachurches are nondenominational, followed by Southern Baptist as the second most frequent type. Megachurches usually do not operate simply as one big worship service but instead include many subgroups doing special activities or involving subsets of congregants. This arrangement offers many routes for recruiting and retaining new adherents, especially because people often get involved in churches as well as unions and other kinds of associations when coworkers, neighbors, or friends draw them in, and they stay to enjoy ongoing interactions. A national survey of megachurch attendees from 2008 shows that most of them initially joined the church because a friend or family member invited them. Megachurches also do community outreach. In survey data that the Hartford Institute collected in 2020, 89 percent of respondents either strongly agreed or agreed that the church was "actively involved in our local community." Fifty-eight percent of respondents said that their congregation put some or a lot of emphasis on some form of advocacy or political involvement.[35]

Megachurch attendance has been growing in recent years, and unionists told us about the involvement of family members or friends in such congregations. One USW interviewee said the following of his home county of Somerset: "Some of my family is Catholic, but today the parishes have been consolidated. There are a lot of churches springing up, but they aren't mainline Protestant or Catholic. I don't have much experience with them, but my assumption is that they're megachurches and that [they are] associated with right-wing politics." Another retired Steelworker affirmed this trajectory of consolidation of churches in a different part of southwestern Pennsylvania: "When I grew up in this town in Charleroi, there were three Catholic churches, one was the Italian one, they were all ethnically different. Now you see what's happening . . . all those churches were condensed. Every week it seemed like they were condensed. Since the demise of the steel mills, the churches have closed left and right." The replacement of many smaller churches or parishes with megachurches furthers the shift away from local community embeddedness not just because larger congregations are replacing smaller ones but also because specialty subgroups within megachurches draw participants from large driving radiuses. A local preservationist to whom we spoke lamented that his town had lost Methodist, Catholic, Slovak, and Protestant congregations, saying, "Lots of young people joined megachurch congregations, and you can't walk to those churches. They don't foster community. [Those churches] took a bunch of our people."

As these shifts have proceeded, many larger churches around industrial towns have gravitated toward fostering moral-political orientations distinct from those nurtured by the smaller, locally embedded churches that predated them. Small churches played a big role in the "save the industry" campaigns of the 1970s and 1980s and were supportive of organized labor, but many of the current megachurches and larger amalgamated churches stress more general outlooks and messages—frequently offering a blend of cultural conservatism and aggressive American patriotism. Sociologists Andrew Whitehead and Samuel Perry argue in *Taking America Back for God* that a specifically right-wing Christian nationalist movement began to gain traction from the 1960s to the 1980s in response to social changes. As they put it, "economic, political, or cultural upheavals cause Americans to fall back on their core identities, traditions, values, and narratives about themselves to bring order out of chaos. . . . Over the last four decades, a host of conservative religious organizations have emerged to warn Americans of the degradation these transitions will bring."[36] By stressing stances such as opposition to abortion and gay marriage or expressing worries about cultural shifts tied to rapid immigration and America's changing economic and geopolitical place in the world, pastors and lay leaders in many churches in western Pennsylvania and other regions of the industrial Midwest are able to appeal in emotionally charged ways to nostalgia for remembered or misremembered pasts that many industrial workers feel after decades of unsettling displacements.

In chapter 2, we discussed how closely intertwined labor and religion have always been. In many midcentury industrial communities, priests, ministers, and other religious leaders were involved with the labor movement, cosponsoring events with local unions and even at times participating on the picket line during strikes. Today, such mutually supportive relationships between local unions and churches have largely disappeared. Clerics and lay-persons often proclaim frankly politically right-wing social values and outlooks—conveying messages that either ignore unions altogether or, in some instances, actively reject them as left-leaning secular influences. To be sure, not all churches, not even all megachurches, operate this way, and even churches located in the same region that have similar congregants and espouse theologically parallel worldviews may stress quite different civic ties and political messages. Variations in interchurch networks likely link sets of pastors and lay leaders to national advocacy hubs. Such issues have not been adequately researched, partly because studies of religion and politics tend to be pigeonholed into separate academic specialties and even more because political scientists who do pay attention to cultural realities tend to rely almost exclusively on surveys of individual attitudes that do not speak to the operations and goals of pastor networks or churches as organizations. More creative research designs are clearly needed. It is apparent, however, that right-wing outlooks are trumpeted by many leaders of the new kinds of churches attended by today's blue-collar workers, including unionists.

INTERNATIONAL UNIONS IN CHANGING TIMES

We conclude this chapter by assessing important variations in the processes of union change that we have summarized so far. Although Big Labor's national influence has undeniably receded since its heyday in the mid-twentieth century, large U.S.-Canadian international labor unions have handled these changes in different ways, with the underlying structures of some unions making it easier for them to adapt to new economic and social realities. Industrial unions like USW have seen their long-standing, plant-based, locally embedded modes of member engagement fundamentally disrupted. But building trades unions such as IBEW have never been as rooted in geographically compact workplaces, making it easier for them to adapt long-standing modes of member engagement to new conditions. Key differences between industrial unions and building trades unions can mean that today's workers in the building trades feel more aligned and loyal to their union than their counterparts in industrial unions.

Workers in Industrial Unions and the Building Trades

Although Steelworkers and other industrial workers were hit hardest by the collapse of steel and the decline of manufacturing that began in the late 1970s, workers in the building trades were also affected because industrial plants in western Pennsylvania were major employers of building trades members, such as electricians and insulators. Whenever mills or plants were installed or expanded during the midcentury heyday of manufacturing, outside contractors from the building trades unions were enlisted to do the construction work. Such projects could last years and employ thousands of tradespeople. Electricians and other building trades workers lost opportunities when major industrial complexes went under, but they could also more readily shift to new jobs than could steelworkers. Whether employment opportunities remained had a major effect on workers' willingness to remain engaged with their unions, no matter the sector. When we consider USW versus IBEW members who remain employed in western Pennsylvania and beyond, however, we can see significant *organizational* variables that influenced ongoing ties between members and unions. Even during and after the period of industrial collapse, there are still thousands of remaining steel and industrial workers in western Pennsylvania and the rest of the Rust Belt—and there are also many building trades workers. Based on the qualitative data that we have gathered from such still-employed people, IBEW clearly seems to have remained more meaningful to its members than other unions, including USW. Noticing this, we have asked why IBEW unions have been able to sustain stronger ties and more of a sense of identity and loyalty among members. There are logical occupational and organizational reasons why the trades manage worker-union ties in distinctive ways. In the building trades, workers are employed based on contracts awarded to the local union by construction managers. "The local union is your hiring hall," multiple building trades interviewees stressed to us. As a building tradesperson, your workplace changes dozens of times throughout your career. As a result, workers do not have loyalty to any particular workplace because they will work at that location for maybe a couple of years before moving on to the next project. Work is determined by the contracts awarded to the local union, and workers therefore look to the local union rather than a company as their source of work and income.

In contrast, industrial workers are hired by companies, and their unions do not serve as hiring halls. "I'm great for conspiracy theories," one steelworker joked. "U.S. Steel doesn't want unions, we know that. So in their hiring practices, do they purposefully look at getting people from various places or regions? I don't know, but I wouldn't rule it out." In many cases, local unions have a say in who is hired by the company, but the company makes the final decision. Another steelworker told us about his experience being on the hiring committee for a U.S. Steel mill:

> I did interviews for the company, as local union president, we had that in our contract, so I got to see what they look for. . . . [The company] is always looking for someone who sides with them, people who are nonunion guys. They would ask if [the person being interviewed] belonged to unions before, they started off there. Then [the company interviewers] got into what [the applicant] would want to do in the mill. If they wanted to get into management, that was a bright spot in their interview process.

Whereas workers in the building trades are loyal to the local union as their hiring hall and the distributor of work, workers in industrial unions are more susceptible to split loyalty between the company as the source of their employment and the union as the advocate for their best interests in the workplace.

For industrial workers, work is usually constant—unless and until there are layoffs. In contrast, employment has always been more episodic in the building trades: one works based on when the union has been awarded contracts, and those contracts depend on regional growth and the ups and downs of market cycles. When a worker finishes a stint on one project, he or she comes into the union hall to sign "the book" to be assigned a new gig. Such assignments occur in chronological order based on who has been waiting the longest and has thus moved to the top of the list. Projects can be as short as several weeks or as long as a couple of years, interviewees told us. Especially in trades such as electrical work, one project can be very different from the next. Our interviewees told us that the fluidity of the work in the building trades was something that was attractive to many workers. Travel and varied projects keep the work interesting, some told us. "If you have a [building trades] union card, you're not tied to a particular employer. You can go wherever," one former electrical worker explained. Many IBEW members from other states, for instance, worked in the western Pennsylvania region prior to the collapse of the steel industry. When steel mills closed, those out-of-town workers were the ones let go—not the Pittsburgh-based IBEW members. One retired IBEW Local 5 member explained it to us this way:

> All the big contractors had all the work they wanted before the mills closed. We had loads of out-of-towners. If you were a Local 5 member, you were never laid off. Between 1939 until 1980 or 1981, there wasn't a single Local 5 union member laid off because we had so many out-of-towners. They were the fluid workforce. Some of those out-of-towners had union tickets from South Carolina or Connecticut or something, but they lived here.

In the building trades, work also moves from one place to another. Workers may apply their skills in one county one day and another state the next. In industrial unions, workers generally remain at a single workplace for their entire time as a member of that local union. If a worker was laid off at one mill represented by a USW local and then got a job at a different USW-organized mill, they often traded in their original local union card for a different one, even if the move was just down the street. This contrast means that building trades unions anchor workers to the union and a trade, while local industrial unions tend to link workers to places and particular company sites.

A final point worth emphasizing is union expansion (or the lack of it) into additional occupational and professional sectors. As we discussed in chapter 3, most industrial international unions have evolved to represent new categories of workers outside their original occupational sectors, but building trades unions have remained intensely trade-specific. The workers represented by each building trades union have not changed much in the last several decades: IBEW still represents communication workers and other types of electrical workers; the International Union of Bricklayers and Allied Craftworkers (BAC) represents bricklayers and masons; the International Association of Heat and Frost Insulators and Allied Workers (HFIAW) represents (you guessed it) thermal insulators.

When we asked various members of the building trades why their unions have kept to their traditional trades, most invoked respect for trade specialties and the often extensive training that a building tradesperson must go through to become a union journeyman. To become a member in a building trades union, one must go through extensive training, which usually includes a multiyear apprenticeship. "The building trades respect each other's expertise, that's why I think they haven't expanded," one member told us. "It would be like stepping on the toes of other unions." Prior to the mid-twentieth century, unionization by trades may have stymied some forms of cross-union labor unity, but the effects today may be the opposite: reinforcing union identity and solidarity. As one insulator explained to us, "I do believe . . . that the extensive training and nature of work in the trades contributes to more pride and unity, despite the decrease in regard to party politics these days. There's a substantial market for Building Trades insignia and tattoos. . . . I also think there is more respect for unionization in general [in the trades]."

The building trades unions have also refused to reach out beyond the construction industry, even when such steps could have avoided stepping on other unions' jurisdictions and could have increased their overall organizational power. The reason for this, many building tradespeople argue, is grounded in the sense of pride in a given skill set that all members of a building trade tend to feel. "Some building tradespeople, at least in my day, really saw themselves as the extension of the craft guilds of the Middle Ages," one retiree told us. "Those people [in the Middle Ages] were free—they weren't serfs—because of their specific skill set in masonry or whatever." Workers in the building trades take pride in the fact that their union membership requires a specific cultivated skill set. One electrician told us of a bird-watching trip she went on where she happened to run into a Canadian union carpenter with whom she immediately connected. "All my friends were amazed because they were like, 'Wow, he was instantly your friend,'" she said, laughing. "You instantly have a bond . . . he called me 'sparky' the rest of the day."

Union Salience and Communications

Key differences between the building trades and industrial unions that we have just summarized—company versus union as the "hiring hall," transitory versus permanent workplaces, and the range of occupations represented by unions—significantly affect union salience for members. We explored this idea in greater detail by focusing on IBEW and USW and coding the content of their international union publications from 1965 to 2015. Although both IBEW and USW sent monthly publications to all American and Canadian members, the content looked very different in the mid-twentieth century.[37] For decades, Steelworker publications were relatively short newspapers of about sixteen pages, while IBEW publications were magazines that could reach ninety pages in length. Topics in midcentury USW magazines generally focused on national happenings or events in the union that were of national consequence—a strike or lockout, for example—perhaps on the assumption that additional publications were regularly issued by locals serving members working and living close to one another. Topics in IBEW magazines were more varied, covering educational or general interest subjects—such as laying out for members what the various federal agencies do. Authors of the content in USW magazines were almost exclusively staff members of the International. In IBEW magazines, rank-and-file input—in the form of reports from local unions in the "Local Lines" section—often took up almost half the publication.

Why did such striking differences exist in the midcentury USW versus IBEW newsletters? IBEW likely sponsored and disseminated lengthy publications not only because its locals were less place-specific but also because members might not be working in the same territorial jurisdiction as their home district at any given time. When work was slow in a certain area, members had to travel to other jurisdictions, sometimes for months at a time. A lengthier, meatier magazine enabled local unions to communicate with their traveling members about the events and affairs of their unit. More space devoted to snippets about individuals also helped leaders keep in touch with union members and members with each other, even when they were working geographically apart.

To compare more precisely how communications from USW and IBEW evolved over decades, we conducted an analysis in which we coded every *mention* of a local union in two months of issues of IBEW and USW newsletters during one year at the midpoint of each decade, from 1965 to 2015. Every time a "Local Union X" was mentioned, we recorded various data points on how it was discussed, including the writer's affiliation, the location of the local, and the categorical relevance of the mention (see appendix D for more details on our methodology). In total,

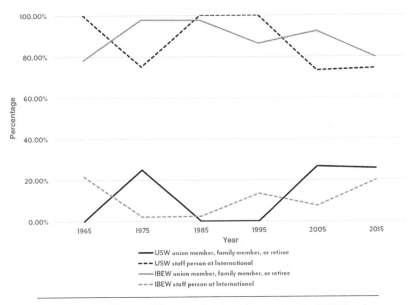

FIGURE 4.4 Writer affiliation of local union mentions in IBEW and USW magazines, 1965 to 2015.

we recorded more than 1,700 mentions of local unions. Our results reveal that when locals were mentioned in USW magazines, it was almost always in segments written by members of the central International staff. In contrast, mentions of locals in IBEW magazines were usually penned by a local union member or retiree writing to the editors (see figure 4.4). In addition, when we analyzed the photographs in IBEW and USW magazines, we found that IBEW consistently featured photos of local union members and their families more frequently than did USW. When aggregating all photos of local union members, family members, district leaders, and International staff, 83 percent of images depicted local union members and their families in IBEW magazines published from 1955, 1985, and 2015—versus just 17 percent of images depicting district or International leaders. By contrast, in USW newsletters, 62 percent of magazine photographs depicted local members and families, and 38 percent showed district or International staffers.[38]

We also examined the actual content of mentions about local unions. In the midcentury, such mentions in both USW and IBEW publications tended to be about personal or community-based matters, but as the decades covered in our coding progressed, the balance between such content and other kinds shifted in different ways in USW versus IBEW publications. We sorted each mention of a local union into the following content categories: social engagement, community engagement and/or charity, news on individual members or family members, union business affairs, and politics or political issues. We consider the first three of these five categories to be evidence of efforts to enhance the union's social salience—by highlighting union involvement in the community or in the personal or family lives of members. As the categories tracked in figures 4.5 and 4.6 show, over the early decades of our analysis, USW and IBEW references to locals placed similar emphasis on social, community, and individual topics—the kinds of references likely to have concrete and personal meaning to members. But over the decades, such emphasis significantly declined in USW publications, even as discussion of union business expanded, especially after the 1980s. In the IBEW publications, references to community involvement declined only marginally—suggestive that this building trades international union has continued to relate to its grassroots members in the same style and with similar personal and community stories over time.

The contrasting trends we have found in USW and IBEW publications make sense, in our view—and indicate different potentials for adaptation to the twenty-first-century conditions

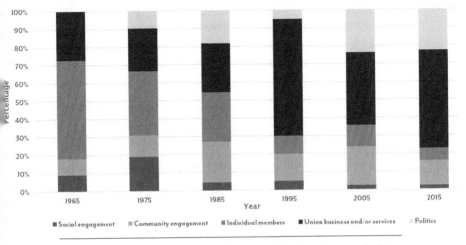

FIGURE 4.5 Emphasis on members/communities versus business/politics in USW magazine stories mentioning locals, 1965 to 2015.

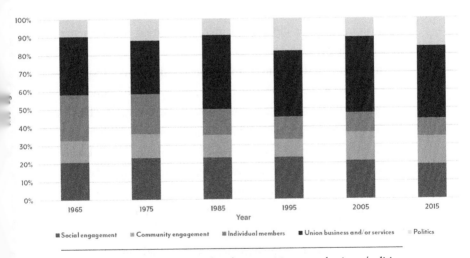

FIGURE 4.6 Emphasis on members/communities versus business/politics in IBEW magazine stories mentioning locals, 1965 to 2015.

faced by major unions. In its heyday, USW could rely on the reinforcement of general union messages to members by horizontal, less formal communication among union members employed in fixed workplaces with many ties among themselves and to neighbors in the immediately surrounding communities. And USW locals sometimes had newsletters of their own. Given such strong local roots, the International could send broader messages in its magazine and presume that personal and community content would reinforce union worldviews. The magazines sent from the International could concentrate on broader messages. When union members moved out of neighborhoods surrounding the surviving plants, local unions no longer had much infrastructure to build and sustain solidarity. Content about union business could still be conveyed in the magazine but not supplemented and reinforced by local communications. Nor would it be realistic to rely on locals and members to send information to magazine editors because many mills closed and many remaining union members have dispersed.

In contrast, IBEW and its magazine editors never presumed that they were reaching members working under the same roof or necessarily living close to one another. For example, IBEW Local 5, headquartered in Pittsburgh, has always represented members across large distances—a May 1978 map in the Local 5 newsletter shows that the jurisdiction covers almost half of the state of Pennsylvania. To create a sense of community, IBEW locals have long relied on publications that include written content submitted by locals and members, along with rotating gatherings held at different places within their jurisdictions. Given the constantly changing nature of work in construction, members of IBEW, even those enrolled in the same locals, do not see the same people at work every day, so they must stay connected to one another through explicit communications about themselves, their families, and union-sponsored events and activities.

In short, it has always been important for IBEW to engineer supralocal ways for members to read about one another's doings and to congregate in settings not in or near workplaces lest union members go years without seeing other members with whom they had become friends on this or that job. Well before the power of Big Labor and related manufacturing industries went into decline in Pennsylvania and beyond, IBEW, as an international and through its area-wide locals, already had infrastructures in place to coordinate gatherings and spread communications to widely scattered members. When storms of economic transformation hit the Rust Belt, it was easier for IBEW officials, magazine editors, and local union leaders to continue and to update long-standing patterns of communication. Maintaining engagement, pride, and unity among members has been significantly easier for IBEW than for USW. The contrasts we have explored in this chapter by tracking IBEW and USW and their magazines could be generalized to other building trades and industrial unions. In any event, it seems clear that IBEW—in some ways an "old fashioned," skill-based trade union—faces twenty-first-century realities with the benefit of already established practices designed to maintain connections and solidarity among members who work and live in widely scattered locales. USW did not have such practices when its local communicating networks collapsed in many places, which resulted in increased disconnection between members and their union.

Having probed several decades worth of changes in blue-collar and union communities in western Pennsylvania, we are ready to move back to the big picture and turn our attention to the ways in which the national and local shifts we have discussed so far are playing out for political loyalties and party fortunes in the current period. Chapter 5 tackles that challenge, tracing how much Pennsylvania's industrial union workers have changed from the days when it was virtually unthinkable for union members to announce support for Republicans.

5

FROM UNION BLUE TO
TRUMP RED

After Donald Trump carried most counties in western Pennsylvania by decisive margins, one Republican county chair to whom we spoke saw the region's current conservative proclivity as a culmination of political changes over the past several decades. "Democrats can say it was Trump, but no. It was a whole lot of things over the years," she told us in an early 2021 interview. "As the Republican Party, we were historically a nonissue here. We couldn't get anybody elected to anything except the offices that were required to go Republican by law." This began to shift in the 1990s, she told us, and electoral change accelerated until, in the 2000s, it seemed to her as if everyone in her county was voting Republican. Trump's distinctive version of GOP appeal simply sealed the partisan shift, she explained. By that time, previously pro-union Democratic strongholds, which included many counties in western Pennsylvania, moved decisively into the red column.

In this chapter, we consider the political reverberations of the changes in social and community ties discussed in the previous chapters. By developing this line of analysis, we further probe and pull together the underpinnings of the momentous Rust Belt political realignment that has played out so dramatically in western Pennsylvania.

NEW POLITICAL REALITIES IN FORMER STEEL COUNTRY

Let's begin by clarifying where and when electoral upheavals have happened—especially in presidential party politics. The GOP county chair quoted above did not have the timing quite right when she offered as an aside that GOP presidential contender Ronald Reagan "won this county in the eighties" because "Reagan won all over, everyone loved him." This was not correct. Despite the Gipper's broad popularity, he did not carry her county, let alone all of western Pennsylvania—not in 1980 and not in 1984. Although 1980 was a year in which more union households across the United States voted Republican than ever before in modern times, eight counties in western Pennsylvania voted for Democrat Jimmy Carter over Republican challenger Reagan—and those western counties added up to eight of just ten Keystone counties statewide that went for the Democratic presidential candidate that year.[1] Four years later, in 1984, ten western Pennsylvania counties voted for the Democratic candidate, Walter Mondale, leaving Philadelphia County in the southeast as the only other Pennsylvania jurisdiction that went blue. Despite erosions, what American studies researcher Taylor E. Dark calls "an enduring alliance" between "the unions and Democrats" persisted through the mid-1980s and, as figure 5.1 shows, even to the close of the twentieth century.[2]

Following Democratic erosions in the 1980s and 1990s, dramatic shifts away from blue candidates accelerated in the early 2000s. By 2016, only one western county—Allegheny, home of Pittsburgh—supported Democrat Hillary Clinton, and in 2020, only one additional western county joined Allegheny in the blue column, when Erie County in the state's northwest corner tipped for Biden. Looking more broadly across the entire twenty-county western region of Pennsylvania in 1984, nine counties, almost half, supported Democratic candidate Mondale. Those included

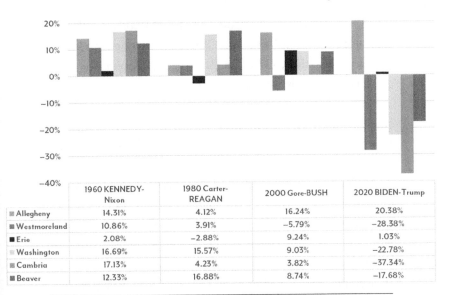

	1960 KENNEDY-Nixon	1980 Carter-REAGAN	2000 Gore-BUSH	2020 BIDEN-Trump
Allegheny	14.31%	4.12%	16.24%	20.38%
Westmoreland	10.86%	3.91%	-5.79%	-28.38%
Erie	2.08%	-2.88%	9.24%	1.03%
Washington	16.69%	15.57%	9.03%	-22.78%
Cambria	17.13%	4.23%	3.82%	-37.34%
Beaver	12.33%	16.88%	8.74%	-17.68%

FIGURE 5.1 Democratic presidential margins in the largest western Pennsylvania counties, 1960 to 2020. Especially since 2000, Republicans have made major gains everywhere except Allegheny County.

not only relatively industrialized Beaver, Cambria, Washington, and Westmoreland counties but also the smaller counties of Armstrong, Fayette, Greene, Lawrence, and Mercer.[3] By 2020, however, all nine of those counties weighed in for Republican Trump by margins ranging from 17.7 to 52.3 percentage points, with an average of a whopping 32.3-percentage-point margin.[4]

In the mid-twentieth century, quite a few rural western Pennsylvania counties were already consistently or occasionally voting Republican—so such counties have just become *more red* since 2000. But recent partisan U-turns have happened more broadly. Heavily unionized, industrial western counties that voted blue even during the early phases of steel's decline started shifting toward the GOP in the 1990s and then moved faster in that direction after the turn of the twenty-first century. Writing in 2014 for the *Beaver County Times*, J. D. Prose observed that

Beaver County, which was "long the home of labor strength and true-blue Democrats," had "two GOP state senators, two GOP state representatives, and a Tea Party–backed Republican congressman who easily won the county."[5]

The upshot is that, beyond Pittsburgh and its immediate environs, most of western Pennsylvania is by now red. Only Erie is truly a swing county. Although we will not provide all the details of political campaigns and elections below the presidential level, the strong swing to the political right has happened up and down the ballot in virtually all western counties—and by now, pro-GOP margins are not close. Nor is any partisan reversion back to the Democrats on the current horizon. Almost everywhere, public animus toward government, cities, and liberals is visibly emblazoned on flags, yard signs, and pickup trucks. Displays of loyalty to Trump and his version of the Republican Party can literally be over the top, as you can see in figure 5.2, which shows a display on a house in northwestern Pennsylvania.

FIGURE 5.2 Trump support signs in a yard in western Pennsylvania.
Photo by authors.

MAKING SENSE OF WORKING-CLASS REORIENTATION

Voters in many groups have shifted right across vast stretches of nonmetropolitan America, within and well beyond the Rust Belt. Working-class families have played an important role in that shift—including still-unionized workers in western Pennsylvania. To explain how and why unionists are involved in the march toward GOP loyalties, we rely necessarily on qualitative as well as quantitative evidence. As we discussed in chapter 1, when long-running national and statewide polls ask about the partisan loyalties of "union members," most ignore consequential distinctions between public versus private-sector unions, and they fail especially to pinpoint variations among union members employed in different specific industries or enrolled in particular international unions. That matters because union membership, even as it dwindles overall, has shifted toward public-sector unions enrolling white-collar employees who tend to be more politically progressive. The varied trades and industries represented by today's large industrial unions, such as the United Auto Workers (UAW) and United Steelworkers of America (USW), would make it difficult to parse political support among trade-specific union subgroups, such as steelworkers. To get at the finer distinctions that matter for our arguments here, we use quantified data about specific sets of union members when we can find them, but otherwise we offer insights and tentative conclusions based on news reports and—above all—the many interviews we have conducted.

Our union interviewees, active and retired, underlined consistently what must have occurred in many places to contribute to the aggregate voting transformations we have just described. "Absolutely" the politics of USW union members has changed, one retired Steelworker and former president of a union local told us. "When I grew up, the Steelworkers were all Democrats. . . . Now I can honestly tell you, from firsthand experience, . . . the majority of Steelworkers are not on the Democratic side anymore. Between Hillary and Trump, 90 or 95 percent [of members in my local] supported Trump. And that's a fact." Although the percentages mentioned by this retired leader cannot be confirmed, other USW members—including officials at the International— agreed on the underlying truth of this and other statements. They acknowledge that many union members went for Trump over Clinton in 2016 and that Trump did almost as well against Biden across western Pennsylvania in 2020. Tim Petrowski of USW Local 1900 was quoted by WBUR radio as saying that, while union management supported Biden, the rank and file in his South Lyon, Michigan, local was divided. "Twenty years ago, this place would have been 95 percent Democrats, and now it's really split. . . . I'd probably have to say something like 60–40 Republican over Democrat now," he said.[6] Such a realignment also held for the United Mine Workers of America (UMWA), with members expressing enthusiastic support for Trump in both 2016 and 2020. One UMWA interviewee had access to some systematic intraunion data but, on the record, was only willing to be quoted saying that "a lot" of his members support Trump, adding "because it's true."

Republican leaders know about the support their candidates get from rank-and-file union members. One of the county political chairs we spoke to estimated that "75 to 80 percent" of the "union people" in his county voted for Trump in 2020. "People are scared," he added. Not only did this Republican chair say that most union people in his county voted for Trump, but he also said that many believed that the election was rigged. "We all know the [2020] election was stolen.

I don't have to be a believer to sit back and look at the facts. It doesn't take a brain surgeon to figure it out, they had four years to plan it."

Multiple factors have played out for years to account for the regional electoral change—including aftershocks from the collapse of the steel industry and subsequent economic shifts, the brute shrinkage in union membership and resources, population and demographic changes, and overall shifts in U.S. politics toward highlighting the cultural clashes that most scholars stress as motivating workers who vote for Republicans. Our contribution here is to acknowledge yet go beyond these factors to focus on the growth of status resentments among workers, including many still unionized, who feel left behind by Democrats, even as they are also attracted to right-leaning causes and GOP loyalties.

To aid our analysis, we extend insights about place-based divisions of the sort political scientist Kathy Cramer developed to explain urban versus rural clashes in Wisconsin.[7] Even in still industrialized areas of western Pennsylvania, we see analogous worker resentments grounded in a sense that they have been "left behind" and are looked down upon by urbanites. Such perceived divisions have partisan implications because, for many remaining Rust Belt workers, unionized or not, the Democratic Party seems increasingly wedded to metropolitan constituents and no longer locally present or attuned to the concerns of other groups once loyal to the party. Along with growing resentment of today's Democratic Party, new ties to right-wing aligned groups and organizations propel many workers into Republican ranks. This happens even though international union leaders continue to argue, as they long have, that Democrats favor public policies more likely to help workers and unions.

Regional Economic Transformation and Resentment

In March 1988, two years after the closure of the once mighty U.S. Steel plant in Homestead, Pennsylvania, His Royal Highness Charles, then Prince of Wales, visited western Pennsylvania to discuss the future of the Monongahela Valley. The prince, now king of Great Britain, had a passion for architectural design and came to Pittsburgh to speak to groups of "architects, academics and others debating ways in which cities and towns could best respond to the brutal realities of post-industrial life."[8] One of the most popular proposals in these circles at the time was to create a "garden festival" where the Homestead steel mill had been (see figure 5.3). Other ideas included building a dock for yachts where the mill had formerly loomed. But many workers were less than thrilled by these notions, and the *Pittsburgh Post-Gazette* cited an especially pointed retort: "We were the

FIGURE 5.3 Postcard view of the entrance to the U.S. Steel Works in Homestead, Pennsylvania, ca. 1960. Theda Skocpol personal collection.

steel-making capital of the world, and they were talking about flowers. We wanted to get back to steel making."[9]

To this day, Pittsburgh uses historic iconography to portray itself as "the Steel City" that "built America." But the reality has become very different: the city has moved past its bygone era of industrial glory.[10] Like the U.S. economy that once thrived on domestically produced goods and materials, the Pittsburgh economy now features—and promotes—services, health care, and knowledge-based industries. This transition has advanced quickly, no matter how much pride still-living workers take in the buildings, bridges, and beltways they constructed not long ago or the chemicals, automobiles, metals, and other industrial goods they produced in factories now mostly shuttered or cleared away for shopping malls or strip malls. The recommendations King Charles offered during his visit spoke to the emerging economy, even if they were jarring to some ears, because they epitomized the chasms many industrial workers felt between an older economy and society and new forms of work and social life. To many working-class people, the emerging economy of western Pennsylvania was beginning to forget and devalue their skills, lives, and accomplishments.

Across America's Rust Belt, the period after the collapse of the steel industry and contraction of many other industries was a time of significant change not only for the family, union, and community, as we have discussed, but also for the economy as a whole. Some parts of the Rust Belt have made only fitful progress and continued to flounder economically, including Youngstown and Toledo, Ohio, and Detroit and Flint, Michigan. But other areas, including Pittsburgh, emerged from years of uncertainty to ride an education and medical transition to a more white-collar-centric workforce. As one interviewee aptly put it, higher education and health care propelled Pittsburgh into the twenty-first century. In some parts of western Pennsylvania, the knowledge and service economy came to replace manufacturing as a source of jobs and market revival. Around Buffalo, New York, too, areas that used to be home to heavy manufacturing facilities now provide jobs in health care, social assistance, or educational services.

However promising this large-scale economic transition looks from afar, for many Rust Belt areas, the transition from an industrial economy to a knowledge- and service-based economy has been wrenching not only fiscally but also socially and psychologically for many workers and community members. In the late 1970s, Pittsburgh mayor Richard Caliguiri launched a planned urban revitalization called Renaissance II to help his city's economy rely less on heavy industry and manufacturing. Saving Pittsburgh's economy from the steel crisis was the goal—not saving the actual steel industry—and from the launch of Renaissance II to the early 2000s, the sites of some of the greatest steel mills of America changed drastically. While some rusted away, others were turned into strip malls, new facilities, or landmarks to attract tourists. The former U.S. Steel building, which had been completed in 1970, became the new headquarters of the internationally acclaimed University of Pittsburgh Medical Center (UPMC) hospital system, while Bakery Square, site of the former Nabisco plant, became a business park home to Google and other technology companies.

The urban center of Pittsburgh may have bounced back from industrial decline, but former industrial towns and small cities outside the city limits kept struggling and decaying. Although some efforts were made to use worker retraining programs to boost communities beyond the big city, many industrial workers who once worked and socialized in places like Clairton and Monongahela felt left behind in a regional economy that had simply moved on in a highly unequal and geographically varied manner. In the midcentury industrial heyday, many steel and other industries' corporate headquarters were located in the city of Pittsburgh. But most of their productive mills and plants operated outside the city limits—and most of their workers lived near the outlying plants. Industrial decline therefore hit the smaller outlying neighborhoods and cities harder. From the mid-1980s, the unemployment rate of Allegheny County became significantly lower than those of the surrounding counties. While Allegheny County's unemployment rate was 13.9 percent in 1983, Westmoreland County's was 19.3, Fayette County's was 24.9, and Beaver County's was 27.1.[11] These unemployment figures do not even account for the thousands who left the region for jobs elsewhere. In the Mon Valley alone, employment in the steel industry decreased from 35,000 in 1979 to less than 1,000 in 1986.[12]

Given these realities before and during the transition from heavy industry to the services and knowledge economy, Renaissance II had some credibility and effectiveness, but "the [region as a whole] really suffered," as a United Electrical, Radio, and Machine Workers (UE) interviewee told us. "We lost a massive amount of people—200,000 from Youngstown to Johnstown. [Those people are] all over the country now." Another interviewee asked us if we knew why there are so many Steeler fans all over the country and went on to explain that it was because of the mass exodus after the industry collapsed. The migrants may have found new jobs elsewhere, but they kept their allegiance to Pittsburgh's heralded football team.

During the Renaissance II period, infrastructure and economic improvement projects unfolded both within Pittsburgh and in surrounding areas—but according to many observers, the distribution was not proportional to need. Public-private partnerships and government tax money funded many projects in well-off suburbs rather than in struggling mill communities. As Robert Erickson and Charles Martoni noted in their 1987 paper for the *Journal of the American Planning Association*, that meant "the affluent southern suburbs of Pittsburgh are served by a new $500 million light rail system while the roads and bridges of the Mon Valley collapse." Only "a few million dollars have been spent in the Mon Valley in recent years to repair the infrastructure and to develop alternative uses for currently abandoned industrial sites."[13] Along with other forces beyond their control, such disparate flows of funding for revitalization left many blue-collar workers feeling understandably left behind and increasingly frustrated with their relegation to the fringes of society.

Hearing from the Bypassed

Resentments about being left behind by recent economic transformations of Pittsburgh permeated many of our discussions with interviewees, young and old. One man recounted a snide remark from Mayor Caliguri that left workers from the original UE and USW locals feeling betrayed:

> When we first came to Pittsburgh, we went to see the [U.S. Steel's] Homestead Works. You got a sense of just how big it was. It was just huge and it was very impressive to see. Then, all of a sudden, it was all empty. When Caliguri was asked one time about Pittsburgh losing a third of its population after the steel collapse, he said, "Well they weren't the best people anyways." Yeah. Can you believe that?

At one time, political and corporate leaders alike had championed the region's heavy industry and its workers, but Caliguri's comment signaled a departure from that. As the area's economy moved on, workers experienced more than economic losses. They felt betrayed by local and regional leaders who seemed prepared to forget or disrespect the earlier foundational contributions of an entire segment of the population. Many felt they were not only abandoned economically but also rejected socially, bypassed as less worthy citizens compared to rising urbanites working in the education and medical fields.

New economic successes in metropolises like Pittsburgh can, in short, encourage optimism among some yet at the same time stoke status resentments for others. Insecurities about employment coupled with feelings of social downgrading led to a new kind of blue-collar social identity and outlook, filled with resentments in sharp contrast to the optimistic "union man" identity of the mid-twentieth century. Where once there was a forward-looking, even triumphalist sense of shared unionized worker power, now mutually reinforced feelings of loss and rejection are widespread. Some interviewees expressed this as frustration with others not knowing the history of the region; others declared outward hostility toward the malls and parks that now stand where mills and plants stood; and some blamed urban centers for attracting resources and talent away from struggling communities outside the city.

Looking at the matter analytically, these clashes of outlook resemble the place- and class-based resentments analyzed by Cramer as "rural consciousness" opposed to urbanism in Wisconsin. Cramer traveled that state and listened to the voices of nonmetropolitan people who expressed despair and anger at being left behind by Madison and Milwaukee.[14] The resentments we witness in western Pennsylvania among blue-collar current and retired workers, including unionists, are similarly grounded in uneven place-based changes. But the resentments against metropolitan areas that we discuss are mostly not "rural." Although some workers and retirees we spoke to do live in rural western Pennsylvania, many live in small towns or working-class suburbs.

Cramer defines the resentments she found in Wisconsin as based on social perceptions that metropolitan "decision makers routinely ignore rural places and fail to give rural communities their fair share of resources, as well as a sense that rural folks are fundamentally different from urbanites in terms of lifestyles, values, and work ethic."[15] We find from interviews with western Pennsylvanians that place-based tensions are front and center, but we also learned that not all interviewees in Pennsylvania actually resent the economic shifts of Pittsburgh and the nation. Some simply express a profound sense of loss—without hostility—for bygone livelihoods and the decline of their own communities. One elderly shopkeeper in Charleroi, Pennsylvania, encapsulated this sense of loss. In a conversation at the checkout, we asked about the shop. She told us it had been there for a long time—"forever," as she said—and we asked if a lot had changed since she had begun working there. "Oh yeah," she replied quietly. "Everything has changed. These streets used to be so busy you could barely walk down them—that was back before the mills closed down. It was the perfect place to live." Some workers and community members, like this shopkeeper, looked at the changes with wistful nostalgia, while others exhibited more pronounced resentment, but almost all of those to whom we spoke either implicitly or explicitly contrasted their communities' present state with that of revamped urban centers.

As in Cramer's observations, the beliefs of many of our interviewees were rooted in place and class.[16] In our case, however, "place" is more about where individuals are *not* located than where they are. These workers share a sense that they have no access to the benefits and opportunities that core city residents often get in both the private and public sectors. One retired Steelworker summarized it eloquently: "I remember the glory days [of the Mon Valley]. That'll never happen again. . . . But at the same time, I know that there are a lot of places in this country that are thriving. And look at Pittsburgh—it went from being a steel mill town to [being] a medical center. So that's how the industry in Pittsburgh flipped. For this valley, we're just rusted, a time gone by in history." The retired Steelworker directly juxtaposes the precipitous decline of the industrial towns in the Monongahela Valley to Pittsburgh's successful transition out of being simply a steelmaking city. His tone reflected loss, not hostility or bitterness.

Earlier in our interview, this same interviewee commented, "Growing up in Charleroi, they called it 'Magic City' because it was the shopping center of the valley. It was jumping, man, back here in the seventies." Having lived in his childhood home of Charleroi his whole life, he could vividly describe how much the area has changed: "Growing up in Charleroi, it was the best. We had seven shoe stores, four movie theaters, you couldn't walk down the street because there were so many people. Now this is one of the drug capitals of the valley. These towns are ghost towns. It's never ever going to get better; they call it the Rust Belt for a reason. It's a shame." Although the changes that came to the valley made residents there feel forgotten and left behind, many are still attached to Pittsburgh and view gains there with minimal resentment and potentially even a bit of pride.

For interviewees who expressed more irritation, the public's lack of awareness about the industrial history of the region informed greater hostility toward the progress of Pittsburgh. Older workers especially, but also some younger ones, are proud of Pittsburgh's industrial history and feel attached to the project of preserving it. As one older but not retired Steelworker put it:

> [People now in southwestern Pennsylvania] don't know the history and what we've gone through over the years, the struggle the valley has gone through. They see all these shops in Homestead, they don't know that was a sprawling mill at one time. Duquesne is a research center, McKeesport is closed. Our history was wiped away. They don't realize what was there and what we struggled for. I don't think they realize why we fight so hard for the couple thousand jobs we have. It's sentimental for a lot of us. They say, "Steel is bad, just realize it," and it's not.

This respondent's "us versus them" and "we versus they" comments are emblematic of how some industrial workers contrast their experiences and understandings with the experiences of outsiders, especially urbanites.

Feelings of loss are compounded by some workers' beliefs that many others in the region seem unmindful that some heavy industry persists in the region. One younger interviewee who works at Irvin Works in West Mifflin, Pennsylvania, told us a story about going into Pittsburgh and doing a boat tour of the city. During the tour, the guide made a comment about steel no longer being made in the region. After the tour concluded, our interviewee approached the tour guide and told him that what he had said was incorrect—there is still some steel being made in western Pennsylvania. He pushed for this correction, he explained to us, because a "lot of people don't get it; they don't think we're still making steel in Pittsburgh. You gotta take pride in that. . . . I come from a whole line of steelworkers and coal miners, you should be proud of where you've come from and what you represent."

Some workers pointed fingers at corporate greed and poor government policies. A couple of older interviewees cited the 1982 decision of U.S. Steel to purchase Marathon Oil rather than modernize its equipment in aging steel mills to compete with foreign-made steel as symbolic of companies' general lack of care for their workers. Such decisions—of companies making large corporate acquisitions instead of investing in the people and places devoted to the American industry—appear to many to be constantly recurring.[17] Workers also placed blame on politicians who catered to corporate interests rather than protecting domestic workers. Not all the politicians who interviewees considered to have left them behind were Republicans; Democrats were equally if not more responsible according to many.

Some workers we spoke to recognized that, toward the end of the twentieth century, class power in politics became even more pronounced and that upper-class influence affected the economic transition of the region. As one former UE member put it, the "politicians were looking to where the money was, which was the Duquesne Club, the corporate people, who were saying, 'We're going to be [a city based on] eds and meds here.'" The Duquesne Club is one of the most elite business and social clubs in Pittsburgh, located for more than a century in the heart of downtown. Its website in 2021 proudly quoted a prominent businessman as saying that "many of the major business transactions in Pittsburgh were negotiated within the walls of this historic club."[18] As Pittsburgh repositioned itself to be a twenty-first-century health-care, technology, and education hub rather than an old mill town, workers' reactions varied, but all agreed that choices by elites to deprioritize heavy industry and its workers contributed to the surrounding region's decline and displacements.

The feelings of regret, displacement, and resentment came through more clearly in our discussions with industrial union members, even as we learned that workers in the electrical fields and building trades often do not feel the same way or with such intensity because their jobs were not as tied to outlying communities. But these blue-collar workers, including those in unions like the International Brotherhood of Electrical Workers (IBEW), also often perceive status-laden social differentness between themselves and core urbanites. In a twenty-first-century America that increasingly touts higher education over manual labor and technical skills, workers in the construction industry experience many of the same realities and feelings as displaced or still employed industrial workers. Interclass interaction is increasingly infrequent, which has contributed to heightened divides between workers in blue-collar fields and their regional neighbors in other social or economic strata, with many political reverberations we will explore later in this chapter. Even if blue-collar workers live or work near a big city, many of these divides, some of them expressed explicitly in shared worldviews, unite them to other similarly situated individuals, setting the stage for tensions and conflicts with white-collar or elite urbanites thought to be out of touch with today's working class and union realities. As one UE retiree summed up, "I think there's a lot of bitterness toward the coasts and the people who shed crocodile tears but don't do anything. The coasts have done just fine, when the rest has suffered."

Of course, Pittsburgh's leaders still memorialize the steel industry. An official video fashioned to persuade Amazon to select Pittsburgh as the location for its second headquarters was entitled "Future. Forged. For All" and started with a voice-over narrator saying, "You've probably heard something about Pittsburgh. The city that built America. The city that built the world. The city that fell so hard."[19] Visuals accompanying this narration—intended to spur a faster shift to a knowledge- and service-based economy—show old clips of the steel mills along the river and steelworkers tipping their hard hats to the camera. Former mayor Bill Peduto tweeted in November 2020 that Pittsburgh is "Rust Belt strong," the "gem of Appalachia."[20] Such statements are common among leaders but can sound awkward to industrial workers in the region. Talk aside, many workers feel left behind by regional elites who they believe have moved on without properly supporting their disrupted lives or truly valuing their work, past or present.

THE LURE OF RIGHT-WING TIES AND LOYALTIES

As divides and vacuums appeared in once-thriving industrial areas of western Pennsylvania, new social involvements and redirected political loyalties have taken their place for many blue-collar workers, unionized or not. Of course, gross demographic shifts have undoubtedly contributed to political rearrangements. A mass exodus of workers from the western Pennsylvania region followed the collapse of Big Steel. Despite overall U.S. population growth, for example, Washington County, home to many once-bustling industrial towns in the Monongahela Valley, had 83,251 voters in the 1976 election but 77,745 voters in 1996. Even Allegheny County, home to the revitalized city of Pittsburgh, went from 647,857 voters in the 1976 presidential election to 538,615 twenty years later. During this same era, economic and population growth occurred in the Philadelphia region, hundreds of miles away in the southeast corner of the state. Over time, western areas become less weighty in Pennsylvania politics overall.

Not only did regional populations shrink but the western Pennsylvanians who moved away also tended to be young. As one retired UE member said, "We lost all five of our children because they just left the area. There was nothing here for young people. The crumbs that were here were pretty much taken [by the unemployed]. The young people fled this area like crazy." Some retired unionists stayed loyal to old ideals of union and Democratic Party solidarity, but political science research indicates that, in general, older individuals vote for conservative candidates at higher rates than younger people do.[21] Thus, regional population losses and aging likely contributed to the conservative turn.

However, political shifts in most of western Pennsylvania are attributable to more than population movements and geographically uneven economic transitions. Community-level reorganizations have also undermined Democrats and bolstered the political right—and in our view, those local reorganizations have been especially important for steelworkers and other industrial unionists, whose lives once revolved around mills, union locals, and nearby associations and churches. That web of community groups reinforced peer ties that fostered the midcentury "union man" outlook and Democratic Party loyalties. As a current Republican Party chair we interviewed acknowledged, "I was a Democrat most of my life . . . because this was a Democratic county. . . . It didn't matter what the person did, [workers] would just vote Democrat. They didn't look at the person, they just voted Democrat." But by now, support for unions and voting for Democrats are no longer automatic. Rank-and-file union members now routinely ignore higher-level union leaders who endorse Democrats and vote instead for Republicans. This has happened, we argue, as workers have become more involved with nonunion community organizations propagating right-wing outlooks that reinforce many simmering resentments of big cities and Democrats. We do not argue that new ties and loyalties matter *instead* of demographic and economic shifts, but we do maintain that social network reorganizations interacted with and reinforced larger macro-level trends and transformations.

Today's locally influential western Pennsylvania groups lean toward conservative priorities. We build on the previous chapter's discussion of churches and gun groups to show that newly intensified and politically charged ties involve gun rights associations and Tea Party affiliations as well as prolife churches and a wider array of more recently expanding far-right networks—all of them increasingly intertwined with energized local GOP organizations. This interlocking array of local groups has a disproportional influence on the social, political, and regional identities of workers, in contrast to the situation decades ago when organized labor had a cornerstone role in the region. As many towns and cities withered and the influence of labor unions (especially industrial unions) advocating for working people declined, many western Pennsylvania workers and their families and neighbors turned elsewhere for social and political connections and inspiration.

Gun Clubs and Networks

In the 2000 election year, the *Los Angeles Times* reported on Rust Belt union members struggling to decide between voting for the Democratic candidate, Al Gore, and the Republican candidate, George Bush Jr. "The gun issue is the issue, definitely," said one United Dairy and Bakery Workers member from Saginaw, Michigan. "If Gore was elected there would be no Second Amendment, cut and dried."[22] In 2000, internal labor polling found that more than 40 percent of union members were sympathetic to the National Rifle Association (NRA).[23] In this same election year, J. J. Barry and Edwin Hill—the international president and international secretary-treasurer of IBEW, respectively—wrote a letter to members in the union's monthly magazine entitled "Your Vote Belongs to You—Use It Well." In it, they recognized the different civic and political allegiances pulling on IBEW members, saying, "Being an IBEW member is only part of our identity. We are active in religious groups, gun clubs, civic organizations, fraternal lodges, and, yes, politics."[24] They end the letter by urging members, first and foremost to vote but to bear in mind the union when making their decision. By 2000, when this letter and the aforementioned *Los Angeles Times* article were written, the NRA and AFL-CIO— contending for workers' attention and loyalties—were the two most influential associations in many industrial communities across the Rust Belt and beyond. Long before the rise of Trump, in short, unions were going head-to-head with the NRA—along with the politically involved local gun clubs to which unionists belonged—to win the votes of those who were often members of both.

Local unions have recently used the tools in their arsenal— such as newsletters and recreational opportunities among members—to push back on the NRA's influence over members' political loyalties. In the fall 2020 issue of the IBEW Local 5 newsletter, business manager Michael Dunleavy addresses the gun issue directly in his recurring column, the "Business Manager's Corner":

> If the Second Amendment is your issue, it has already been affirmed by the Supreme Court that you have the right to bear arms. With the current six to three majority and the younger age of the conservative members of the Court, this right is guaranteed going forward so there is no need to vote against what is best for you, your family and your fellow Union Members economically.

An interesting fact is that guns have only been confiscated two times in American history; both times under Republican Presidents most recently during Hurricane Katrina in New Orleans when George Bush (43) was President and Louisiana had a Republican Governor.[25]

This column nicely epitomizes a kind of defensive union accommodation to progun politics. In a sense, contemporary unions are trying to push guns back into the more apolitical social space they once held for many of their members. Although long part of working-class social life, guns were not always a top political flashpoint, and gun organizations were historically not able to rival or replace union influences. Indeed, for much of the first century of its existence, the NRA itself was mainly concerned with instructing gun owners on how to shoot accurately and even had other priorities, such as wildlife conservation.[26]

The NRA's mission abruptly changed in the late 1970s, however, when a dissatisfied contingent of the organization overthrew the traditional leadership at the 1977 annual conference.[27] Since then, the organization has become increasingly political and more closely tied to gun manufacturers looking to sell more powerful armaments, guns, and gear, and aligning almost exclusively to a more rightward-leaning Republican Party. The NRA now gives huge donations to political candidates, spends millions on legislative lobbying, gives "grades" to elected officials based on their stance on gun rights, and encourages its members to prioritize gun issues when they go to the polls. In addition, ethnographic research on NRA-sponsored gun safety training and recreational activities finds that these programs convey important moral messages about the meaning of good citizenship, portraying gun enthusiasts as citizens who care about protecting their communities, families, and the nation.[28] Just as unions once did much more effectively than they do today, the NRA links national and state politics and policies to local socially embedded identities and moral outlooks.

As we learned in chapter 4, gun clubs in western Pennsylvania have become more central as alternative community institutions have dwindled. They continue to teach and promote safe gun stewardship, and they also help keep people in touch with one another. As one retired steelworker said:

> I see [the guys I used to work with] every so often. I saw one guy over at the gun club, every time [we see each other] we tell stories [about the mill], we just laugh our butts off. . . . The gun club I went to was up in Washington Township in Belle Vernon. But the whole part about it was that it was basically a big bar, you basically go there to socialize. It's not because it was a gun club, it could've been anything.

From this interviewee's perspective, the function of the gun club is not as important as the fact that it brought people together. He went on to say that the gun club might as well have been a Lithuanian club. Because many ethnic and other community-oriented organizations are no longer present in the region, gun clubs have become a hub for community engagement. The current Democratic Party chair in a western Pennsylvania county—who is a former building trades union member and from a family of coal miners—affirmed that gun clubs function as social gathering places. "The gun clubs are a place to go to drink on Sundays when the bar is closed. [Many] people who belong are social members. It's kind of a drinking club," he explained. Many gun clubs have capitalized on their recent role of fostering member-to-member relationships by broadening the scope of the club to include other activities.

It might seem innocuous that community social interactions are now occurring at gun clubs rather than in union halls or ethnic clubs, but there are critical political side effects of this transition. Many of the hundreds of gun clubs in the western Pennsylvania region receive grant money or other perks from the NRA or its Pennsylvania affiliate, and their websites often include links to the NRA website or provide instructions about how to join. In chapter 4, we gave the example of one western Pennsylvania gun club that requires individual membership in the NRA in order to be eligible to join the gun club. Hand in hand with such links go political messages because many club mission statements now tout the importance of protecting Second Amendment rights. The increasing relevance of NRA-linked gun clubs as hubs for community interconnectivity means that "America's gun culture is about a lot more than individuals, because gun ownership is connected to cultural understandings and to social networks of kin and friends who do activities together."[29] According to one recent study, more than one of every five gun owners feel that "guns are part of their social lives with family and friends."[30] For some workers, guns also serve as a reminder and remnant of their service in the nation's military—in this sense, guns function both as a patriotic emblem and as a social symbol that connects them to other veterans. As gun ownership came to represent more than just recreation, the nonliteral connotations and emblematic meaning of guns became just as important as their functionality.

To spell out one obvious channel of influence, gun clubs often host events for candidates running for local or state office, and those events help to make guns—as well as so-called social issues such as abortion—what one county Democratic Party chair in western Pennsylvania calls "dead-end issues." Gun clubs and right-leaning churches alike urge members to make their

188 • FROM UNION BLUE TO TRUMP RED

selections at the ballot boxes based nearly exclusively on these two politically polarized issues. According to this Democratic Party chair, Republican candidates for local and state offices often tout progun and antiabortion loyalties in visits to gun clubs for campaign events. Although some Democratic candidates try to visit gun clubs as well, "[they] have to work really hard to feel accepted." For Republican candidates, the Democratic Party chair said, "there are more natural inroads."

More broadly, gun clubs intensify industrial workers' sense of cultural nostalgia. As sociology and government professor Jennifer Carlson points out in *Citizen-Protectors*, NRA-sponsored courses and events affirm the traditional white male interpretation of being a good citizen obligated to use guns and knowledge about them to protect those who are ostensibly less able to protect themselves.[31] A good example of this outlook lies in popular right-wing support for Kyle Rittenhouse following the Kenosha, Wisconsin, incident in which he killed two men in what he claimed was self-defense after he traveled there purportedly to protect small businesses.[32] Rittenhouse may have been just barely beyond boyhood, but he was enacting a celebrated male role for the political right—the role of the armed protector.

Changes in gender and race relations may also explain why gun ownership and club ties are so attractive to blue-collar white men, including current and former industrial unionists. Based on name data from gun clubs' websites, club leadership in western Pennsylvania is almost entirely male, and given the demographics of western Pennsylvania counties and American gun owners, we can safely assume that club membership skews significantly male (and white) as well.[33] As psychiatrist and sociologist Jonathan Metzl argues, "working-class white men long benefited from racial and gender systems that gave them a monopoly over manufacturing and construction jobs," but recent "changes in the economic and social order left working-class white men feeling bypassed . . . [by] women and people of color."[34] White men more often work with or for women and people of color than in previous generations, and, of course, family roles have also changed in ways that require many men to share duties once left to homemaking wives. Participation in gun clubs thus serves to reestablish and reaffirm the otherwise receding male role as the source of family protection and leadership within the community. Guns themselves may symbolize the remaining power and authority that many white men wish to assert and preserve as their other sources of social leverage recede. Gun clubs and pro-Second Amendment associations can therefore tap into powerful yearnings felt consciously or subconsciously.

Many if not most gun clubs have Facebook pages or websites that not only keep members informed of events at the club but also encourage engagement on policy issues that affect gun rights. For example, the Ambridge District Sportsmen's Association, a club claiming about 1,200 members in Beaver County near the former location of the Jones and Laughlin Aliquippa Works steel mill, has what it calls "legislation alerts" on its webpage, which also declares, "We are strong supporters of the Second Amendment. . . . We thank you in advance for helping to make Pennsylvania a strong Pro-Second Amendment state and our Nation a strong Pro-Second Amendment nation."[35] During the 2020 election cycle, this association publicized get-out-the-vote events organized by the Firearms Owners Against Crime organization, which featured guests including Donald Trump Jr., and it also shared a poster-like image entitled, "Stand Your Ground Against Socialism" with details about a rally in Harrisburg to protect gun rights. Some clubs, such as this one, are overtly conservative and support the Second Amendment; some are less forceful. Either way, gun club proclamations of

conservative values often silence both in-person and online dis-
senters. As one retired Steelworker and Democrat said, "I know
to keep my mouth shut when I go to the [gun] clubs. There are
certain unwritten rules because if people started talking [about
politics], there could be a serious problem." Gun clubs encourage members, either explicitly or implicitly, to prioritize voting
for candidates based on the gun issue.

Of course, the processes we have just summarized are unfolding far beyond western Pennsylvania and even the Rust Belt,
where gun and hunting clubs have long been present. (The
Ambridge District Sportsmen's Association in Beaver County,
for instance, was founded in 1935.[36]) In recent years, however, the
significantly right-leaning political mobilization of the NRA and
other organized gun networks, combined with the reduced influence of labor unions, has shifted the source of network-grounded
political information and peer influences for members and neighbors of these clubs. Gun ownership in the United States peaked
in the 1990s, during which 51 percent of respondents to a Gallup
survey reported having a gun in the house.[37] As of 2017, 85 percent
of surveyed Americans felt that gun laws were an "important
issue" to their voting choices, with 25 percent of respondents saying that, in order for them to cast a ballot for a candidate, that
candidate "must share their views on gun control."[38] Second only
to building a wall on the U.S.-Mexico border, Americans as of
2017 were most polarized on the issue of gun control legislation.
Since the 1990s, Republicans have become more monotonically
progun and opposed to virtually any limits on gun purchases, in
contrast to previous commonsense gun control regulations that
Republicans of generations past supported.[39] In 1995 only about
45 percent of surveyed Republicans believed that the government
should prioritize protecting gun rights over gun control legislation, but in 2017, that number was about 80 percent.[40]

For many, gun ownership is a way of life: an intergenerational hobby, a valuable way to collect old and new objects, and the means to defend one's family against harm. Many working-class men feel proud of their guns, which represent their power to protect themselves and others. Guns are "made of real mass and . . . draw real blood, and [they function] as connotative cyphers whose associations trigger themes such as protection, danger, safety, identity, race, gender, class, erotics, oppression, or revulsion."[41] Gun clubs and the companies that sell guns and gear to individuals and clubs play on men's desire to be seen as protective and powerful agents within the family and community, running advertisements with statements such as that the gun restores the "balance of power" in the family and a man's "confidence to live [his] life."[42] Membership in gun clubs and ownership of guns themselves today represent social and civic commitments as much as recreational interests.

From Union Halls to Local Tea Parties

In his fall 2012 column in the newsletter, the business manager of IBEW Local 5, Michael Dunleavy, wrote about seeing Tea Party bumper stickers in the parking lots of the local union. "This morning when returning from a downtown meeting, I pulled into the Local Union parking lot behind a vehicle with multiple bumper stickers touting the Tea Party," he said. "This member came to sign the book [to get assigned a job] and obviously didn't see the correlation between his unemployment and [the Tea Party's] policies."[43] As this anecdote suggests, western Pennsylvania sprouted Tea Party–affiliated groups in the early 2010s, and as Dunleavy noticed, Tea Party participation or sympathy and union membership overlapped.

The Tea Party was a massive political reaction against the results of the November 2008 election. Barack Obama was elected America's first Black president and Democrats won both houses of Congress. Within weeks of Obama's inauguration amid a deepening major economic recession, an MSNBC commentator, Rick Santelli, used his show to call for "Tea Party protests" against Democratic mortgage assistance and other economic recovery policies.[44] Days to weeks later, street protests spread, featuring largely older white individuals dressed in colonial costumes symbolizing Revolutionary-era resistance against government "tyranny." Many carried signs denouncing President Obama, some with racist slogans or pictures. Ultraright national advocacy organizations and Fox News and other right-leaning media outlets jumped on the bandwagon, calling for coordinated nationwide protests against Obama and the Democrats. Waves of such protests occurred in the ensuing weeks and months, including hundreds of Tea Party demonstrations around Tax Day in April 2009 (and subsequent years) as well as coordinated protests around the Fourth of July and a massive march on Washington in September 2009.[45] Starting in the spring of 2009, self-proclaimed Tea Party conservatives opposed to President Obama and health-care reform and climate change bills making their way through Congress went beyond street protests and Beltway lobbying to organize what eventually became some 2,000 to 3,000 local, voluntarily led Tea Party groups. Spearheaded by volunteer leaders and boasting membership numbers ranging from the dozens to the thousands, local Tea Party affiliates spread across all fifty U.S. states and met regularly—weekly, biweekly, or monthly—in towns, suburbs, and cities all over America.[46]

Scholars studying the Tea Party at first tended to accept the word of national professional free-market advocacy groups like Americans for Prosperity that this was a movement of fiscally conservative people opposed to social spending and federal government deficits.[47] But eventually attitude studies and ethnographic and interview-based studies established that, at the grassroots, most local Tea Party groups were more intensely animated by cultural conservative causes such as opposition to immigration and resentment of social programs that might help Black, Hispanic, low-income, and young Americans.[48] Gun rights advocates, sometimes even armed militia men, joined Tea Party groups, and about half of grassroots participants were also already active Christian right adherents opposed to abortion and gay rights.[49] These men and women, usually middle-income white people in their fifties or older, were often prepared to pressure Republican officeholders—including many for whom they voted—to take hard-right stands on both fiscal and cultural issues. Above all, they demanded that Republicans refuse any and all governing compromises with the Democrats and President Obama. Studies show that Tea Party members tended to hold more racist and anti-immigrant views than other conservatives and Republican supporters.[50]

Buoyed by grassroots activists and determined voters, Tea Party–aligned Republican candidates made major gains in the November 2010 elections for Congress and state legislatures; afterward, they intensified their clout in and around the GOP, even when many of them stopped attending regular Tea Party meetings or referring to themselves explicitly as "Tea Partiers." Ideas and angry political styles spawned by the Tea Party movement have been a persistent and growing force in the GOP ever since.[51] In Pennsylvania specifically, many Republicans benefitted from and were influenced by the Tea Party upsurge. In 2012, for instance, Pennsylvania's Beaver County, once a union-heavy Democratic stronghold, elected a Tea Party–endorsed GOP candidate, Keith Rothfus, to the (then) twelfth congressional district seat in Congress. With continued funding and support from the far right, Rothfus was reelected until defeated by Democrat Conor Lamb in a very close November 2018 race.

Theda Skocpol and her associates have long worked to develop lists as complete as possible of named local Tea Parties that functioned as organized groups between the spring of 2009 and 2013. From this work it is possible to calculate the relative density of local Tea Party affiliates across the fifty U.S. states, normalized for population. In such calculations, the state of Pennsylvania falls close to the median. Skocpol and colleagues have developed county-by-county rosters of local Tea Party affiliates for a half dozen key states, one of which is Pennsylvania. From that work, we know that Tea Party groups were especially numerous per capita in the twenty counties of the western region of the Keystone state. By late 2010, western counties that included 27.3 percent of Pennsylvania's population had twenty-seven Tea Party groups, close to two-fifths (38 percent) of all Tea Party groups in the state. This outsized Tea Party share in western Pennsylvania stands in comparison to forty-four Tea Party affiliates (62 percent of the state total) spread across the remaining forty-seven counties, where 72.7 percent of the population in Pennsylvania lived. Normalized against population, in short, western Pennsylvania was a relative hotbed for organized Tea Party affiliation.

Nor was this just a matter of western Pennsylvania being more rural. Of course, western Pennsylvania, as we define it, includes some rural counties (such as tiny Forest County) and some only spottily industrialized counties (such as Crawford County, once home to a thriving oil industry around Titusville). But Tea Party groups were numerous in previously heavily industrialized counties such as Beaver and Westmoreland. In fact, our calculations show that the number of Tea Party groups as of 2010 were moderately highly correlated with the number of USW union halls in 1960.

To be sure, moderately strong correlations between different organizational densities does not mean that the same people were involved. Some anecdotal observations from our interviews suggest, in the current period, union and Tea Party memberships have overlapped to some degree. But the important point about 1960 versus 2010 is that politically salient and visibly active *organized hubs* shifted markedly. This was most obviously the case in Beaver County, where in 1960 USW brick-and-mortar halls were located in Aliquippa, Beaver Falls, Midland, and Monaca. All but one of these USW halls was gone by 2010, when Tea Party groups were meeting regularly in Baden, Beaver Falls, and New Brighton. After the Tea Party organizing waves spread across the nation, Tea Party groups served some of the same functions that union locals and community halls once did in western Pennsylvania—including hosting overtly political events. Union locals and their halls have long sponsored meetings and forums that let election candidates—usually Democrats—meet and speak with potential voters. More recently, Tea Party groups did the same—this time, to highlight conservatives, in very local contests as well as in high-profile state and national elections.

A good example happened in May 2013 at Uniontown, in Pennsylvania's southwest corner. According to the *Herald-Standard,* the Fayette County Tea Party hosted a meeting at their headquarters to hear from four candidates in a judicial election for the County Court of Common Pleas.[52] Queries focused on right-wing, hot-button issues that local judges would be unlikely to encounter, including abortion, the death penalty, and whether Islamic sharia law could be enforced in America. All candidates gave the proper right-wing assurances; some wooed attendees by denouncing the Supreme Court's 2012 decision to uphold the Affordable Care Act.

Although the local election was ostensibly nonpartisan, candidates were also quizzed about their party registrations. Two acknowledged registering as Democrats long ago when that was de rigueur in the area, but by 2013, they signaled that they had long distanced themselves from that affiliation.

Although most of Pennsylvania's local Tea Party affiliates have ceased official organizational activities, their activists carry on as Trump GOP enthusiasts and often as leaders in conservative organizations—including as recently installed local Republican officials or aligned volunteers. A county Republican chair in southwestern Pennsylvania said that her involvement in the GOP was the result of being opposed to the passage of the Affordable Care Act and pointed out that "Obama brought a lot of people around here into the Republican Party." In her county, the GOP grew rapidly in the early 2010s along with the Tea Party movement. In another interview, the Democratic chair of a different county recounted a story about her husband observing a Tea Party meeting at the courthouse and staying when it was finished to see where the folding chairs had come from. The source was the county Republican Party headquarters, which she saw as a clear indication that the Tea Party movement was closely intertwined with the official county GOP.[53] The Democratic chair of a county northeast of Pittsburgh told us in 2021 that there had recently been an upsurge in the number and types of right-wing extremist groups in the county—and she implied that some of them were likely present at the Capitol insurrection on January 6, 2021, saying that she had heard about "buses" being organized in her county by Republican activists to drive people to Washington.

Driving through western Pennsylvania, one sees clear remnants of the Tea Party movement. "Don't Tread on Me" flags, adopted as the Tea Party's unofficial banner, can be spotted on cars and houses. Some were also plastered on vehicles in the employee parking lots of the steel mills we checked out (where we tallied such flags in the "Republican" category). National polls make it clear that Tea Party participants and sympathizers went on to favor Donald Trump overwhelmingly, and that is surely true in Pennsylvania.[54] Indeed, at least four Tea Party groups still exist in the western region; they may not have held regular meetings throughout the COVID-19 pandemic, but they still serve as hubs of information for community members on social media. The Facebook pages of these groups are still active and are frequently updated. Some Tea Party groups were still holding events as of the 2020 election and into 2021. On April 8, 2021, the Cambria-Somerset Tea Party held an event in Johnstown for elected officials to discuss voting "fraud" and "security" issues in the wake of Donald Trump's false claims about the stolen November 2020 election.[55] The *Daily American* reported that the director of the Pennsylvania Americans for Prosperity network—the dark money group tied to the Koch brothers, Fred Koch Jr. and Charles Koch—also distributed literature on voting laws at this event. This meeting, like many of the Cambria-Somerset Tea Party, was held at the Freemasons' Temple in Somerset, Pennsylvania, a fraternal group outpost that was once likely tightly intertwined with local unions in the region.

New Energy for Far-Right and GOP Organizations

Ample scholarship suggests that union membership reduces racial resentment among white workers. But it is likely that, in the mid- to late-twentieth century, not only did union membership decrease racial resentment in the abstract sense but it also

prevented *affirmative* prejudicial action by members. One interviewee who had worked with union and nonunion miners in
Pennsylvania and West Virginia for more than fifty years told us
a story that he prefaced as "kind of funny but dark":

> A while back, now this was a while ago, I was talking to a guy, and
> he said that he had recently asked a miner he had a lot of respect for
> about the KKK [Ku Klux Klan]. The miner gave a very right-on
> talk about how in the [United] Mine Workers, we don't care about
> color, we believe in equality and all that. And then when he was
> done, he said, "but if it wasn't for all that, I'd probably join the KKK."

Of course, the miner in this anecdote *clearly* had prejudicial views. But there is something to be said for the fact that
his social and political needs were satiated by his membership
in the progressive organization of the UMWA. Because of the
union, he did not join an abhorrent extremist organization, and
even though he was not convinced by the UMWA's positions on
equality, his devotion to his union prevailed over his potential
desire to deviate from the union stance.

Today, with fidelity to unions among such groups having
nearly evaporated, an intervening organization or entity often
cannot prevent a similarly situated individual from making the
leap to join an extremist organization. In the aftermath of the
Capitol insurrection on January 6, 2021, pundits and popular
media began to take stock of how groups such as the Proud Boys
and the Oath Keepers formed and gained traction. In many
cases, the genesis of far-right nationalist or white supremacist
groups was social in nature. Both in person and online groups
provided space for mostly white men to express their frustration with perceived social relegation. The founder of the Proud
Boys, Gavin McInnes, explained on his podcast "The Gavin

McInnes Show" that the Proud Boys began as a "drinking club" in which like-minded men would meet at bars in New York City and gripe about politics and social progress. McInnes once told Alan Feuer from the *New York Times* that Proud Boys meetings were quite like those that "the Shriners or the Elks might do," as Feuer recounted.[56]

Crucial differences, of course, set the Shriners well apart from the Proud Boys and the Elks in a different space from the Oath Keepers. Fraternal organizations have always been structured in alignment with basic tenets of American democracy—beyond being federated and having constitutions and elections, fraternal organizations elect top leaders and have long encouraged and even at times required active participation in democratic and civic affairs by their members. A reverence and appreciation for U.S. institutions is instilled in members. The Proud Boys and Oath Keepers, clearly, were not established with such groundings in American constitutional democracy. Nevertheless, it matters that today's far-right nationalist groups compare themselves to fraternal organizations of years past and deploy twisted versions of traditional fraternal ideals. Workers of yesteryear socialized with others within the context of shared membership in fraternal organizations rooted in American constitutional values or at union halls that encouraged working-class coalitions. Today's disillusioned white workers do not turn to fraternal groups or union communities when they are frustrated with the system—such institutions simply do not have the standing in the community that they used to. Instead, a small but an increasing number of white male workers today turn to dangerous fringe groups that harbor resentment toward women, people of color, immigrants, and others—and those groups claim, however unconvincingly, that they are furthering "true American" values and solidarities.

The GOP establishment has also made distinct efforts to rope in industrial workers who previously voted for Democrats. Various western Pennsylvania Republican officials have told us that communicating their message to industrial workers, including union members, is an essential part of their regional strategy. Two of the Republican committee chairs to whom we spoke came from industrial backgrounds, and each described workplace dynamics on both sides of the union-management divide. They agreed—and claimed that union workers they know also believe—that the union amounts to outdated and unnecessary bureaucracy because of the existing protective labor rules enforced by the Occupational Safety and Health Act (OSHA) and even the Environmental Protection Agency (EPA). From their perspective, and surely in their political messaging, union members are forced to send their hard-earned dollars to a bureaucracy that does not align with their political views. In essence, they are trying to tell workers that unions are unnecessary now, in the process taking advantage of the already institutionalized gains unions made in the past.

Similar to gun clubs, local Republican Party headquarters sponsor get-togethers and aim to serve as gathering places for community members. According to one GOP official, having a brick-and-mortar location within the county was highly beneficial for the party because people would come, get to know one another, and become more likely to participate in political events. This Republican official described the utility of the headquarters building as a gathering space in language similar to the way union halls were described as community hubs. According to this county Republican Party leader, union workers stop by the office and discuss their resentment about paying union dues.

Workers once reflexively voted Democrat because their fellow workers and neighbors did the same, and similar processes seem to encourage working-class people in industrial and ex-industrial communities today to vote automatically for Republicans. GOP officials described union members as having "woken up" in recent years by realizing that their values no longer align with the Democratic Party. "God-fearing, gun-bearing workers have realized that if they don't change what they're doing, their rights are going to go away," explained one local GOP leader. "They see that [Democrats] are going to take [their] rights away. . . . They're going to lose the life that they know if they don't change their vote."

"Lose the life that they know" clearly refers to more than just workers' fears about losing jobs and benefits. It alludes more broadly—and with real emotional punch—to the social and economic displacement felt by many non-college-educated, nonurban individuals in a fast-evolving American society. The Republican official just cited told us that he believed the vast majority of industrial union workers in his county are now voting for GOP rather than Democratic candidates because many now feel that the Republican Party better represents their way of life and "who they are."

UNION WORKERS AND THE DEMOCRATIC PARTY

In response to the Trump presidency, some liberal pundits repeated the adage that when fascism comes to America, it will be "wrapped in the flag and carrying a cross."[57] One of our interviewees, a retired steelworker and former Democrat, had a different version. "When fascism comes to America, it's going to be wearing a suit and a Democrat Party pin," he told us emphatically. We prodded a little. "You're less worried about the Trump contingent, even after January 6, than about the Democrats?" Yes, he responded. "The Democrats are more dangerous because they act like they're for you—like they're for the working people—but they're not." He is now a member of neither party. The Democrats have lost huge swaths of working-class voters in the Rust Belt, including this steelworker who is now so outwardly suspicious of the Democratic Party that he trusts it less than the GOP (many of whose candidates he still says he despises).

After the presidential election of 2016, union leaders expressed distress that their official endorsements of Hillary Clinton failed to persuade many of their members to vote for the Democratic ticket. As they had for decades, the top officials of almost all America's major unions told their members that Democrats supported economic policies that were more likely to help wage earners and modest-salary earners and also protect or expand the legal rights of unions. Yet even more obviously in 2016 than in preceding presidential contests, Republican contender Donald Trump attracted large shares of blue-collar votes, including from unions. Indeed, Trump received more union support than any Republican nominee since Ronald Reagan.[58] Still, Trump benefited from the fruits of shifts that our research indicates started decades ago.

Trump did well with unionized voters despite the fact that surveys tracking the (overly) broad category of "union members" now sample a much more diverse population than they did in earlier decades. As private-sector unions have lost ground to those in the public sector, and as formerly blue-collar unions like USW and UAW have recruited in new economic sectors, white male industrial "union men" have ceased to be a majority of the overall union population. Because "the demographics of union membership have shifted a lot over the last 30 years," explained the *Washington Post*, "Trump probably did better than

Reagan with . . . white union members."[59] Compared to unions in general, white males comprise a higher share of USW membership (about 70 percent according to an estimate from a USW leader we interviewed), so it seems likely that an outright majority of this demographic of USW members must have turned away from Democrat Hillary Clinton to support the Trump-Pence GOP ticket.

From 2016 to November 2020, Trump retained much of his blue-collar support. *Politico* reported in late September 2020 that union leaders were struggling to convince blue-collar members to follow their endorsement of the Democratic ticket. "It doesn't seem like there's anybody changing their minds," Don Furko, president of USW Local 1557 in Clairton, Pennsylvania, told the *Politico* reporter, who wrote that "the majority of his membership is backing Trump."[60] High-level union leaders expressed frustration about the Democratic Party's lack of response to the disproportionate number of union members who voted for Trump in 2016. One international executive told us that she was exasperated with the party because there was "no discussion of why 2016 happened and how we are going to change the party." She explained that her members "don't believe in the Democratic Party anymore" and that the party was not doing enough to win back "the more than 50 percent of [her] members who voted for Trump in 2016."

Much of the evidence in this book helps to explain why rank-and-file USW members have become estranged from the Democratic Party and suggests why so many turn a deaf ear to the continuing official endorsements that top USW leaders deliver to Democratic candidates. Since its rise as a powerful Congress of Industrial Organizations (CIO) international in the mid-twentieth century, USW has always taken a relatively centralized approach to electioneering and policy lobbying—and such centralization may have increased after the 1980s as overall membership declined. Union officials surrounded by professionals in Washington, DC, may not always see their rank-and-file members clearly—a malady common to many DC-based staff operations. One current county Republican chair—who was a longtime Democrat and former union member—told us that the bureaucratization of unions today has fundamentally changed them. "It's not the union *that it was*," he said. "It's a big business." As unions have moved from being directed largely from the ground up to being managed from the top down, members may have felt that the union's interests became increasingly removed from their own.

There are additional reasons for the growing disconnect between supralocal union officials and rank-and-file USW members. During the heyday of Big Steel, USW was a vast network of interconnected units, and regional and national offices enjoyed strong connections to thousands of union locals in widely dispersed mill communities. In USW and other industrial unions, rank-and-file members got information and opinions about elections and policy issues from peers in their local unions, not just (or even primarily) from top-level USW executives arguing from above for the union's endorsements. Across the Rust Belt and certainly in western Pennsylvania, many USW locals issued their own newsletters to convey information about candidates. Candidates made the rounds at union-owned halls and other community institutions, and cycles of social events created space for casual, peer-to-peer political talk.

We have already detailed how such community webs sustained cultural understandings and outlooks of the midcentury union man. The point to stress here is that the same webs also linked rank-and-file members to one another, to union leaders, and to locally present party organizations, which overwhelmingly benefitted Democrats. Almost all these local networks were disrupted or closed after the contraction of steel and other heavy industries. From the 1990s into the 2000s, even as gun clubs, megachurches, Tea Party groups, and revitalized local GOP offices drew blue-collar people into their orbits, industrial union leaders at all levels, from local to regional, to national, experienced communication gaps because of dwindling ties to local groups embedded in informal networks that once kept them directly or indirectly in touch with rank-and-file members.

This way of thinking about the shifting ground for blue-collar politics can help make sense of much of what we learned from interviews about many workers turning away from taken-for-granted support for Democrats. In addition, this perspective suggests why not all unionized blue-collar sectors have necessarily moved the same way. In the following subsections, we first gain added understanding about why our steelworker interviewees so often report distancing from and feeling abandoned by the Democratic Party. Then we look at why political developments may differ among blue-collar tradespeople enrolled in unions like IBEW that have never been as dependent as USW on geographically fixed workplaces or union locals.

Industrial Worker Estrangement Is Not Just About Policies

Perceived contrasts between Democratic metropolitan areas and troubled industrial and ex-industrial towns surely have contributed to worker disillusionment with their own union leaders and the Democratic Party. Surveys and our own Pennsylvania interviews suggest that, in the minds of many blue-collar workers, the two major U.S. political parties have adopted opposite national platform stances on many cultural issues—such as those dead-end issues of guns and abortion—that resonate quite differently across the metropolitan versus nonmetropolitan divide. But economic and social questions can spark skepticism about otherwise well-known Democrats, too. Especially since the election of President Barack Obama, some blue-collar white workers dislike that Democrats push programs like the Affordable Care Act because some of them believe that such programs disproportionately help minorities and hurt their own union-negotiated private-sector health insurance benefits.

The requisite for today's Democratic Party to assemble electoral coalitions that bridge between big cities and nonmetropolitan areas opens the party to right-wing claims that this or that favored economic policy or social benefit may disproportionately benefit one kind of community over another or one racial, ethnic, or generational group over another. In addition, frequent debates over energy and trade policy can put stress on big-umbrella Democratic coalitions because, as we learned in various interviews, many industrial union workers worry that new initiatives can hurt their jobs, families, and communities. Most basic of all, however, is that many blue-collar workers, including union members, simply worry about the overall outlook of the Democratic Party today and suspect that the party's core values and plans for the future may leave them behind.

Energy and environmental issues are important to workers not just in policy terms but also on this larger worldview dimension—and our interviewees had opinions on these topics. Many stressed that they were *not* unilaterally against climate-related regulations. In the words of one current UMWA member, the "guys [I work with] are hunters and fishers, and they don't want to hunt and fish with sulfur in the streams. But we just don't want to be left behind. I think that we see that we have to be part of the solution, which could be anything. . . . These guys live in these communities and fish and hunt, but they don't want to be left behind." Multiple interviewees specifically referenced Hillary Clinton's infelicitous 2016 aside that she was "going to put a lot of coal miners and coal companies out of business" as a clear indicator of the willingness of the Democratic Party to leave industrial workers behind.[61] Although policies to protect the region's natural resources are not necessarily anathema to industrial union workers in western Pennsylvania, many are concerned about the criticism of workers themselves or targeted attacks on the industries that still support many of them. Union leaders thus adopt a goal to "make climate more understandable to our members" based on the "regional impacts of climate change," according to one international leader to whom we spoke.

Many steelworkers seem tepidly supportive of measures intended to protect the region's environment, to get well beyond Pittsburgh's history as a city laden with smog and covered with dust by midday. According to members of the international executive board of USW, one of the union's main priorities is ensuring that the plants at which their members work are complying with environmental policies. One retired Steelworker told us:

> I'm seventy-nine, and I remember everything was covered with a red dust when I was a kid. I'm 100 percent an environmentalist, I seriously am. . . . I have six kids, thirteen grandchildren, and seven great-grandchildren. I want them to be able to see a tree one day. I remember driving through the Liberty tubes [the Liberty Tunnel south of downtown Pittsburgh] with my dad, you couldn't see anything. And to be able to drive through that now and see the clean air and everything, I think it's great.

Such general acceptance of environmental regulations might seem like good news for Democrats, who often must appeal to both blue-collar unionists and college-educated voters who prioritize a stepped-up fight against climate change. Advocates and Democratic candidates themselves try to find a sweet spot by stressing new investments in job-creating clean energy projects. But they often meet worker skepticism. When asked about the potential of clean energy jobs, many of our interviewees expressed frustration at what seems to be more of a useful political buzz phrase rather than the promise of real economic revival. One interviewee, a retired miner, became quite incensed:

> What jobs? They're not in southwestern Pennsylvania or West Virginia. They're not here! The only jobs that are available in those industries are a couple of things: the manufacturing of the parts of the solar panels or wind turbines or the erection of those. Those jobs don't last for a long time. See when they talk about those green jobs, when someone makes a hot water tank, they consider that a green job. We're in a bad place, kid!

Part of the problem is recent historical experience, and union leaders are attuned to the skepticism with which workers view such policies. A top-level union executive explained to us that they "don't say 'green jobs'" because for workers, "it's a fallacy." People in communities who have witnessed so much job loss already feel abandoned by policymakers—including Democrats—who have repeatedly held out the promise of new jobs for the region. They have heard talk of clean energy jobs but have not seen many of those jobs appear, much less experienced the promised return to community prosperity.

This brings us to ways in which workers speak about the general mentality they attribute to each party, to the kind of views and values the parties intentionally or unintentionally communicate to this part of the electorate. Many workers suggest that the Republican Party has a tough attitude, and they complain that the Democratic Party is whiney or overly concerned with political correctness. Some workers may interpret efforts to help the poor, minorities, or women as falling into this category of policymaking. Some interviewees also criticized Democrats for supposed plans to force certain measures, like health insurance, on people who may not want them. As one current younger Steelworker said, "I agree 100 percent with the Democratic platform, but I don't like how they want to shove it down [our] throats. When I registered Republican, I was thinking that you just have to let people be." Many see the Democratic Party as too pushy, especially in its moral stances on certain issues, and feel that the excessively woke segments of the party are tiring and irritating. This wariness about being pushed around by politicians may shift as the GOP becomes more identified with coercive regulations on matters such as denying abortion access. In the wake of the 2022 Supreme Court *Dobbs* decision overturning *Roe v. Wade*, it has become increasingly clear that Americans across income and partisan lines do not like politicians of any stripe telling them what to do as individuals.

Last but hardly least, any given party loyalty is more than an individual's isolated stance because it feels to most people like a matter of joining with others to push back against obvious enemies. Conservatives have had success in spreading the notion that the Democratic Party stands in lockstep with and advocates for coastal elites rather than the working class. Multiple interviewees commented that they do not see "people like them" in the Democratic Party. As a mine inspector explained to us about former mining towns in western Pennsylvania and West Virginia, the difference is that

fifty years ago, the UMWA was everywhere, and in those days, the union was able to make it about an economic elite that people were up against. On the face of it, it looks like a change of heart, but I don't see it that way. I think that when you talk to working-class West Virginians, I don't think their view of the world has changed that much over the last fifty years. They see themselves as being left out and looked down upon. . . . When unions started to fade, you started to get that line from the NRA instead—it's a sophisticated, Eastern, intellectual elite that looks down on them. . . . It's not really a change of worldview.

The union made wealthy corporate conservatives into the enemy—this was the group that did not understand or appreciate the labor of working-class Appalachians. The enemy shifted as conservative influences became the reigning regional narrative and the union's "us versus them" framing dissipated.

Much of the growing disconnect between Democrats and remaining industrial unionists comes from frayed local union and party ties along with new links to community-based conservative networks. In turn, such shifts in community ties encourage changes in shared identities, worldviews, and beliefs about social and political friends and foes. After Tea Party ideas, Trump, and Trumpism moved to the fore in GOP politics, messaging about the out-of-touch nature of the Democrats became even more explicit and emotionally resonant. Regardless of this or that issue stand, Democrats are often seen as aloof, absent, and threatening to workers, especially those outside big metropolitan areas. Worker-citizens who feel overlooked or abandoned—or worse, looked down on—become open to messages from the right that their real political enemies are no longer economic elites but instead are liberals or the so-called radical left Democrats. Through powerful national media operations spewing messages linked to local social networks, the right paints its Democratic enemies as trying to tell working people how to talk or reform their way of life. And because the U.S. is a two-party system, where many voters cast their ballot for "the other guy" or the "lesser of two evils," the GOP benefits when Democrats are demonized for being opposed to everyday workers, particularly those in the electorally important Midwest. It is impossible to know what proportion of industrial union members actually believe and act electorally on such ideas, but we can be sure that the proportion of unionists who believe these demonizing claims about Democrats has shifted markedly in favor of conservatives in recent years.

The Politics of Steelworkers Versus Electrical Workers

So far in this chapter—and for most of this book—we have focused on the changing local lives and associational and political involvements of *industrial* blue-collar workers, such as the Steel-workers, and have used western Pennsylvania as a window into America's Rust Belt. Here and there we have drawn parallels or contrasts to IBEW, a major construction trade union historically part of the American Federation of Labor (AFL) that coordinates electrical workers at dispersed and ever-shifting worksites. In contrast to USW's reliance on a dense network of locals tied to mills and mill towns, IBEW has fostered member-to-member ties in other ways, including regularly featuring large numbers of local and member reports in its lengthy monthly news magazine. As we now examine shifting union involvements in electoral and partisan politics, are there reasons to believe that the contrasting USW and IBEW structures and community-building strategies we have already highlighted also influence the choices these two sets of blue-collar unionists make at the ballot box?

We realized as our research comparing USW and IBEW progressed that, logically speaking, there *could* be organizationally conditioned political consequences as a result of the unions' differing structures. From the mid-twentieth century to the present, supralocal union leaders in both IBEW and USW have, for the most part, continued to ally with and officially endorse and donate to Democrats. Their capacities to influence the rank-and-file, though, may have regressed. As major industries fell and rose in Pennsylvania and beyond, with devastating consequences for neighborhoods and smaller cities, USW International leaders and the subnational leaders lost many channels linking them to localized rank-and-file clusters. A trade union like IBEW, which was already accustomed to communicating with dispersed members who moved around in shifting teams, might have maintained closer communications with local and regional leaders and rank-and-file members. Many rank-and-file steelworkers became detached from their union and were drawn into alternative community groups and loyalties, but perhaps the shifts have not been as great for IBEW workers and their union, leaving IBEW officials in a better position to keep communicating credible political information to their rank-and-file members and achieving more success in persuading members to follow official union electoral endorsements.

If this is true, it would be ironic. The AFL building trades were tagged by scholars and analysts as more conservative than the CIO industrial unions. As complex, relatively decentralized federations of skilled occupations, the AFL building trades unions had a long history of accepting varied stances by locals and district leaders aligned to prevailing partisan winds in different states and cities and towns. When issues of gender and racial diversity came to the fore after the 1950s, AFL leaders dragged their feet about integration and equality more than CIO leaders did.[62] During the mid to late twentieth century, these variations did not prevent the leaders of most building trade unions from joining leaders of industrial unions in encouraging members to vote for Democrats, especially in national elections, but it is still fair to say that the trade unions and their members had a reputation for supporting Republicans more often than, say, autoworkers, steelworkers, or miners.

By now, however, old industrial union organizational linkages have broken down, and many rank-and-file blue-collar union members feel much less invested in their unions, which are today recruiting new members in very different occupations. As we have described, western Pennsylvania nominal union members still working in steel and other heavy industries are generally not paying much heed to their international union's voting recommendations. In contrast, as we discussed in chapter 4, IBEW members—and likely building trades workers at large—still feel considerable *occupational pride* and express positive feelings of belonging and ownership of unions that sustain their skills and job opportunities. Long-standing communication channels within IBEW have not been as disrupted as in USW, so rank-and-file members might remain more politically in tune with their union's national and regional leaders.

We cannot quantitatively test this hypothesis because publicly available surveys about trends in workers' partisan identifications and reported voting choices do not include union-specific breakdowns. Surveys generally compare union members to nonunion members on voter turnout or partisanship, but interesting as these general findings may be, the data behind them are of no use for testing the precise sectoral and organizational hypotheses we have put forward.[63] In the absence of ideal data, we note varied pieces of evidence pointing to different political trajectories for USW and IBEW unionists.

Although we certainly cannot predict everyone's political views from the evidence that we found, our western Pennsylvania interviewees from IBEW were relatively optimistic that their immediate co-unionists continued to lean left in their basic political orientations. "I don't know exactly how it is," said one IBEW retiree, "but I know the leadership [of my local] has always been progressive. . . . [I would say the local] is 60 to 70 percent Democratic. Maybe not by party but in terms of left-wing, right-wing. When people openly put stickers on their cars for Republicans, a lot of guys were angry about it. If there were guys who vocally spoke up for Republicans, they were in the minority." In contrast, our USW member interviewees talked about their local union leaders openly supporting Republican candidates and encouraging members to do the same. As we quoted earlier, one former USW local president told us that he believed "90 to 95 percent" of his members voted for Trump over Hillary Clinton. Another USW unionist talked about frustration among members over not being allowed to put up 2016 Trump yard signs outside their union hall. Union leaders said no to members who wanted to do this because the International had endorsed Clinton. Obviously, such divergences fuel additional rank-and-file dissatisfactions with USW's high-level leadership.

Even as national IBEW and USW officials consistently endorse Democratic candidates, for many grassroots union members, union support means more than the International's preferences. At the crucial local and subnational levels, local IBEW unions appear to be both more politically involved and more liberal-leaning than USW's remaining steelworker locals. As the hub for Pittsburgh and a wide swathe of the surrounding area, IBEW Local 5 regularly hosts candidates at its local union hall and makes political comments and endorsements in its monthly newsletter. In July 2021, IBEW Local 5 hosted a roundtable with

Vice President Kamala Harris and Secretary of Labor Marty Walsh on labor organizing.[64] A month later, the Democratic congressional representative from western Pennsylvania Conor Lamb announced his run for Senate outside Local 5.[65]

In contrast, most of the western Pennsylvania USW locals are rather inactive politically. Whether leaders in the remaining USW locals comprised of industrial workers try to reinforce USW International's endorsements of Democrats, rank-and-file members have proclaimed themselves "Steelworkers for Trump" in western Pennsylvania and beyond. A well-publicized instance happened in northwest Indiana in September 2020, when USW members paid for a billboard trumpeting "Steelworkers of NW Indiana for Trump."[66] Before long, the International demanded it be reworded in order to avoid misleading people about the union's official endorsement. In response—and likely fooling no one—the billboard was simply reworded to read "Blue Collar Workers of NW Indiana for Trump."

Another version of the same locals-versus-officials drama played out when scores of members intervened on posts on USW's Facebook page promoting the 2020 Biden-Harris ticket to post their own personal versions of the USW logo declaring, "I am a member of the United Steelworkers and I am voting for Trump" (see figure 5.4).

Beyond interview comments, billboards, and news accounts, additional evidence about possible USW versus IBEW differences comes from a pathbreaking statistical study conducted by political scientists Sun Eun Kim and Yatam Margalit on unions' capacities to influence policy attitudes of members.[67] Using evidence about the public stances of major unions on international trade issues, this innovative study included workers in a range of sectors to see whether unionized workers are more likely than their nonunionized counterparts to know and reflect official union trade positions.

FIGURE 5.4 Image used on social media, especially Facebook, to declare support among USW members for Trump during the 2020 election.

With a variety of sophisticated statistical techniques and controls, the study shows that, indeed, unions do influence their members' attitudes about the benefits and harms of international trade—and the results are not simply due to the types of people who join or do not join unions in each economic sector. Beyond asking the workers who responded to their survey about views on trade, these investigators also gathered information on demographic characteristics and partisan identifications (on a scale ranging from "strong Democrat" to "strong Republican"), and they included an open-ended question that prompted each respondent to "please list the three issues that the union discussed most frequently in its communications to you." Substantive answers were then coded into eight topical categories (politics, trade, immigration, health care, job security, wages, union benefits, and contracts) so that the investigators could calculate the shares of each set of unionists who named issues in each area (the researchers' immediate goal was to learn whether workers heard their union's position on trade and reflected it in their answers).

We obtained the underlying data from this interesting study, including the survey results from 500 of the 4,000 respondents who said they belonged to specific, named major unions. For us, blue-collar unions were the ones that mattered, and among the unions these respondents named were IBEW and USW as well as four other blue-collar unions in the private sector: UAW, International Brotherhood of Teamsters (IBT), United Brotherhood of Carpenters (UBC), and International Association of Machinists (IAM). Because the actual number of each set of respondents who identified with a union in this survey is small, we can only note some comparative tendencies. But those are intriguing and in line with our qualitative evidence.

Across the six sets of industrial unionists just named, we calculated the ratio of members who said they were "strong Democrats" to "strong Republicans" as a rough measure of clear-cut partisan tilt. Both the sixteen IBEW respondents and the fourteen USW respondents ranged across the full partisan spectrum, but the IBEW respondents had five self-proclaimed "strong Democrats" and one of the more left-tilted strong Democrat to strong Republican ratios. (The UAW respondents were by far the most Democratic-leaning, perhaps because this survey was taken soon after the Obama administration bailed out the Midwestern auto industry.) Five USW members said they were "strong Republicans" and tilted clearly rightward overall (as did the respondents from IBT).

Open-ended responses in this survey were even more suggestive. In their lists of three major issues discussed in union communications, the IBEW respondents named "political" topics—having to do with elections and voting. Compared to answers from *all* the public- and private-sector unionists included in this survey, the IBEW respondents were more likely to cite "political" communications from their union than were respondents from any other named union except the UAW respondents. In contrast, the USW respondents did *not* cite political communications; they were more likely than the other respondent sets either *not* to list any issues they heard about from their union or to offer irrelevant snide remarks. One Steelworker mocked his union, claiming it communicated "jack shit" and about "how they'll take my money." Another Steelworker caustically wrote that his union communicated about "bowing to Obama the king." This was quite different from what the IBEW respondents had to say. Beyond one nonresponse and an apolitical joking comment, IBEW respondents listed union-relevant economic concerns or mentioned that they had heard from their union about "supporting Obamacare," and voting or "electing Democrats." These response patterns are congruent with the hypothesis that, as of the 2010s, IBEW members hear regularly from their union about a range of issues, not just union-relevant economic topics but also Democratic-leaning political matters. They also hint that IBEW members may be less dismissive than USW members about politically relevant messages from their unions.

We should be clear that we are *not* claiming any definitive findings about IBEW compared to USW from the interview segments, public reports, and 2010 survey excerpts just discussed. The union man mentality and unquestioned Democratic Party loyalties so pervasive across many blue-collar unions in the mid-twentieth century have since fractured in the building trades as well as in manufacturing and industry. Unionized or not, workers in all these areas, including many IBEW members, have changed their party registrations or political outlooks. Our claim is simply that the structures, communication procedures, and national-subnational linkages distinctive to particular unions may well have made a difference for union responses and adaptations to economic and social upheavals since the 1980s—with at times divergent political consequences.

Democratic Party loyalties and votes for the party's candidates have clearly lost ground across all of blue-collar America, but the rates, locales, and degrees of change in union-party ties have varied. The sorts of organizational hypotheses we have suggested here underline why USW's alliance with Democrats was probably especially brittle, while IBEW members as well as officials have probably been less likely to shift toward the right and the GOP. Imperfect as it is, the evidence in this subsection of the chapter underlines why future research on unions and politics needs to consider the varying organizational structures in geographical groundings of different unions.

"A LIE IS BETTER THAN NOTHING"

As we conclude this chapter, we note that, in the once-mighty western Pennsylvania "workshop of America" so many area denizens recall with pride, electoral upending reached a new crescendo between 2010 to 2020. By 2016 especially, regional voters—including a big plurality if not an outright majority of remaining unionized steelworkers—had turned away still further from the Democrats that they or their regional predecessors once considered close partners and allies. Growing majorities of western Pennsylvanians embraced GOP candidates and Donald J. Trump. Trump's issue gestures were certainly part of this—as one expert on union politics commented to us, USW was especially tense about Democratic involvements with international trade pacts its members saw as hammering good jobs and wages in their region. But a lot more than party or candidate issue positions went into partisan transformations. For years, conservative groups had offered new ties and worldviews in place of shuttered union halls and traditional associations. Then the flamboyant Trump heard and spoke to the anger and abandonment felt by so many western Pennsylvanians—and offered at least emotionally satisfying ripostes to supposed villains, coupled with vague but alluring promises of a better future that would recapture glories of the past.

The Trump contingent of the Republican Party paid attention to working-class people in the Rust Belt in a way that few candidates have in recent times. Trump held rallies in their regions, spoke directly to these workers, and matched their frustration with his own endless resentments. He pointed a finger in a way that was comforting to people whose communities have suffered, ridiculing and blaming "bad trade deals," China, and the "swamp" of insiders in Washington for treating working-class people in the Rust Belt poorly. Trump's invectives resonated with workers in western Pennsylvania in a way that previous Republican candidates, such as Mitt Romney, were not able to match. In the words of one GOP county chair in the region, "Let's face it, Mitt Romney was not relatable. . . . Previous Republicans [to Trump] didn't get it. Sometimes you just have to have a conversation with people. I've been to a couple of Trump's rallies, and he just spoke off-the-cuff and reacted to the people who were there. People like that around here." Trump recognized these workers, paid attention to what they wanted, and incorporated those wants into his rhetoric.

Trump's recognition of workers in southwestern Pennsylvania is clear from the map of his campaign stops in both 2016 and 2020. Between June 11 and November 7, 2016, there were a total of nine appearances by either Trump or Pence in the region, and eight by Democratic candidates Clinton and Kaine. Whereas Trump and Pence campaigned in historically industrial towns such as Youngstown (in Westmoreland County, Pennsylvania), Monessen, and Johnstown, Clinton and Kaine primarily visited the city of Pittsburgh.[68] Clinton's campaign stumps, coupled with her comments about coal and her other policy stances, understandably made industrial workers feel as though she was only focused on getting out the urban vote.

Trump's strategy was the opposite: he relied on getting out the vote in white, working-class regions of the country, particularly in the Rust Belt. In July 2016, Trump visited Monessen in Westmoreland County, a former steelmaking hub in the Monongahela Valley. At the rally, Trump said to the crowd, "We are going to put American-produced steel back into the backbone of our country. This alone will create massive numbers of jobs."[69] No other candidate had made a similar promise since the 1970s. Not everyone believed what Trump said about bringing back jobs in the steel industry but, according to workers, at least he paid attention to their needs and at least he spoke to them. Many industrial workers have been yearning to be recognized in political discourse for their labor and struggles. Candidate Trump was willing to do this.

Recognizing the importance of tightening the margin in the counties of western Pennsylvania, the Biden 2020 campaign made more stops in various locations in the region than the Clinton campaign did. From September 1 to November 5, 2020,

Biden or Harris stumped a total of seven times in the twenty-county region of western Pennsylvania: in Pittsburgh twice, Greensburg, New Alexandria, Johnstown, Shanksville, and Erie. The Trump ticket visited the region ten times during this period: twice in Erie, and once each in Butler, Export, Moon Township, West Mifflin, Monroeville, Latrobe, Johnstown, and Shanksville.[70] Because of her gender, Clinton was at a disadvantage in appealing to many members of the working-class population in the Rust Belt. This was salient in the 2020 race as well but not to the same extent. From one Democratic Party chair's perspective, Harris's half-Black identity did play a role in dampening support in various parts of western Pennsylvania in 2020 because workers "didn't want to see a Black woman on the ticket, and they didn't want to see a woman as president [in 2016]." Joe Biden himself constantly invoked his own working-class family roots and sensibilities.

Of course, waning Democratic fortunes are not just a matter of who does a better job of siting rallies or rhetorically invoking blue-collar concerns. In addition to paying attention to the "forgotten" and "overlooked" class of industrial workers by visiting those regions, Trump projected a tough-guy, in-your-face attitude that also resonated with many in western Pennsylvania. As one recently retired pro-Trump Steelworker said, "There's a lot of people who can relate to Trump. It's the same mentality, it's just the way these people think." Many workers felt that Trump's ostensible honesty and bluntness were refreshing. When driving around the western Pennsylvania region, we saw dozens of signs and flags that read "Trump 2020: No More Bullshit," and later on, flags that read "Don't Blame Me, I Voted for Trump," "Let's Go Brandon," or "Trump 2024: Save America." Does much of this have an implicit prejudicial edge to it? Yes, it does. Tough-guy rhetoric also appeals to threatened "manliness," even to the point of allowing voters to blink at Trump's recurrent viciousness toward women.

After he squeaked through the 2016 Electoral College and moved into the White House, President Trump did, to some degree, deliver on his promise to do something to help the American steel industry. In March 2018, the Trump administration imposed a set of tariffs on imported steel and aluminum products to bolster domestic industries.[71] USW members told us that they had been lobbying for such tariffs for years. In an analysis of the Trump administration's steel tariffs, economic law professor Rachel Brewster states that "the Trump campaign sought to frame this issue as one regarding the loss of traditional forms of male employment . . . the optics of 'bringing back' stereotypically masculine jobs powers this trade policy forward."[72] This is presumably a large part of the reason Trump was so supportive of the steel and coal industries—they represented the old social hierarchy, before women and racial minorities "displaced" white men. Despite the social implications, the tariffs were understandably popular among advocates of the steel industry, including USW and lobbying groups representing American steel corporations, because they propped up domestic steel production. Many Pennsylvanians, in contrast to the rest of the American public—as well as the majority of both the Democratic and Republican contingents of Congress—were supportive of imposing the tariffs, even though they were not a long-term panacea to the declining American steel industry.[73] Many pundits pointed to unfavorable consequences of the tariffs as reasons that they should be revoked, such as exacerbating the already tense relationship between Washington and Beijing and equating to one of the largest tax increases in recent U.S. history.[74]

American industry and manufacturing did not magically revitalize under the four years of the Trump administration.

Manufacturing continued to decline, and the coal industry, despite Trump's promises, did not rebound.[75] Part of the reason why many industrial workers stuck with Trump even in 2020 has to do with the title of this subsection, their sense that "a lie is better than nothing." This striking sentiment is what one interviewee said was appealing about Trump's pitch. Even if Trump's promises were not fulfilled, at least he was paying attention—and talking—to the working class in the Rust Belt. Many of his supporters see him as on their side and trying to do what needs to be done, even if he does not succeed. That matters to many more than the fact that, in his business dealings, Trump has usually silenced workers and deliberately employed nonunion labor, including the undocumented immigrants he so often demonizes. None of it matters because Trump, as the politician of nostalgia and resentment, reaffirmed displaced workers in the most rudimentary way: by recognizing them. In return, many working-class people in western Pennsylvania felt—and still feel—a profound sense of loyalty to this billionaire reality-show salesman from New York City. Many in turn are also increasingly loyal to the Republican Party that Trump successfully remade in his image.

We have offered a socially grounded perspective on the partisan realignment Trump has driven and symbolized in blue-collar Rust Belt America, focusing on western Pennsylvania as representative of this trend. Over the last half century, the political influences present in this region have shifted dramatically. Whereas in the mid-twentieth century unions with many locals tied to workplaces and surrounding neighborhoods provided the underlying organizational structure that made taken-for-granted social and political loyalties plausible, today the old ties and structures are mostly dissolved. Organizations with broader territories and conservative moral frames have now gained social and political influence in most of the region. Gun clubs serve as a communal hub, functioning both as gathering places and as centers where displaced white men can assert physical dominance and familial superiority. Tea Party groups—and other far-right successor groups—also gained ground in the region, pulling local workers farther to the right. County Republican committees have prioritized speaking directly to the remaining industrial workers in the region and emphasizing feelings of economic nostalgia by placing blame on other groups.

Workers have developed a new sense of shared identity rooted in working-class resentments against the places and constituencies they see now at the core of the Democratic Party. Many workers feel estranged from Democrats, which they see as urban elites or as dominated by big-city interests. Industrial workers especially no longer think of unions as "theirs"—and they no longer see them as indispensable to their livelihoods. This is especially true for unions that are no longer present locally. To many workers, unions are simply bureaucratic organizations that take money out of their pockets and channel some of that money to politicians, usually Democrats, who do not seem to offer good solutions. Workers worry about new kinds of Democratic priorities, such as environmental goals, that they fear could leave them even further behind.

After Democrats and the Clinton campaign mostly ignored Rust Belt regions in the 2016 presidential election, a costly mistake, the Biden 2020 campaign visited more Rust Belt locations, including in western Pennsylvania. Biden was able to tighten the margins somewhat in most western counties and flipped Erie County, just barely, back to the blue column. But from what we have learned and reported here, most industrial workers seem to have remained loyal to Trump because the grounding of

Trump's appeal lies not in his policies but rather in his aggressive recognition of blue-collar whites' resentments and yearning to be respected. Candidate and presidential visits are part of this, but only part, and they have to continue and be backed up over months and years. Trump has accelerated such changes by and for Republicans because he both visits repeatedly and tells western Pennsylvanians and others in the Rust Belt that worsened economic and social conditions are not their fault—and that he is going to fix them. Even if most know they are lies, or at least dreams not likely to be realized, Trump told blue-collar people what they wanted to hear. For many who feel politics has long failed them, the Trump promise, however empty, has been better than nothing.

6

ON UNION DECLINE AND THE
POTENTIAL FOR RESURGENCE

Public perceptions and media portrayals today make it seem natural—maybe even inevitable—that many blue-collar men, including union members, cast their ballots for Republican candidates. In actuality, this is a recent development, one that this book has helped to illuminate. Not long ago, unionized industrial workers in western Pennsylvania took for granted that Democrats were much more often on their side than were Republicans. In turn, such unionists lent their support to Democratic candidates. Even when Ronald Reagan attracted more working-class voters than was usual for Republicans in his day, most heavily unionized areas of western Pennsylvania remained in the Democratic presidential column.

But a drift away from Democratic loyalties was steady and perceptible starting in the 1980s, as once-mighty industries were devastated and plants closed across much of America's Rust Belt. Once a more popularly attuned and resentful style of GOP politics took hold in the 2000s, the rightward turn of many of western Pennsylvania's workers sped up—including the turn toward the GOP of many unionized workers still employed in remaining steel and industrial jobs.

A FOCUS ON BOTTOM-UP EROSIONS

In this book, we have both built on and gone beyond previous analyses of the shrinkage of union resources that accompanied the decline of America's once-mighty industrial sectors and the related waning of Democratic electoral fortunes. As numbers of dues-paying members declined, national and regional union officials certainly had less money and person-power to back up electoral endorsements and legislative lobbying efforts. Yet the ties between unionized industrial workers and the Democratic Party were never only, or even primarily, a matter of top union officials writing checks or issuing directives to local union leaders and members. As we learned from retiree interviews and the internal United Steelworkers (USW) survey conducted in 1955, rank-and-file members were not necessarily enthusiastic about formal politicking by central union officials. Instead, they supported active community involvements by their unions and activities involving their locals, themselves, their families, and their neighbors. Political loyalties were part of that larger picture of socially engaged workplace and community activities— and we have argued that the entire ensemble of interactions and loyalties underpinned the powerful midcentury social identity of the so-called union man.

We have also fleshed out an argument that blue-collar workers of the mid-twentieth century heeded the political advice of their local and international unions not so much because they were told to do so but because being part of a working-class coalition was central to their peer networks and shared identity. Midcentury industrial union members overwhelmingly backed Democratic candidates because members and local leaders saw Democrats as allies opposing Republican and corporate enemies in ongoing battles between elite interests and working

Americans looking to build better lives for themselves, their families, and their neighborhood communities. Voting for Democrats and backing the party's policy goals were part of "who you were" and even a matter of loyalty to one's coworkers and friends. Electoral political involvements were part of multiple social ties and loyalties that unionized industrial workers took for granted on the job and in the neighborhoods that encircled the big industrial facilities across western Pennsylvania—from Erie to Uniontown; from Aliquippa to Johnstown; and, of course, on the outskirts of the city of Pittsburgh.

Using western Pennsylvania as a laboratory of changing Rust Belt realities from 1960 to the present, this book has attempted to further our understanding of the social grounding of the identities and loyalties of union members, particularly those of blue-collar men doing heavy industrial work. We have tracked changes in communities and social ties to better understand why organizational and political involvements have shifted markedly since the 1980s and especially during the early twenty-first century.

We started by redefining what economic transformation meant. Industrial contraction, massive job losses, and attacks on Big Labor did more than just weaken the political power and resource capabilities of the international leaderships of USW and other major industrial unions. Erosion also happened from the bottom-up as, community by community, local union chapters and union halls closed or merged, as organizational connections between unions and surrounding community groups frayed or disappeared. Some steel mills and other industrial plants remain in western Pennsylvania, and many of those surviving steel producers still have unionized workforces. But even in those workforces, unions are no longer the centerpieces of societal webs. As union enrollees began to see that their union could not reliably protect them from plant closures and unemployment, worker loyalties pivoted over time from the union to the company, which many came to see as the sole source of any remaining job security. The union man of yesteryear—united against employers by mutual commitment, historical awareness, and occupational pride—is largely a lost identity.

Beyond the decline of good-paying jobs and union clout, families and communities have also changed. More of workers' energy and attention goes to home life and social organizations other than the union locals and connected churches and clubs that used to enmesh blue-collar participants. Even if it means driving some distance, gun clubs and megachurches have become more central to workers' off-hours. And those involvements link worker participants to supralocal associations like the National Rifle Association (NRA) that foster very different moral sensibilities and different political ideologies than union-connected groups once did.

Industrial workers in western Pennsylvania still feel a deep sense of regional identity. But today, this sense of identity is grounded in different ties and revamped "us versus them" perspectives. Past unionized industrial workers felt part of a united "we" that opposed a powerful "them" linked with corporate elites and often their business-oriented Republican political allies. These same midcentury union members also felt loyal to ethnic, church, and community groups they perceived to be on their side, both politically and in all of life's vagaries. Now they or their successors either simply feel more on their own as individual employees, or they consider themselves part of neglected categories of workers struggling in places and industries left behind and looked down upon by metropolitan people. Party polarization has become tied up in this shift of perceived societal fault lines because many industrial workers think of Democrats as metropolitans who have abandoned or even betrayed nonurban industries and communities. The intertwined workplaces, communities, places of worship, and social lives that many retirees fondly remember as centerpieces of the heyday of labor no longer exist except in romanticized memories. Instead of a shared sense of interconnectedness, workers today who feel replaced and marginalized may share a sense of resentment and even anger.

We treat economic and societal transformations as intersections of supralocal and local reorganizations, and we look at partisan shifts the same way. Although the economic collapse of big industries gathered force in the late twentieth century, the Republican Party did not immediately become the full beneficiary of growing worker alienation or simmering anger about Democrats either not being able or not wanting to prevent economic disruptions. Democratic voting habits waned slowly, and it is likely that many workers just switched back and forth or stayed home during elections. But once an aggressive brand of conservatism gathered steam during the Barack Obama presidency and once GOP candidates emerged who pointed to new villains for the woes of working-class communities, larger numbers of industrial union members moved enthusiastically into the Republican column. Then came Donald Trump, who stoked resentments and gave them a racial and prejudicial edge. Trump told workers seeking recognition that he was on their side and visited their regions repeatedly. He gave focus and new force to the working-class feelings of betrayal and helped forge new links between such voters and a reoriented Republican Party. It is unclear whether Trump himself is crucial to this political revamping, but it does seem likely that changes in the Republican Party, its voter base, and its contrasts with Democrats will persist for years in western Pennsylvania and other working-class regions.

Both preceding and following Trump, worker-citizens were shifting away from the Democratic Party and becoming more open to Republican appeals. At the start of this book, we quoted western Pennsylvanian retirees who told us that, fifty years ago, we would be hard-pressed to find a union member who would cast his ballot for a Republican candidate. Today, as we have described, the stickers on cars and trucks in the parking lots of plants with remaining USW members tell a different story. Instead of touting the union or Democratic Party loyalties, today's bumper stickers proclaim deep concern for gun rights, remnants of Tea Party sympathies, and proud enthusiasm for Trump. We claim that such refocused concerns are bound up with changes in associational and political influences in the region. Workers may have formerly gathered at ethnic clubs, union halls, or nearby churches with prolabor clergy, but such institutions hardly exist anymore. Workers often live far from work and drive from long distances to their workplaces. Regional gun clubs have enlarged their functions; they no longer provide only ranges for shooters to practice but also spaces for members to gather, for community and family social events, and for meetings with politicians making pitches to voters. Activities that local union halls once hosted in industrial communities now may happen at gun clubs or in conservative churches that similarly structure social life for many workers' families.

Workers' decisions at the ballot box are affected in turn by such changed local and regional social infrastructures. Republican fortunes have improved in tandem with shifts in workers' community lives and associational involvements—a set of changes that have also happened in other regions, including areas in Michigan, Ohio, West Virginia, upstate New York, and Wisconsin. Because Democratic candidates and officeholders in these areas still usually stress economic policies that they say can help workers and unions, liberals and pundits alike have wondered why such workers are now seemingly voting "against their own economic self-interest." But our findings from interviews and community observations suggest that this way of posing the question is myopic: voters' interests are not determined via cold perusals of policy issues.

It is more fruitful to suppose that the inclinations of all subgroups of voters, not just those of blue-collar citizens, move in tandem with peers as new life experiences and mutual involvements highlight certain values and realities over others. Many scholars, such as political scientist Leonie Huddy, have already demonstrated that group identity is central to voting behavior.[1] Building on such insights, we have probed the ways in which changing social relationships have encouraged transformations in local and regional identities and political loyalties among industrial union members. Today's political views among workers are not *purely* based on local influences—that is not what we are saying—but local forces certainly play a significant role in determining which election messages, party stances, and political ideologies voters accept.

CONTRIBUTIONS TO UNDERSTANDING U.S. CIVIC ENGAGEMENT

Our work contributes to scholarship showing that social identities are constructed, reinforced, or undermined by face-to-face and often localized social interactions, even as they are informed by macro-level demographic trends. In the union communities of the mid-twentieth century, workers mutually influenced each other, reinforcing both shared loyalty to their union and the widespread belief that the Democratic Party was more effective for workers' interests than the Republican Party. Yet when we look beyond the union members in western Pennsylvania, the evidence we have presented in this book falls in line with accumulating scholarship on the decline of U.S. civic engagement and community involvement. Especially in less economically privileged places with larger shares of residents who do not have college degrees, U.S. society is less civically interconnected than it was in the mid-twentieth century, when most Americans belonged to at least a couple of associations, clubs, leagues, or lodges.[2] Civic associations directly or indirectly fostered an appreciation for group solidarity and basic democratic values among diverse members and also gave people a sense that their local activities connected to two-way communication with entire regions, states, and the country as a whole. Many organizations paralleled the federated structure of the United States and required members to abide by their organization's constitutional rules such as paying dues and voting on measures, officers, and delegates to regional or national conventions. Major labor unions had slightly different forms of federated organization but included many of these same features for members. Of course, such mass membership organizations were far from egalitarian and inclusive by today's standards, especially when it comes to differences of race and gender. But there were many parallels in the ways they operated—and the civic lessons they conveyed—even across such social divides. The unions that grew in mass memberships and organizational clout in the mid-twentieth century were integral parts of this larger civic universe.

Much of the scholarship on civic decline and growing citizen isolation in the United States glosses over changes in the surrounding civic organizational infrastructure we have just summarized and thus overlooks some important mechanisms that connect civic changes to political shifts. In this book, we have argued that the decline of socially interconnected local unions has contributed to the political realignment of workers. Most of the available literature on unions and partisanship abstracts away from the organizational, community, and network factors we have highlighted and relies on demographic and attitude surveys alone to document parallels between the declines in national union memberships, shrinking union monetary investments in politics, and erosions in Democratic vote margins. Resource mobilization theories are invoked to explain why these correlated shifts have occurred—and the resources highlighted are aggregates of votes and money contributions. Relational ties, including the local roots of eroding union political sway and shifts in workers' voting patterns, are often ignored. Our contribution has been to offer new evidence and outline suggestive hypotheses about previously understudied ways in which changing civic and social involvements have contributed to declines in both union political influence and Democratic vote margins. Our claim is that workers in the past and those today do not make choices at the ballot box simply via cost-benefit analyses of candidates or policy positions, nor have they ever simply responded to top-down union directives. We argue that workers' political reorientations happened at least as much through shifting understandings of "who we are" and upended perceptions of which major U.S. political party is "on our side" in publicly declared stances as well as policy promises.

Beyond friendly arguments with resource mobilization theorists, we have also taken issue with self-styled culturally oriented scholars who stress globally characterized identity politics and race relations. Although racial animosity among members of the white working class cannot be dismissed, what we have shown here is that votes for Republicans among union members are not solely a product of changing race relations and power dynamics in the United States. White industrial workers may now respond to angry politicians pushing implicit or blatant racist messages, but their predecessors and even some of them in their youth were surely exposed to similar feelings and racial stereotypes yet nonetheless supported progressive candidates and policies. Race-based generalizations thus do not account for unionists in the past *prioritizing* union-backed stances over other kinds of messaging they received. Invoking racism in an essentialist way cannot tell us why, in the same region with similar population demographics over time, unionists have *given less priority* to union-backed stances compared to other sorts of political messaging. For that, we must look at organizational, workplace, and social changes that have happened in communities over time.

Blue-collar western Pennsylvanians who once voted for Democrats and responded to messages from unions are now responding to politicians and messages with vicious racist, sexist, and anti-immigrant edges—and that shift cannot be happening simply because the informal actuality and public potential for such social resentments were always there. Of course, as we noted, the egalitarian nature of unions functioned to decrease racial animosity among members, and muting such tensions may have induced members to be more likely to vote progressive.[3] We heard firsthand accounts reinforcing this theory about union ties mitigating racial divisions and even heard testimony about unions keeping some workers away from extremist organizations, such as the Ku Klux Klan (KKK). But we also believe that in order for unions to function as bridging organizations between Americans of different creeds and racial and ethnic backgrounds, workers must not only belong to unions; they must also *buy into their particular union*.

Union membership and union credibility are not abstract concepts. As we have demonstrated in part by looking closely at the USW versus the International Brotherhood of Electrical Workers (IBEW), unions of all sorts lack sway and meaning for members if their procedures, power, and leaders are not seen as credible by grassroots members. Today, many industrial workers are disengaged and removed from their unions. This alienation likely undercuts the capacities of some unions to build bridges across races, and it certainly renders their national political endorsements less effective in an era when overall U.S. partisan polarization increasingly pits Republicans against Democrats on overtly cultural lines.

WHAT NEXT?

Given what we have found in our research, the question becomes, is there any way to recreate faith in union solidarity and effectiveness, or would such attempts simply be exercises in nostalgia? People still crave a sense of belonging to groups, and research shows that people will go to great lengths to achieve a sense of social reciprocity.[4] Many people satisfy their need for belonging in other ways, including potentially those men we have discussed who have become more directly involved in their children's lives than in generations past. Although more stress on family involvement for working men and women alike can be seen as an obstacle to worker socializing outside workplaces, new family realities also offer opportunities for unions to engage more fully with community events and associations built around children. Family members supported union men of the mid-twentieth century by attending union-sponsored get-togethers, running auxiliary groups, participating in campaigns to buy union-made goods, and having children follow in their father's footsteps in the same unionized trade. Although roles are certainly different today and locals are often less deeply embedded in communities, families and their needs can still be put front and center in local and regional union programs and events. Local unions could, and some perhaps do, sponsor new kinds of family support services as selective benefits for members. Possibilities for innovation abound, but the underlying idea is a reinvention of tradition, making unions vital supports for family and community needs above and beyond boosting take-home pay and employer-provided benefits.

Social gatherings and celebrations have always been crucial tools for building union solidarity, as we have seen. Unions like IBEW that are not as tied to specific workplaces continue to feature more personal and family narratives in their publications, and some union networks continue to hold events to celebrate and announce career and family transitions for members. No matter how strapped for resources unions may be, high-level leaders need to realize that efforts to build and reinforce buy-in and community ties beyond as well as within workplaces are not an expendable luxury; such efforts are vital to the member solidarity that is a core ingredient of organized labor clout in the economy and politics. A shared sense of pride among existing union members is also important to new member recruitment; new members need to hear not only that unions collect dues but also that they offer a community of brothers and sisters who "have each other's back" for contract negotiations and much more. Pride, connectedness, and loyalty are invaluable for groups of all types—and more so for organizations like unions that aim to increase the insufficient leverage isolated individuals have against powerful forces in the corporate and political world.

Efforts to increase member engagement cannot happen solely at the behest of top union executives in national or regional offices. High-level elected officers can certainly champion the cause and lead the way at conventions and meetings, but ground-level leadership and activism, through ongoing, routine efforts by local officials and their members, are vital. Today, as we have discussed, breakdowns occur often in communication and teamwork between top union officials and local leaders who receive pressure from their rank-and-file members—especially when it comes to electoral messaging. Local union leaders who manage to keep their members socially engaged and involved in more than just dues-paying and union business affairs are more likely to be able to advance labor's political priorities—even in Rust Belt regions where most of the messages that workers hear from acquaintances in the community might be conservative in nature. The local leadership of IBEW Local 5, for example, is not afraid to speak out frankly through their regular newsletter about hot political topics such as gun rights and abortion. These local leaders are involved in their members' personal and family lives as well, so even when their political arguments do not tap into as much automatic loyalty as union messages once did, at least the local IBEW leaders can put the union's priorities into direct competition with those pushed by conservative groups.

Over the past six decades, unions and many American associations have either lost their face-to-face components altogether or have evolved from membership-grounded federations with strong local roots into staff-run fund-raising, lobbying, and communications organizations operating out of Washington, DC, or other metropolitan hubs. Although unions still have dues-paying members and multitiered leadership, many of them have also shifted shrinking resources to staff-heavy national operations while doing less to build vibrant activities for existing members and their communities. Today, many of the DC-based arms of labor unions have large staffs and budgets, which are often used for political purposes as well as to manage union contracts. But sheer staff growth and more money shoveled into political campaigns do not necessarily translate into rank-and-file votes for the political candidates endorsed by Internationals. Donations from unions to Democratic candidates help fund television ads and get-out-the-vote efforts, but such input cannot substitute for longer-term, locally rooted efforts to foster ties and shared identity among union workers and families. Such ties and loyalties are the basis for union leaders and activists to keep in touch with members and their families and neighbors in ways that can counterbalance opposing political siren calls.

We are not labor historians, nor do we claim to know all there is to know about effective union building—or even about various creative new engagement initiatives now underway in unions such as USW. But we have spent hundreds of hours listening to workers talk about their unions and reading through reports and firsthand accounts of union life in the past, and our findings in this book reflect those conversations and data. Many upper-level international union leaders know that many of their rank-and-file have abandoned the union cause. Union leadership often tries to compensate through PAC activity, sending communications to union households, and even funding full-time campaigners to go door to door on behalf of political campaigns. Our conclusion is that it might be more useful to reallocate some of those resources to longer-term community-building efforts among networks of union families and communities as well as in workplaces.

International union officials cannot avoid all situations in which local union members, even local officials, support even the most conservative Republicans. High-level International union leaders may worry that further empowering local unions could simply facilitate such defections. Empowering local union leadership nonetheless makes sense for the longer run, especially if that includes building multistrand union connections. By handing over some of the international's power to local leadership—and giving local leadership the resources and tools necessary to build social networks and communicate with and educate their members about public issues—the stage could be set for increased union clout over time.

Deeper involvement in the local union does not mean that workers will automatically follow partisan endorsements because, as many of our interviewees told us, a lot of the rank-and-file members now feel that the Democratic Party overall has abandoned the working class. In an era of fast-rising economic inequality and erosion of working conditions and community institutions for many workers, the Democratic Party establishment has as much or more work to do as top union officials to overcome growing working-class alienation. Occasional appearances by candidates at events with top union leaders does not suffice. It would be better for vibrant locals and credible local politicians to work with one another on specific, shared year-round concerns, not just assume that brief election season initiatives will build mutual trust. Democrats also have to establish an ongoing, cooperative presence in states and districts where electoral wins seem impossible in the near term. Indeed, the meaning of electoral success itself should be redefined to include running locally attuned candidates in every contest at every level, doing community outreach everywhere, and aiming to improve Democratic electoral margins even in defeat. To do this at local, state, and regional levels, Democrats cannot just send in operatives from afar every four years for presidential contests; there must be an ongoing progressive presence through credible local voices. And Democrats must prove to workers and others that they understand and are committed to meeting community needs well beyond the big cities and affluent suburbs. Subnational party officials and activists as well as nominated candidates can do that in part simply by being present, listening, and championing even small public policy steps that could make a difference.

Aside from the electoral benefits, an increased Democratic presence in areas other than urban centers also functions to chip away at rampant levels of party polarization in today's political climate. This means building the party even in the regions of the country that have become solidly red, like many of the western Pennsylvania counties. It also means finding candidates and party leaders who represent the workers of the region—not simply members of the intellectual elite. Gains from an increased Democratic presence in such areas will not be felt immediately, but a long-standing commitment to such regions has the power to reshape political loyalties. As we've shown in this book, western Pennsylvania was not a Republican region four decades ago. It is possible to imagine that, in another several decades, western Pennsylvania and other Rust Belt regions might again be friendly terrain for Democrats who have proven to be effective advocates for those regions and their workers.

To foster union political loyalty at all, unions must *exist*. Today, an upsurge of labor organizing is occurring across the United States, and support for unionization is at its highest point since the 1960s.[5] Recent organizing victories have provoked questions about whether labor could be on the precipice of reversing its decades-long decline. Despite positive momentum, most analysts think it is unlikely that American workers will reach levels of unionization such as those in the mid-1950s anytime soon. Even modest upticks, though, have the potential to make a long-term electoral difference, especially if blue-collar workers in the Midwest can be made part of new unionization waves. Most of today's unionization efforts are not occurring, however, at the type of workplace that we have focused on throughout this book. Making organizing inroads outside major cities during this period of union momentum could go a long way toward reestablishing a competitive balance of progressive and conservative community ties in nonurban areas.

Let us end, finally, on a note about additional research that scholars and observers should do on unions and their involvement in U.S. democracy. The findings and arguments we have presented here are not the usual statistical aggregations about union members in general. Nor are our findings about unions as national resource-wielding organizations that lobby and channel money into elections. We have benefitted from and used findings from both kinds of long-standing research, but we have mostly offered new kinds of evidence to support hypotheses about community-level and regional organizational and social dynamics that interact with and help to explain votes and resource flows in politics. Because we have looked mostly at major unions in one region, and because many kinds of useful data about particular union organizations and memberships are simply unavailable, our findings do not lend themselves to statistical certainty or causal generalizations. Nevertheless, we believe we have drawn important new insights from our organizational analysis and from our rich interviews with current and retired workers. The arguments we have offered here should be further explored in fresh kinds of research on the changing role of unions in American politics.

Much more scholarship needs to be done on particular unions, workforces, and industries, not just on unions and members in general. America's unionized workforce is both shrinking and growing in dynamically varied ways. Unionization drives are making headway in new industries and in professional as well as blue-collar workforces, and today's union organizers and leaders operate in many different ways—all of which will likely have intended and unintended effects. Workers' civic and political involvements depend on evolving social relationships and organizational dynamics that cannot be understood at a distance. To make sense of what is happening and to discern possibilities for the future, observers must marry broad demographic and statistical analyses with insight from workers' own experiences with their unions, workplaces, and communities. Political outlooks and choices are shaped and take effect in those places, with often reverberating consequences for electoral outcomes at the local, state, and national levels. The Democratic Party's future and the future of American democracy more generally depend not only on working people's choices and fortunes but also on how well leaders and researchers understand union potential in an era of unsettling economic transformation and high-stakes political clashes.

APPENDIX A

Voting Patterns in Western Pennsylvania

T he line graph in Figure A.1 shows the *average* vote percentages attained by Democratic and Republican presidential candidates across the twenty-county region from 1976 to 2020. Table A.1 provides basic details about each of these counties, including vote percentages comparing the elections of 1960 to 2020. Those counties shaded grey in the table on the right represent Democratic victories in 1960 versus 2020.

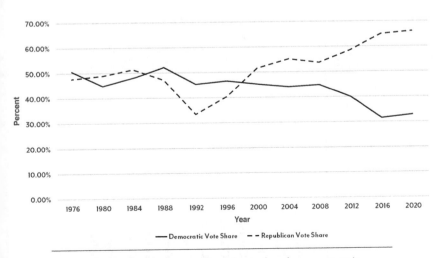

FIGURE A.1 Average presidential vote share by percentage in twenty-county western Pennsylvania region.

TABLE A.1

County Name	Population, 1960	Population, 2020	Number of Local Unions, 1960*	Democrat Presidential Vote, 1960	Republican Presidential Vote, 1960	Democrat Presidential Vote, 2020	Republican Presidential Vote, 2020
Allegheny	1,628,587	1,250,578	202	57.07%	42.76%	59.61%	39.23%
Armstrong	79,524	65,558	6	42.59%	57.23%	23.25%	75.58%
Beaver	206,948	168,215	19	56.04%	43.71%	40.50%	58.18%
Butler	114,639	193,851	20	38.45%	61.22%	33.10%	65.63%
Cambria	203,283	133,472	32	58.48%	41.35%	30.79%	68.13%
Clarion	37,480	37,241	0	34.74%	65.04%	24.00%	74.79%
Crawford	77,956	83,938	27	38.99%	60.68%	30.77%	67.99%
Erie	250,682	270,876	105	50.90%	48.82%	49.81%	48.78%
Fayette	169,340	128,804	5	60.35%	39.38%	32.90%	66.35%
Forest	4,485	6,973	0	35.51%	64.19%	27.51%	71.13%
Greene	39,457	35,954	1	56.21%	43.70%	27.79%	71.19%
Indiana	75,366	83,246	0	41.15%	58.59%	30.67%	68.18%
Jefferson	46,792	44,492	5	36.01%	63.82%	19.83%	78.69%

Lawrence	112,965	86,070	23	50.58%	49.20%	34.68%	64.24%
Mercer	127,519	110,652	27	45.33%	54.43%	36.35%	62.36%
Somerset	77,450	74,129	0	41.71%	58.17%	21.35%	77.61%
Venango	65,295	50,454	50	31.90%	68.01%	28.59%	70.00%
Warren	45,582	38,587	1	35.86%	63.81%	29.38%	68.94%
Washington	217,271	209,349	14	58.28%	41.59%	38.06%	60.84%
Westmorel and	352,629	354,663	31	55.31%	44.45%	35.24%	63.62%
Totals for the twenty-county region	3,933,250	3,427,102	568				

*Estimates based on data collected from city directories and Yellow Pages circa 1960 via Ancestry.com and the Library of Congress.

APPENDIX B

Sample Interview Questions

The following list is not exhaustive. Questions differed based on the age of union members so not all the following questions were asked to any given interviewee. Interviews with community members and county political party chairs often involved questions about how individuals had perceived changes in their communities over time. All interviews were semistructured. We would often ask follow-up questions based on interviewees' responses.

1. Tell me a little bit about your career history. How long have you been a member of [union]? What local?
2. Where did you grow up? Where do you live now?
3. How has [community] changed throughout your life?
4. What got you involved in the ___ industry?
5. What are your memories of the region from when you were young?
6. Do you remember the collapse of the steel industry?
7. What did your friends and coworkers do after the steel collapse?
8. How would you say most people felt about the union and company back then? How did you feel about them?

9. What were the political beliefs of most workers when you began in the [industry/union]? Do you think those views have changed?

10. Are members today engaged with union activities? Would you say more or less, or the same, compared to before?

11. How often do you hear about, or attend, union-sponsored events, such as social events?

12. Does your local union often communicate to you? If so, how? Via Facebook, paper newsletter, for example?

13. How do you feel about the International? How about other members?

14. How do you feel about the political orientation of the union/International?

15. What would you say is the enemy of steelworkers right now?

16. What groups are/were you a part of outside work? Sports clubs, religious organizations, for example?

17. How often do you see other workers/retirees outside work?

18. What did you think of the 2020 election?

19. What did you think of the Capitol insurrection of January 6, 2021?

20. How do you think the majority of [industry/union workers] feel about politics right now?

21. What are the biggest political issues for [industry/union workers] right now?

22. What would you say your political orientation is?

APPENDIX C

Photographs in IBEW and USW Newsletters

n order to understand how representations of women and people of color have changed over time in International Brotherhood of Electrical Workers (IBEW) and United Steelworkers (USW) newsletters, we coded all photographs printed in IBEW and USW magazines from 1955, 1985, and 2015. We used the January and July issues of the magazines from each of these years. The purpose of this analysis was both to probe how women and people of color were being depicted in union publications and to understand how the magazines were depicting local and International leaders.

Our methodology for this analysis was quite simple. We looked at every photograph in the magazines and coded it for its various qualities. The first question we answered about each photograph was whether it was of a person or people or an inanimate object(s). If a person or people were in the photograph, we coded answers to a series of questions about the image:

- Title of the article that goes with the photograph (or the photograph headline).
- How many people are in the photograph? If indiscernible, respond "many."
- What is the union affiliation of the person/people in the photograph? Options:

- International leaders or people who work at the International
- District leaders
- Local union members (including local union leadership)
- Family of union members
- Individuals *not* identified as members of the union
- In what context was the photograph taken? Select only one of the following options:
  - Union business affairs (i.e., negotiations)
  - Community engagement (i.e., with members of other unions or participating in charity)
  - Political (i.e., with candidates, politicians, etc.)
  - Photograph of member(s) being honored (i.e., someone who retired, died, etc.)
  - Social or activity (i.e., bowling or fishing)
- How many white men are in the photograph?
- How many white women are in the photograph?
- How many Black men are in the photograph?
- How many Black women are in the photograph?
- How many men/women of other races are in the photograph?

It is crucial to note here that we coded racial and gender identification of individuals in the photographs only when we could be relatively certain of their phenotypical presentation. When in doubt about an individual's racial or gender identification—due to poor photograph quality or any other reason—we did not count that individual in any race or gender category.

Table C.1 shows how representation of people of color and white women evolved over time in the IBEW and the USW magazines, rounded to the nearest percentage. Table C.2 shows the union affiliation of people in newsletter images, differentiated by local union members and family versus International leaders and district staff members.

TABLE C.1

Minority Representation	1955		1985		2015	
	IBEW	USW	IBEW	USW	IBEW	USW
Nonwhite individuals pictured in union magazines	0.3%	5%	4%	11%	13%	22%
White women pictured in union magazines	13%	6%	9%	9%	12%	10%

TABLE C.2

Union Affiliation of People in Newsletter Photographs	1955		1985		2015	
	IBEW	USW	IBEW	USW	IBEW	USW
Local union members or family	78%	40%	93%	65%	78%	80%
International or district staff/leaders	22%	60%	7%	35%	22%	20%

APPENDIX D

Local Union Mentions in IBEW and USW Newsletters

I n order to understand the activities, concerns, and priorities for local unions over time, we systematically recorded and analyzed all mentions of local unions from select magazines of the United Steelworkers (USW) and the International Brotherhood of Electrical Workers (IBEW). These magazines, which were distributed internationally to all members, were key ways in which members received information and signaling from USW and IBEW, respectively. Both unions sent out monthly newsletters through the twentieth century. More recently, publication of newsletters by the unions has not been quite as regular.

Important differences between the USW and the IBEW magazines exist. In the mid-twentieth century, IBEW magazines were significantly longer than USW counterparts. The July 1965 IBEW magazine was eighty-nine pages long, and the USW magazine, then called "Steel Labor," was sixteen pages. IBEW magazines have become shorter and more like newsletters over time. In January 2015, the IBEW magazine was twenty pages. Until the 1980s, the USW magazine was organized more like a newspaper. The USW magazine—which went from being called "Steel Labor" to "Steelabor," to "USW@Work" in 2006—has become longer. By 2005, USW was issuing seasonal magazines rather than monthly magazines, and they were usually around thirty-five pages in length. Through the mid-1980s, USW distributed different regional issues, which included the regular edition, Southern edition, Western edition, Midwest edition, and Canadian edition. For our analysis, we used copies of the regular edition. Both IBEW and USW still issue newsletters, now available online and on paper.

We selected two months—January and July—per decade of the magazines to analyze systematically. We chose to analyze nonelection years—1955, 1965, and so on, through 2015—so that our results were not skewed overly political. For each magazine, we recorded every mention of a local union. Mentions of local unions appeared in different capacities in international newsletters: in articles that discussed individual members, in individual member write-ins or letters to the editor, in reports on local union affairs, and more. We recorded the type of writer of each mention—primarily whether he or she was a staff person at the international union or a local union member, family member, or retiree—and what category the mention fell into: an individual write-in, a report on a union, or the mention of a local union in an article in the magazine. Finally, but this was very important, we classified in what context(s) the local union was being discussed. We created content-based categories based on the primary contexts in which local unions were mentioned. Our content-based categories include the following: the local's social engagement efforts, community engagement efforts, business affairs, politics, and news on individual members or their families.

These five main categories comprised the vast majority of local union mentions in international union magazines or newsletters. Other types of mentions included local union mentions related to life advice or general interests, but because there were not many mentions that fell into these categories, we omit them from our overall analysis. In order to understand how we classified these five categories, brief definitions of the terms follow.

The Local's Social Engagement Efforts

Local union mentions related to social engagement efforts are those that discuss efforts on behalf of the union to bring union members—and sometimes their families—together for purely or primarily recreational purposes. Types of local union mentions included in this category are local union reports on hosting dinners or dances for members, updates on the local's bowling league, or an article about a particular local union's conservation club for members who like to hunt and fish. These union mentions generally serve the purpose of strengthening relationships between members of the union, not with outside community members. It is important to note, however, that events can be both bonding and bridging if, for example, the event can be classified as both a social engagement effort and a community engagement effort.

The Local's Community Engagement Efforts

Local union mentions related to community engagement are those that discuss the local union's nonpolitical activities in the context of the broader community or locality. Local mentions that we classified as community engagement efforts include reports on the local union's float in the annual Labor Day parade; an article that discussed donating blood locally; and local union mentions that include crossover events with other types of civic organizations, such as Elks Lodges or ethnic clubs. Community engagement efforts are those that strengthen the bonds between the local union and its larger community or region in some capacity.

The Local's Business Affairs

Local union mentions that we classified as the union's business affairs were those that concerned the operational, fiscal, or internal responsibilities of the local. Examples of local union mentions that we classified as business affairs include reports on contract negotiations, discussion of training or safety classes, announcements regarding a local's credit union, and reports on union officer elections. The union business affairs category also encompassed logistical and fiscal aspects of union activity.

Politics

The politics category includes any context in which a local union is mentioned in relation to local, state, or federal politics, including in relation to candidates or policy. Examples include a local politician attending a union event; a letter to the editor about an individual's political views; reports on a local union participating in get-out-the-vote campaigns for a candidate; and efforts to support or oppose a particular piece of local, state, or federal legislation. Some mentions that were categorized as politics were also categorized as community engagement efforts, such as a local union sponsoring a voter registration drive or hosting a debate for local city council candidates.

News on Individual Members or Their Families

We classified local union mentions as "news on individual members or their families" if the mention reported on the personal or professional news of a particular member or members. Frequent examples include announcements of retirement, passing, or hospitalization. But other examples include reports on members' hobbies (such as rock or coin collection), their hunting trophies, or information on their children's lives. When lists of many members' names were provided, such as those who graduated an apprenticeship course, we generally did *not* classify this as news on individual members unless the list was relatively short and details were provided about the individual members mentioned. Our rule of thumb was that, to be categorized as "news on individual members or their family," there had to be some detail provided about an individual person.

Local union mentions often concerned more than one of the categories described above. When an individual wrote to their union magazine or when a local union reported on its activities, writers generally discussed multiple topics. For example, the following report was submitted by IBEW Local 1362 of Cedar Rapids, Iowa, to the January 1965 IBEW international magazine, the *Electrical Workers' Journal*:

> Our members voted to have a Family Fun Day at Cemar Amusement Park held on Saturday, October 3. The park was available from 1 P.M. to 10, with an estimated 4,000 members and their children enjoying a bout on roller skates, ferris wheels, and various other rides directed at entertaining the younger children. . . .
> Saturday, October 10, was the big night set for our annual fall

dinner dance at Armar Ballroom. . . . A recently retired employe [*sic*] who long served as our recording secretary and who had twenty years with our local, was also at the door, still doing his job in offering unselfishly of his services to his fellow man, and welcoming friends at the dinner dance. We all definitely feel deep gratitude to Brother Bill Willson for all he contributed to our local. . . . A special meeting was called on Sunday, November 8, for the purpose of voting on the contract proposal between Collins Radio Company and our local. . . . What with the elections over and many of our members actively contributing time to "Get Out the Vote" drives and working at the polls, we wish to thank all who contributed their time and talents accordingly.

This excerpt comes from a single local union report and, as such, was coded as one local union mention—it only states "Local 1362" once at the top of the report. Clearly, however, this local union mention covers multiple categories: social engagement, union business affairs, news on an individual member, and politics. It was thus coded as belonging to each of these categories. As a result, there are many more categorical references than there are local union mentions in our data because many local union mentions fall into multiple categories.

In our analysis, we group social engagement efforts, community engagement efforts, and news on individual members or their families together as proxies for efforts by the union to strengthen members' sense of union identity. These types of mentions deviate from the union's explicit responsibilities and function to enhance the bonds between unionists and, outside the union, with the external community. The categories of politics and business affairs, in contrast, are more formalist and less personal than the other three.

NOTES

1. UNDERSTANDING SOCIAL AND POLITICAL CHANGE IN THE RUST BELT

1. Lara Putnam, "Rust Belt in Transition," *Democracy Journal*, June 12, 2020, https://democracyjournal.org/magazine/57/rust-belt-in-transition/.

2. David Macdonald, "Labor Unions and White Democratic Partisanship," *Political Behavior* 43, no. 2 (June 2021): 859–79, https://doi.org/10.1007/s11109-020-09624-3, 863.

3. Timothy J. Minchin, "A Pivotal Role? The AFL–CIO and the 2008 Presidential Election," *Labor History* 57, no. 3 (July 2016): 299–322, https://doi.org/10.1080/0023656X.2016.1164380.

4. Sung Eun Kim and Yotam Margalit, "Informed Preferences? The Impact of Unions on Workers' Policy Views," *American Journal of Political Science* 61, no. 3 (2017): 728–43, https://doi.org/10.1111/ajps.12280.

5. James Feigenbaum, Alexander Hertel-Fernandez, and Vanessa Williamson, *From the Bargaining Table to the Ballot Box: Political Effects of Right to Work Laws* (Cambridge, MA: National Bureau of Economic Research, January 2018), https://doi.org/10.3386/w24259.

6. Drew Desilver, "The Polarization in Today's Congress Has Roots That Go Back Decades," *Pew Research Center* (blog), accessed May 18, 2022, https://www.pewresearch.org/fact-tank/2022/03/10/the-polarization-in-todays-congress-has-roots-that-go-back-decades/.

7. John F. Camobreco and Michelle A. Barnello, "The Changing Face of Unions and White Labor Support for the Democratic Party," *Forum*

13, no. 2 (July 1, 2015): 209–22, https://doi.org/10.1515/for-2015-0018; Donald W. Beachler, "Race, God, and Guns: Union Voting in the 2004 Presidential Election," *WorkingUSA* 10, no. 3 (2007): 311–25, https://doi .org/10.1111/j.1743-4580.2007.00164.x.

8. Daniel G. Gallagher and George Strauss, "Union Membership Attitudes and Participation," Institute for Research on Labor and Employment (IRLE) Working Paper (University of California, Berkeley, May 1, 1991).

9. Robert D. Putnam, *Bowling Alone: The Collapse and Revival of American Community* (New York: Simon & Schuster, 2000); Dan Clawson, "Union Density and Bowling Leagues: Declining Together? Review of Robert Putnam's 'Bowling Alone,'" ed. Robert Putnam, *New Labor Forum*, no. 9 (2001): 73–77.

10. Matthew J. Lacombe, *Firepower: How the NRA Turned Gun Owners into a Political Force* (Princeton, NJ: Princeton University Press, 2021).

11. Lawrence Mishel, Lynn Rhinehart, and Lane Windham, *Explaining the Erosion of Private-Sector Unions: How Corporate Practices and Legal Changes Have Undercut the Ability of Workers to Organize and Bargain* (Washington, DC: Economic Policy Institute, November 18, 2020), https://www.epi.org/unequalpower/publications/private-sector-unions -corporate-legal-erosion/.

12. "Industrial Unionism," LII/Legal Information Institute, accessed May 18, 2022, https://www.law.cornell.edu/wex/industrial_unionism.

2. THE SOCIAL UNDERPINNINGS OF THE "UNION MAN"

1. Joe Glazer, "Bricklayin' Union Man" (Washington, DC: Smithsonian Folkways Recordings, 1987), https://folkways.si.edu/joe-glazer/bricklayin -union-man/american-folk/music/album/smithsonian.

2. Blue Highway, "Union Man" (Nashville, TN: Rounder Records, 2001), https://open.spotify.com/track/1dUnlxfjj3PGcHTCiYvZfi.

3. "Andy Johnson Honored" (Local 5 Newsletter: International Brotherhood of Electrical Workers, October 1980), IBEW Local 5 Archives, Pittsburgh, PA.

4. "Local Lines: Brother Trivitt Retires After 35 Years," *IBEW Journal* (July 1985), IBEW Media Center. Local 639, San Obispo, CA. Sent in by Stan Garland, P. S.

5. "Local Lines: Philbert Axton Mourned by Local 605 Brothers," *Electrical Workers' Journal* (September 1970), IBEW Media Center. Local 605, Jackson, MS. Sent in by J. W. Russell, P. S.

6. "Aliquippa Steelworker" (United Steelworkers Local 1211, July 1967), United Steelworkers Archives.

7. "Local Lines: Past Articles Indicate History Repeats Itself," *IBEW Journal* (July 1985), IBEW Media Center. Local 995, Baton Rouge, LA. Sent in by Pete Macaluso, R. S.

8. "United Steel Workers of America Convention Proceedings of 1958," September 18, 1958, authors' collections.

9. "Local Lines: Scribe Tells of Non-Union Contractors," *IBEW Journal* (July 1975), IBEW Media Center. Local 309, Collinsville, IL. Sent in by John Lorentzen, P. S.

10. "Local Lines: New Jersey Local Holds Christmas Party," *Electrical Workers' Journal* (February 1970), IBEW Media Center. Local 675, Elizabeth, NJ. Sent in by Edward "Ted" Hanna, P. S.

11. Matthew J. Lacombe, *Firepower: How the NRA Turned Gun Owners into a Political Force* (Princeton, NJ: Princeton University Press, 2021), 22.

12. "Local Lines: Local 1579 Is Host for State Convention," *IBEW Journal* (July 1965), IBEW Media Center.

13. Tom Waselski, "Why I Came to Work Today," *Pittsburgh Post-Gazette*, July 28, 1992, Newspapers.com.

14. "Local Lines: Letter to Russell on Labor's Political Role," *Electrical Workers' Journal* (July 1955), IBEW Media Center. Local 613, Atlanta, GA. Sent in by O. B. Crenshaw, P. S.

15. "Local Lines: Work Picture Appears Brighter in Fairmont," *Electrical Workers' Journal* (January 1970), IBEW Media Center. Local 425, Fairmont, WV. Sent in by Charles T. McGee, P. S.

16. "Andy Johnson Honored."

17. "More Life-Saving Awards," *Electrical Workers' Journal* (January 1965), IBEW Media Center.

18. "Pittsburgh Pirate," *Economist*, January 30, 2003, https://www.economist.com/books-and-arts/2003/01/30/pittsburgh-pirate.

19. Jessica Learish, "The 20 Deadliest Jobs in America, Ranked," *CBS News*, July 19, 2017, https://www.cbsnews.com/pictures/the-20-deadliest-jobs-in-america-ranked/.

20. As many interviewees told us, it was typical in the building trades and other unions not to be able to get into the industry unless you had a family connection to it. Although not an explicit rule at the steel mill or coal mine, most workers had fathers and grandfathers in the industry as well. Being an insulator, steamfitter, steelworker, or miner, therefore, was often highly associated not only with the broader community and region but also with one's own family history.

21. Harry P. Cohany, "Membership of American Trade Unions, 1960," *Monthly Labor Review* 84, no. 12 (1961): 1299–1308.

22. Lee Sustar, "Black Power at the Point of Production, 1968–73," *International Socialist Review*, Center for Economic Research and Social Change ISR, accessed May 18, 2022, https://isreview.org/issue/111/black-power-point-production-1968-73/index.html.

23. Sustar, "Black Power at the Point of Production."

24. Sustar, "Black Power at the Point of Production."

25. Sustar, "Black Power at the Point of Production."

26. Thomas J. Sugrue, "Affirmative Action from Below: Civil Rights, the Building Trades, and the Politics of Racial Equality in the Urban North, 1945–1969," *Journal of American History* 91, no. 1 (2004): 145–73, https://doi.org/10.2307/3659618.

27. Sugrue, "Affirmative Action from Below," 160.

28. "African-American's Rights: Unions Making History in America," University of Maryland, University Libraries, accessed June 10, 2022, https://exhibitions.lib.umd.edu/unions/social/african-americans-rights.

29. Herbert Hill, "The Problem of Race in American Labor History," *Reviews in American History* 24, no. 2 (1996): 189–208, https://doi.org/10.1353/rah.1996.0037, 195.

30. Paul Frymer and Jacob M. Grumbach, "Labor Unions and White Racial Politics," *American Journal of Political Science* 65, no. 1 (January 2021): 225–40, https://doi.org/10.1111/ajps.12537.

31. Raymond Henderson and Tony Buba, *Struggles in Steel: A Story of African-American Steel Workers* (Braddock, PA: Braddock Films, 1996).

32. Henderson and Buba, *Struggles in Steel.*

33. Henderson and Buba, *Struggles in Steel.*

34. Henderson and Buba, *Struggles in Steel.*

35. Henderson and Buba, *Struggles in Steel.*

36. "Local Lines: Ladies Auxiliary Holds 41st Anniversary Dinner," *Electrical Workers' Journal* (July 1965), IBEW Media Center. Local 716, Houston, TX. Sent in by Bob Louvier, P. S.

37. "Local Lines: Local Active on Legislative Program," *IBEW Journal* (July 1965), IBEW Media Center. Local 111, Oklahoma City, OK. Sent in by O. O. Pennington, P. S.

38. "Local Lines: Elections Held; Negotiations in Progress," *IBEW Journal* (July 1975), IBEW Media Center. Local 1837, Portsmouth, NH. Sent in by David Adams, P. S. and David Bostrom, P. S.

39. "With the Ladies: Take a Tip from a Song," *Electrical Workers' Journal* (January 1955), IBEW Media Center.

40. "Voice of Local 306" (United Auto Workers Local 306, May 17, 1967), Walter P. Reuther Library, Voice of Local 306 Archives, Wayne State University, Detroit, MI.

41. John W. McCollum and Hazel M. West, eds., "Report on Union Member Attitude Survey" (United Steelworkers of America District 13 and the Union Research and Education Project at the University of Chicago, 1955), Box 9, John P. Hoerr papers at Pennsylvania State University.

42. "Aliquippa, PA Population," accessed May 18, 2022, https://population.us/pa/aliquippa/.

43. Joshua M. Penrod, *Johnstown Industry*, Images of America (Charleston, SC: Arcadia, 2021).

44. In fact, along with major unions, the Fraternal Order of Eagles worked for new public social insurance policies, and the Grand Eagle himself was present when President Franklin Roosevelt signed the Social Security Act of 1935 into law.

45. We draw especially on the trends and research reported in chapters 1–3 of Theda Skocpol, *Diminished Democracy: From Membership to Management in American Civic Life* (Norman: University of Oklahoma Press, 2003).

46. United Steelworkers of America, "The 1959 Steel Strike," Pamphlet No. PR-112 (Pittsburgh, PA: United Steelworkers of America, ca. 1960), from T. Skocpol private ephemera collection.

47. Steel Workers Organizing Committee, *Manual of Common Procedure for Local Unions* (Pittsburgh, PA: Steel Workers Organizing Committee, n.d., ca. 1940s), from T. Skocpol private ephemera collection.

48. "Aliquippa Steelworker"(United Steelworkers Local 1211, August 1966), United Steelworkers Archives.
49. "Annual Labor Celebration," 1983, UMWA District 2, Box 472, "Labor Celebrations,"Indiana University of Pennsylvania Special Collections 52.
50. David J. Dodson, "Letter to the Johnstown Tribune Democrat," September 5, 1980, UMWA District 2, Box 472, "Labor Celebrations," Indiana University of Pennsylvania Special Collections 52.
51. "About These 'Right-to-Work' Laws," *Electrical Workers' Journal* (January 1955), IBEW Media Center.
52. "Pamphlet for a Seminar Hosted by the Tri-State Conference on Steel," May 1982, Series I, Box 3, "TSC/SVA Internal Documents," Indiana University of Pennsylvania Special Collections 62.
53. Staughton Lynd, "The Genesis of the Idea of a Community Right to Industrial Property in Youngstown and Pittsburgh, 1977–86," n.d., Series I, Box 3, "TSC/SVA Internal Documents," Indiana University of Pennsylvania Special Collections 62.
54. Pat Cloonan, "Religion vs. Lost Jobs," *Freemont News-Messenger,* January 2, 1985, Series I, Box 3, "TSC/SVA Internal Documents," Indiana University of Pennsylvania Special Collections 62.
55. "Aliquippa Steelworker" (United Steelworkers Local 1211, February 1983), United Steelworkers Archives.
56. "Aliquippa Steelworker" (United Steelworkers Local 1211, September 1964), United Steelworkers Archives.
57. "Local Lines: Assistance Programs Offered to Members," *IBEW Journal* (July 1985), IBEW Media Center. Local 332, San Jose, CA. Sent in by Richard R. Conway, P. S.
58. "Union Labor Temple Webster Avenue and Washington Place," University of Pittsburgh, Labor Legacy, November 27, 2018, http://exhibit.library.pitt.edu/labor_legacy/LaborTemple.html.
59. "Union Labor Temple Webster Avenue and Washington Place."
60. "Where Citizens Meet the Union" (booklet), (United Steelworkers of America, n.d.), Historical Collections and Labor Archives, USWA President's Office Records, 1916–1980 (01961), Eberly Family Special Collections Library at the Pennsylvania State University.
61. "United Steelworkers Local #1211 Union Hall," National Park Service, August 16, 2021, https://www.nps.gov/places/united-steelworkers-local-1211-union-hall.htm.

62. "Where Citizens Meet the Union."

63. "Where Citizens Meet the Union."

64. "Here's How USWA Dues Work for You!" (United Steelworkers of America, n.d.), Historical Collections and Labor Archives, USWA President's Office Records, 1916–1980 (01961), Eberly Family Special Collections Library at the Pennsylvania State University.

65. McCollum and West, "Report on Union Member Attitude Survey."

66. "Aliquippa Steelworker" (United Steelworkers Local 1211, August 1966), United Steelworkers Archives.

67. "This Is Your Government: The Department of Justice," *Electrical Workers' Journal* (January 1955), IBEW Media Center.

68. "Aliquippa Steelworker" (United Steelworkers Local 1211, November 1966), United Steelworkers Archives.

69. "Racine Labor Paper Photographs, 1922–1979," Archival Resources in Wisconsin, accessed June 15, 2022, https://digicoll.library.wisc.edu/cgi/f/findaid/findaid-idx?c=wiarchives;view=reslist;subview=standard;didno=uw-pks-uwpksmc006.

70. Betsy Sinclair, *The Social Citizen: Peer Networks and Political Behavior*, Chicago Studies in American Politics (Chicago: University of Chicago Press, 2012).

71. McCollum and West, "Report on Union Member Attitude Survey."

72. Ziad W. Munson, *The Making of Pro-Life Activists: How Social Movement Mobilization Works* (Chicago: University of Chicago Press, 2008).

73. "District 20 Hosts 4th International Bowling Tournament," *Steel Labor* (July 1975), United Steelworkers Archives.

3. THE ECONOMIC BREAKDOWN OF BIG LABOR FROM WITHOUT AND WITHIN

1. Walter P. Reuther, "Walter Reuther Labor Day Radio Address 1958" (News from the UAW, September 1, 1958), UAW President's Office, Walter P. Reuther Collection, Wayne State University, Detroit, Michigan, http://reuther100.wayne.edu/pdf/Labor_Day_Address.pdf.

2. Noam Fishman and Alyssa Davis, "Americans Still See Big Government as Top Threat," Gallup.com, January 5, 2017, https://news.gallup.com/poll/201629/americans-big-government-top-threat.aspx.

3. Jake Rosenfeld, *What Unions No Longer Do*, 1st ed. (Cambridge, MA: Harvard University Press, 2014), 1.

4. Harry P. Cohany, "Union Membership, 1958: A Survey of Membership and Membership Trends in National and International Unions with Headquarters in the United States," *Monthly Labor Review* 83, no. 1 (1960): 9.

5. Cohany, "Union Membership, 1958."

6. Quoctrung Bui, "50 Years of Shrinking Union Membership, in One Map," *NPR*, February 23, 2015, https://www.npr.org/sections/money/2015/02/23/385843576/50-years-of-shrinking-union-membership-in-one-map; "1960 Census: Population, Supplementary Reports: Employment Status, Weeks Worked, and Year Last Worked," Census.gov, December 21, 1962, https://www.census.gov/library/publications/1962/dec/population-pc-s1-35.html.

7. "Census 2000 Brief: Employment Status: 2000," Census.gov, August 2003, https://www.census.gov/library/publications/2003/dec/c2kbr-18.html. Note that the American labor force refers to both employed and unemployed (job-seeking) U.S. civilians, plus members of the U.S. Armed Services.

8. Andrew Wallender, "Teamsters Membership Drops While SEIU Numbers Rise in 2019," *Bloomberg Law*, April 23, 2020, https://news.bloomberglaw.com/daily-labor-report/teamsters-membership-drops-while-seiu-numbers-rise-in-2019.

9. "Labor Unions During the Great Depression and New Deal," web page, Library of Congress, Washington, DC, accessed May 25, 2022, https://www.loc.gov/classroom-materials/united-states-history-primary-source-timeline/great-depression-and-world-war-ii-1929-1945/labor-unions-during-great-depression-and-new-deal/.

10. Cameron Molyneux, "UAW Locals Map—Mapping American Social Movements," Mapping American Social Movements, accessed May 25, 2022, https://depts.washington.edu/moves/CIO_UAW_locals.shtml.

11. Rosenfeld, *What Unions No Longer Do*.

12. Bruce Western and Jake Rosenfeld, "Unions, Norms, and the Rise in U.S. Wage Inequality," *American Sociological Review* 76, no. 4 (2011): 513–37.

13. Daniel Schlozman, *When Movements Anchor Parties: Electoral Alignments in American History*, 2015, https://doi.org/10.1515/9781400873838.

14. Herbert B. Asher, Eric S. Heberlig, Randall B. Ripley, and Karen Snyder, *American Labor Unions in the Electoral Arena*, People, Passions, and Power: Social Movements, Interest Organizations and the Political Process (Lanham, MD: Rowman & Littlefield, 2001), 42.

15. Asher et al., *American Labor Unions in the Electoral Arena*, 136.

16. Steven Greenhouse, "Opinion: When Republicans and Unions Got Along," *New York Times*, September 6, 2020, sec. Opinion, https://www.nytimes.com/2020/09/06/opinion/labor-unions-republicans.html.

17. Andrew Glass, "Nixon Signs Workplace Safety Bill, Dec. 29, 1970," *Politico*, December 29, 2018, https://www.politico.com/story/2018/12/29/this-day-in-politics-dec-29-1970-1074961.

18. Greenhouse, "Opinion: When Republicans and Unions Got Along."

19. Drew Desilver, "American Unions Membership Declines as Public Support Fluctuates," *Pew Research Center* (blog), accessed June 14, 2022, https://www.pewresearch.org/fact-tank/2014/02/20/for-american-unions-membership-trails-far-behind-public-support/.

20. Michael Harrington, *The Other America: Poverty in the United States*, 1st ed. (New York: Collier Books, 1994).

21. Dennis C. Dickerson, *Out of the Crucible: Black Steelworkers in Western Pennsylvania, 1875–1880* (Albany: State University of New York Press, 1986), chaps. 7–9.

22. John Talton, "How the American Steel Industry Nearly Committed Suicide—and Not from Trade," *Seattle Times*, March 13, 2018, https://www.seattletimes.com/business/economy/how-the-american-steel-industry-nearly-committed-suicide-and-not-from-trade/.

23. Daniel Rowe, "Lessons from the Steel Crisis of the 1980s," *The Conversation*, accessed May 25, 2022, http://theconversation.com/lessons-from-the-steel-crisis-of-the-1980s-57751.

24. Sebastien Bell, "Toyota and Honda Oppose Proposed U.S. Bill That Would Favor Union-Made EVs," *Carscoops*, September 13, 2021, https://www.carscoops.com/2021/09/toyota-and-honda-oppose-proposed-u-s-bill-that-would-favor-union-made-evs/.

25. Prince Ghosh, "The Exodus of Chinese Manufacturing: Shutting Down 'The World's Factory,'" *Forbes*, September 18, 2020, https://www.forbes.com/sites/princeghosh/2020/09/18/the-exodus-of-chinese-manufacturing-shutting-down-the-worlds-factory/?sh=3b119a87c2f2.

26. Charles D. Kolstad, "What Is Killing the US Coal Industry?," Stanford Institute for Economic Policy Research (SIEPR), March 2017, https://siepr.stanford.edu/publications/policy-brief/what-killing -us-coal-industry.

27. Jon Greenberg, "Did President Obama Save the Auto Industry?," PolitiFact: The Poynter Institute, September 6, 2012, https://www.politifact .com/article/2012/sep/06/did-obama-save-us-automobile-industry/.

28. Rowe, "Lessons from the Steel Crisis of the 1980s."

29. Roger Wilkins, "Carter Rejects a Plan to Reopen Steel Plant in Ohio," *New York Times*, March 31, 1979, https://www.nytimes.com/1979/03/31 /archives/carter-rejects-a-plan-to-reopen-steel-plant-in-ohio-agreement -with.html.

30. Prateek Goorha, "Modernization Theory," *Oxford Research Encyclopedia of International Studies*, March 1, 2010, https://doi.org/10.1093 /acrefore/9780190846626.013.266.

31. Andrew Glass, "Reagan Fires 11,000 Striking Air Traffic Controllers, Aug. 5, 1981," *Politico*, August 5, 2017, https://www.politico.com/story/2017/08/05 /reagan-fires-11-000-striking-air-traffic-controllers-aug-5-1981-241252.

32. Joseph A. McCartin, "WCP: The Downward Path We've Trod: Reflections on an Ominous Anniversary," *Kalmanovitz Initiative for Labor and the Working Poor* (blog), August 5, 2021, https://lwp.georgetown.edu /news/wcp-the-downward-path-weve-trod-reflections-on-an-ominous -anniversary/.

33. "Major Work Stoppages: Annual Summary Data," Bureau of Labor Statistics, February 23, 2022, https://www.bls.gov/web/wkstp/annual-listing .htm.

34. "Major Work Stoppages."

35. Moshe Z. Marvit, "For 60 Years, This Powerful Conservative Group Has Worked to Crush Labor," *The Nation*, July 5, 2018, https://www.thenation .com/article/archive/group-turned-right-work-crusade-crush-labor/.

36. "About NLRB: 1947 Taft-Hartley Substantive Provisions," National Labor Relations Board, accessed May 25, 2022, https://www.nlrb.gov/about-nlrb /who-we-are/our-history/1947-taft-hartley-substantive-provisions.

37. Dan Kaufman, "Scott Walker and the Fate of the Union," *New York Times*, June 12, 2015, https://www.nytimes.com/2015/06/14/magazine /scott-walker-and-the-fate-of-the-union.html.

38. Marvit, "For 60 Years, This Powerful Conservative Group Has Worked to Crush Labor."
39. John Savage, "The John Birch Society Is Back," *Politico Magazine*, accessed May 25, 2022, https://www.politico.com/magazine/story/2017/07/16/the-john-birch-society-is-alive-and-well-in-the-lone-star-state-215377/.
40. Mary Bottari, "Who Is Behind the National Right to Work Committee and Its Anti-Union Crusade?," *PR Watch*, June 3, 2014, https://www.prwatch.org/news/2014/06/12498/who-behind-national-right-work-committee-and-its-anti-union-crusade.
41. "An Interview with President Emeritus Edwin D. Hill," *IBEW Journal* (June 2015), IBEW Media Center, 3.
42. William Greider, "They Had an American Dream," *Rolling Stone*, June 20, 1985, https://www.rollingstone.com/culture/culture-news/they-had-an-american-dream-66277/.
43. Mike Stout, *Homestead Steel Mill—the Final 10 Years: Local 1397 and the Fight for Union Democracy* (Oakland, CA: PM Press, 2020), 114.
44. "Pamphlet for a Seminar Hosted by the Tri-State Conference on Steel" (Tri-State Conference on Steel, May 1982), "United Steel Workers of America Local Union 1397, 1950–1990," Series I, Box 3, "TCS/SVA Internal Documents," Indiana University of Pennsylvania Special Collections 62.
45. Irwin M. Marcus, "An Experiment in Reindustrialization: The Tri-State Conference on Steel and the Creation of the Steel Valley Authority," *Pennsylvania History: A Journal of Mid-Atlantic Studies* (1987): 179–96, 184.
46. "Pamphlet for a Seminar."
47. "Copy of 'An Interview with Mike Stout, Grievance Chairman for Local 1397 of the United Steelworkers,'" July 9, 1986, "United Steel Workers of America Local Union 1397, 1950–1990," Series I, Box 3, "TCS/SVA Internal Documents," Indiana University of Pennsylvania Special Collections 62.
48. Staughton Lynd, "The Genesis of the Idea of a Community Right to Industrial Property in Youngstown and Pittsburgh, 1977–86," n.d., Series I, Box 3, "TSC/SVA Internal Documents," Indiana University of Pennsylvania Special Collections 62.
49. Marcus, "An Experiment in Reindustrialization," 182.

50. "Copy of *Pittsburgh Post-Gazette* Article Entitled 'Union Food Banks Facing Financial Dilemma' " (*Pittsburgh Post-Gazette*, February 16, 1984), "United Steel Workers of America Local Union 1397, 1950–1990," Series I, Box 8, "Unemployment Committee Documents," Indiana University of Pennsylvania Special Collections 62.

51. Reginald Stuart, "Ford, G.M. Laying Off 30,000 More," *New York Times*, November 9, 1979, https://www.nytimes.com/1979/11/09/archives/ford -gm-laying-off-30000-more-car-makers-cut-production-plans-for .html; Steven Prokesch, "General Motors to Shut 11 Plants; 29,000 Workers Will Be Affected," *New York Times*, November 7, 1986, sec. Business, https://www.nytimes.com/1986/11/07/business/general-motors-to-shut -11-plants-29000-workers-will-be-affected.html.

52. Wendy Zhang, "Manufacturing Employment in the Southeast: Examining the Last 30 Years," *Monthly Labor Review* (July 2021), https://www .bls.gov/opub/mlr/2021/article/manufacturing-employment-in-the -southeast-examining-the-last-30-years.htm.

53. Howard Schneider, "U.S. South, Not Just Mexico, Stands in Way of Rust Belt Jobs Revival," *Reuters*, April 7, 2017, sec. Aerospace and Defense, https://www.reuters.com/article/us-usa-trump-south-insight /u-s-south-not-just-mexico-stands-in-way-of-rust-belt-jobs-revival -idUSKBN1790HO.

54. Asher et al., *American Labor Unions in the Electoral Arena*, 36.

55. Asher et al., *American Labor Unions in the Electoral Arena*, 35.

56. "Local Lines: Scribe Quotes Letter, Local Helps Charity," *IBEW Journal* (January 1985), IBEW Media Center. Local 2145, Vallejo, CA. Sent in by Joseph Scavone Jr., P. S.

57. Valerio L. Scarton, "Letter to Junior Troutman," November 24, 1980, "UMWA District 2," Box 472, "Labor Celebrations," Indiana University of Pennsylvania Special Collections 52.

58. Jim Reisler, "AFL-CIO Chief Warns of High-Tech Job Push," *Johnstown Tribune-Democrat*, n.d., "UMWA District 2," Box 472, "Labor Celebrations," Indiana University of Pennsylvania Special Collections 52.

59. "Handwritten Meeting Notes Entitled 'Labor [/] Clergy,'" May 10, 1991, "UMWA District 2," Box 472, "Labor Celebrations," Indiana University of Pennsylvania Special Collections 52.

60. "Handwritten Meeting Notes Entitled 'Labor [/] Clergy.'"

61. Mayor Fox, *United We Stand: The United Mine Workers of America, 1890–1990* (Triangle, VA: United Mine Workers of America, 1990), 540.
62. Mike Stout, "When the Heyday Was Here," *We Are All Brothers and Sisters*, 2015.
63. Greider, "They Had an American Dream."
64. Greg Braknis, "Labor Unions Struggle Against Rising Tide of Skepticism," *Pittsburgh Press*, September 1, 1991, "UMWA District 2," Box 471, "Solidarity Day," Indiana University of Pennsylvania Special Collections 52.
65. Gary Harki, "From Blue to Red: How the Decline of the Coal Union Helped Republicans Have a Stronghold in West Virginia," *100 Days in Appalachia* (blog), February 15, 2017, https://www.100daysinappalachia.com/2017/02/blue-red-decline-coal-union-helped-west-virginia-become-republican-stronghold/.

4. UNION MEMBERSHIP TRANSFORMED

1. Herbert B. Asher, Eric S. Heberlig, Randall B. Ripley, and Karen Snyder, *American Labor Unions in the Electoral Arena*, People, Passions, and Power: Social Movements, Interest Organizations and the Political Process (Lanham, MD: Rowman & Littlefield, 2001), 32.
2. Asher et al., *American Labor Unions in the Electoral Arena.*
3. The President's Commission on Coal, "Report: Survey of Community Conditions in Coal Producing Areas," 1980, "UMWA District 5," Box 66, Elections and Conventions, Miscellaneous Publications, Indiana University of Pennsylvania Special Collections 52.
4. "Steel Valley Authority: Final Report: Economic Development Employment Survey," n.d., "United Steel Workers of America Local Union 1397, 1950–1990," Series I, Box 5, "Dislocated Workers' Skill Surveys," Indiana University of Pennsylvania Special Collections 62.
5. "Steel Valley Authority: Final Report."
6. "Steel Valley Authority: Final Report."
7. "Aliquippa Update: A Pittsburgh Milltown Struggles to Come Back, 1984–86" (Rivers Communities Project, School of Social Work, University of Pittsburgh, 1986), 23.
8. "Steel Valley Authority: Final Report."
9. "Steel Valley Authority: Final Report."

10. Stephanie Pappas, "The Toll of Job Loss," *American Psychological Association* 51, no. 7 (October 1, 2020): 54.

11. Christopher Byron, "Business: The Idle Army of Unemployed," *Time*, August 11, 1980, http://content.time.com/time/subscriber/article/0,33009 ,924362-8,00.html.

12. Byron, "Business: The Idle Army of Unemployed."

13. Janet L. Yellen, "The History of Women's Work and Wages and How It Has Created Success for Us All," *Brookings* (blog), May 7, 2020, https:// www.brookings.edu/essay/the-history-of-womens-work-and-wages -and-how-it-has-created-success-for-us-all/.

14. "Employment Characteristics of Families Summary," U.S. Bureau of Labor Statistics, April 20, 2022, https://www.bls.gov/news.release/famee .nro.htm.

15. Campbell Robertson, "In Coal Country, the Mines Shut Down, the Women Went to Work and the World Quietly Changed," *New York Times*, September 14, 2019, https://www.nytimes.com/2019/09/14/us /appalachia-coal-women-work-.html.

16. Robertson, "In Coal Country, the Mines Shut Down."

17. "Image 658 of Pennsylvania White and Yellow Pages Zelienople February 1961 Through April 1963," Library of Congress, Washington, DC, 65, accessed June 1, 2022, https://www.loc.gov/resource/usteledirec .usteledireco8518/?sp=658.

18. "Monongahela, Pennsylvania Population 2022 (Demographics, Maps, Graphs)," accessed June 7, 2022, https://worldpopulationreview.com/us -cities/monongahela-pa-population.

19. Theda Skocpol, *Diminished Democracy: From Membership to Management in American Civic Life* (Norman: University of Oklahoma Press, 2003).

20. William Greider, "They Had an American Dream," *Rolling Stone*, June 20, 1985, https://www.rollingstone.com/culture/culture-news/they-had-an -american-dream-66277/.

21. According to two internal rough estimates, only about 20 to 30 percent of today's USW members are steelworkers.

22. Skocpol, *Diminished Democracy*.

23. Robert D. Putnam, *Bowling Alone: The Collapse and Revival of American Community* (New York: Simon & Schuster, 2000).

24. Charley Hannagan, "Central NY Police Cars Display Marvel Anti-Hero Punisher's Logo with a Twist," *Syracuse.com*, April 12, 2017,

https://www.syracuse.com/news/2017/04/central_new_york_police_cars
_sport_punisher_skull_decals_in_blue_lives_matter_tw.html; Sarah Cascone, "Police Have Embraced the Punisher Skull as an Unofficial Logo.
Now the Character's Creator Is Asking Artists of Color to Reclaim It,"
Artnet News, June 10, 2020, https://news.artnet.com/art-world/punishe
r-black-lives-matter-1883013.

25. Cascone, "Police Have Embraced the Punisher Skull."
26. Christina Capatides, "How Heavily Armed Is Your State?," *CBS News*,
December 4, 2015, https://www.cbsnews.com/pictures/most-heavily
-armed-states-in-america/.
27. "Castle Pistol Club," accessed June 1, 2022, https://castlepistolclub
.com/.
28. "Local Lines: Local 177 Work Holding Its Own," *IBEW Journal* (July
1975), IBEW Media Center. Local 177, Jacksonville, FL. Sent in by
W. G. "Bill" Gehm, P. S.
29. "East Monongahela Sportsmen's Club," accessed June 15, 2022, https://
www.emsportsmen.com/.
30. "USA's Mission," *Union Sportsmen's Alliance* (blog), accessed June 3,
2022, https://unionsportsmen.org/about/mission/.
31. Roy Gunter, " 'Letters to the Editor': USA: You Belong," *Electrical
Worker* (January 2015), IBEW Media Center.
32. "Western Pennsylvania Coalfields," accessed March 4, 2021, http://
coalcampusa.com/westpa/index.htm.
33. "Megachurch Search Results—Hartford Institute for Religion Research,"
accessed June 3, 2022, http://hirr.hartsem.edu/cgi-bin/mega/db.pl?db
=default&uid=default&view_records=1&ID=*&sb=4&State=PA.
34. "The Definition of a Megachurch from Hartford Institute for Religion
Research," accessed June 7, 2022, http://hirr.hartsem.edu/megachurch
/definition.html.
35. Scott Thumma and Warren Bird, "Not Who You Think They Are: A
Profile of the People Who Attend America's Megachurches," Hartford Institute for Religion Research, Hartford Seminary, accessed
November 26, 2022, http://hirr.hartsem.edu/megachurch/megachurch
_attender_report.htm.
36. Andrew L. Whitehead and Samuel L. Perry, *Taking America Back for
God: Christian Nationalism in the United States* (New York: Oxford University Press, 2020), 124.

37. As time went on, IBEW and USW outlets became somewhat more similar because USW transitioned to a magazine form in the 1980s.
38. For more details about this breakdown, please see appendix C.

5. FROM UNION BLUE TO TRUMP RED

1. Philip Bump, "Donald Trump Got Reagan-Like Support from Union Households," *Washington Post*, accessed March 4, 2021, https://www.washingtonpost.com/news/the-fix/wp/2016/11/10/donald-trump-got-reagan-like-support-from-union-households/.
2. Taylor E. Dark, *The Unions and the Democrats: An Enduring Alliance*, updated ed. (Ithaca, NY: ILR Press, 2001).
3. "1984 Presidential General Election Results—Pennsylvania," accessed June 8, 2022, https://uselectionatlas.org/RESULTS/state.php?fips=42&year=1984&f=0&off=0&elect=0.
4. "Pennsylvania Election Results 2020: Live Results by County," *NBC News*, accessed June 8, 2022, https://www.nbcnews.com/politics/2020-elections/pennsylvania-results.
5. Louis Jacobson, "The Political Evolution of Southwest PA," *https://www.politicspa.com/* (blog), December 1, 2014, https://www.politicspa.com/the-political-evolution-of-southwest-pa/62105/.
6. Peter O'Dowd and Samantha Raphelson, "A Shop Divided: Union Members Split Over Biden and Trump," *WBUR*, October 1, 2020, https://www.wbur.org/hereandnow/2020/10/01/union-members-biden-trump.
7. Katherine J. Cramer, *The Politics of Resentment: Rural Consciousness in Wisconsin and the Rise of Scott Walker*, Chicago Studies in American Politics (Chicago: University of Chicago Press, 2016).
8. Steve Mellon, "The Digs: The Day a Prince Visited the Mon Valley," *Pittsburgh Post-Gazette*, March 3, 2021, https://www.post-gazette.com/life/lifestyle/2021/03/03/Prince-Charles-visit-Mon-Valley-Pittsburgh-March-1988-The-Digs-photos/stories/202102260126.
9. Mellon, "The Digs."
10. For overviews of these transformations, see William Serrin, *Homestead: The Glory and Tragedy of an American Steel Town* (New York: Times Books, 1992); and Gabriel Winant, *The Next Shift: The Fall of Industry and the Rise of Health Care in Rust Belt America* (Cambridge, MA: Harvard University Press, 2021).

11. Bill Toland, "In Desperate 1983, There Was Nowhere for Pittsburgh's Economy to Go but Up," *Pittsburgh Post-Gazette*, December 23, 2012, https://www.post-gazette.com/business/businessnews/2012/12/23 /In-desperate-1983-there-was-nowhere-for-Pittsburgh-s-economy-to -go-but-up/stories/201212230258.

12. "Copy of Robert Erickson and Charles Martoni's 'Steel Valley Authority: A Labor/Government Partnership,' " n.d., "United Steel Workers of America Local Union 1397, 1950–1990," Series I, Box 4, "SVA Internal Documents," Indiana University of Pennsylvania Special Collections 62.

13. "Copy of Robert Erickson and Charles Martoni's 'Steel Valley Authority.' "

14. Cramer, *The Politics of Resentment*.

15. Cramer, *The Politics of Resentment*, 5–6.

16. Cramer, *The Politics of Resentment*.

17. Robert J. Cole, "U.S. Steel Agrees to Pay $6.3 Billion for Marathon Oil," *New York Times*, November 20, 1981, https://www.nytimes.com /1981/11/20/business/us-steel-agrees-to-pay-6.3-billion-for-marathon -oil.html.

18. "About: Duquesne Club," accessed June 8, 2022, https://www.duquesne .org/about/.

19. City Channel Pittsburgh, *Future. Forged. For All.*, 2017, https://www .youtube.com/watch?v=XEw2Ky5XxDM.

20. Bill Peduto [@billpeduto], "We Are the Gem of Appalachia. Rust Belt Strong," *Twitter*, November 5, 2020, https://twitter.com/billpeduto/status /1324173114943721476.

21. Johnathan C. Peterson, Kevin B. Smith, and John R. Hibbing, "Do People Really Become More Conservative as They Age?," *Journal of Politics* 82, no. 2 (April 2020): 600–611, https://doi.org/10.1086/706889.

22. Ronald Brownstein, "NRA, Unions Fight for Blue-Collar Voters," *Los Angeles Times*, October 22, 2000, https://www.latimes.com/archives/la-xpm -2000-oct-22-mn-40287-story.html.

23. Brownstein, "NRA, Unions Fight for Blue-Collar Voters."

24. J. J. Barry and Edwin D. Hill, "Your Vote Belongs to You—Use It Well," *IBEW Journal* (October 2000), IBEW Media Center.

25. Michael Dunleavy, "IBEW Local 5 News and Views: The Business Manager's Corner," October 2020, IBEW Local Union 5: Professional Electricians, https://ibew5.org/.

26. Hope Reese, "How the NRA Grew from a Marksmanship Group to a Controversial Political Powerhouse," *Vox*, March 24, 2020, https://www.vox.com/the-highlight/2020/3/24/21191524/nra-national-rifle-association-history-frank-smyth-wayne-la-pierre.

27. Ron Elving, "The NRA Wasn't Always Against Gun Restrictions," *NPR*, October 10, 2017, sec. Analysis, https://www.npr.org/2017/10/10/556578593/the-nra-wasnt-always-against-gun-restrictions.

28. Matthew J. Lacombe, *Firepower: How the NRA Turned Gun Owners into a Political Force* (Princeton, NJ: Princeton University Press, 2021).

29. Theda Skocpol and Caroline Tervo, eds., *Upending American Politics: Polarizing Parties, Ideological Elites, and Citizen Activists from the Tea Party to the Anti-Trump Resistance* (New York: Oxford University Press, 2020), 89.

30. Skocpol and Tervo, *Upending American Politics*, 90.

31. Jennifer Carlson, *Citizen-Protectors: The Everyday Politics of Guns in an Age of Decline* (Oxford: Oxford University Press, 2015).

32. Ryan Bort, "How the Right Found a Hero in Kyle Rittenhouse," *Rolling Stone* (blog), November 19, 2021, https://www.rollingstone.com/culture/culture-news/kyle-rittenhouse-right-wing-violence-1257856/.

33. Kim Parker et al., "1. The Demographics of Gun Ownership," *Pew Research Center's Social & Demographic Trends Project* (blog), June 22, 2017, https://www.pewresearch.org/social-trends/2017/06/22/the-demographics-of-gun-ownership/.

34. Jonathan M. Metzl, "What Guns Mean: The Symbolic Lives of Firearms," *Palgrave Communications* 5, no. 1 (April 2, 2019): 1–5, https://doi.org/10.1057/s41599-019-0240-y.

35. "Legislation Alerts—Ambridge District Sportsmen's Assoc.," accessed March 4, 2021, http://www.adsa.club/legislation-alerts.

36. "Aliquippa Bucktails," accessed June 3, 2022, http://www.bucktails.us/.

37. Gallup Inc., "Guns," *Gallup.com*, May 18, 2007, https://news.gallup.com/poll/1645/Guns.aspx.

38. Gallup Inc., "Gun Control Remains an Important Factor for U.S. Voters," *Gallup.com*, October 23, 2017, https://news.gallup.com/poll/220748/gun-control-remains-important-factor-voters.aspx.

39. Clare Kim, "A Look Back at Gun Control History," *MSNBC*, January 23, 2013, https://www.msnbc.com/the-last-word/look-back-gun-control-history-msna18083.

40. Harry Enten, "The U.S. Has Never Been So Polarized on Guns," *FiveThirtyEight*, October 4, 2017, https://fivethirtyeight.com/features /the-u-s-has-never-been-so-polarized-on-guns/.

41. Metzl, "What Guns Mean."

42. Metzl, "What Guns Mean."

43. Michael Dunleavy, "IBEW Local 5 News and Views: The Business Manager's Corner," 2012, IBEW Local Union 5: Professional Electricians, https://ibew5.org/.

44. Jeff Cox, "5 Years Later, Rick Santelli 'Tea Party' Rant Revisited," *CNBC*, February 24, 2014, https://www.cnbc.com/2014/02/24/5-years -later-rick-santelli-tea-party-rant-revisited.html.

45. Theda Skocpol and Vanessa Williamson, *The Tea Party and the Remaking of Republican Conservatism* (New York: Oxford University Press, 2012).

46. Further research on the Tea Party and additional counts of local groups appear in Skocpol and Tervo, *Upending American Politics*; and Theda Skocpol, Caroline Tervo, and Kirsten Walters, "Citizen Organizing and Partisan Polarization from the Tea Party to the Anti-Trump Resistance," in *Democratic Resilience: Can the United States Withstand Rising Polarization?*, ed. Robert C. Lieberman, Suzanne Mettler, and Kenneth M. Roberts (New York: Cambridge University Press, 2021).

47. John Tamny, "A Monetary Policy for the Tea Party Movement," *Forbes*, accessed June 8, 2022, https://www.forbes.com/sites/johntamny/2010 /11/03/a-monetary-policy-for-the-tea-party-movement/.

48. Skocpol and Williamson, *The Tea Party and the Remaking of Republican Conservatism*. See also Christopher S. Parker and Matt A. Barreto, *Change They Can't Believe In: The Tea Party and Reactionary Politics in America*, updated ed. (Princeton, NJ: Princeton University Press, 2014).

49. Skocpol and Williamson, *The Tea Party and the Remaking of Republican Conservatism*.

50. Parker and Barreto, *Change They Can't Believe In*; Angie Maxwell, "How Southern Racism Found a Home in the Tea Party," *Vox*, July 7, 2016, https://www.vox.com/2016/7/7/12118872/southern-racism-tea-party -trump.

51. Bryan Gervais and Irwin L. Morris, *Reactionary Republicanism: How the Tea Party in the House Paved the Way for Trump's Victory* (New York: Oxford University Press, 2018).

52. Susy Kelly, "Tea Party Asks Judge Candidates to Discuss Views," *Herald-Standard*, May 5, 2013, https://www.heraldstandard.com/election /tea-party-asks-judge-candidates-to-discuss-views/article_1351669e-0d03 -5e85-b4d7-6e2d76f8a212.html.

53. This same person acknowledged that, after the 2016 election, local Democrats were closely aligned with Women's March participants in the anti-Trump resistance.

54. Suite 800, "Trump's Staunch GOP Supporters Have Roots in the Tea Party," *Pew Research Center—U.S. Politics & Policy* (blog), May 16, 2019, https://www.pewresearch.org/politics/2019/05/16/trumps-staunch -gop-supporters-have-roots-in-the-tea-party/.

55. "Legislators, Public to Discuss Voting Reform at Public Forum," *Daily American*, accessed June 8, 2022, https://www.dailyamerican.com/story /news/local/2021/04/02/legislators-public-to-discuss-voting-reform-at -public-forum/43690543/.

56. Michael Barbaro and Alan Feuer, "The Proud Boys' Path to Jan. 6," *The Daily* (podcast), June 9, 2022, https://www.nytimes.com/2022/06/09 /podcasts/the-daily/proud-boys-jan-6.html.

57. Kirk Swearingen, "So Fascism Came to America—but What Was It Wearing?," *Salon*, December 20, 2020, https://www.salon.com/2020/12 /20/so-fascism-came-to-america—but-what-was-it-wearing/.

58. Bump, "Donald Trump Got Reagan-Like Support."

59. Bump, "Donald Trump Got Reagan-Like Support."

60. Holly Otterbein and Megan Cassella, "Rank-and-File Union Members Snub Biden for Trump," *Politico*, September 22, 2020, https://www .politico.com/news/2020/09/22/donald-trump-union-support-snub -joe-biden-418329; Ian Kullgren, "Union Workers Weren't a Lock for Biden . . .," *Bloomberg Daily Labor Report*, November 10, 2020.

61. David Roberts, "Hillary Clinton's 'Coal Gaffe' Is a Microcosm of Her Twisted Treatment by the Media," *Vox*, September 20, 2017, https:// www.vox.com/energy-and-environment/2017/9/15/16306158/hillary -clinton-hall-of-mirrors.

62. Stacy Kinlock Sewell, "Left on the Bench: The New York Construction Trades and Racial Integration, 1960–1972," *New York History* 83, no. 2 (2002): 203–16.

63. Aurelia Glass, Roy Teixeira, and David Madland, "Unions Are Critical to the Democratic Party's Electoral Success," *Center for American Progress Action* (blog), December 21, 2021, https://www.americanprogressaction

.org/article/unions-critical-democratic-partys-electoral-success/; Herbert B. Asher, Eric S. Heberlig, and Randall B. Ripley, *American Labor Unions in the Electoral Arena, People, Passions, and Power: Social Movements, Interest Organizations and the Political Process* (Lanham, MD: Rowman & Littlefield, 2001); David Macdonald, "Labor Unions and White Democratic Partisanship," *Political Behavior* 43, no. 2 (June 2021): 859–79, https://doi.org/10.1007/s11109-020-09624-3.

64. "Pittsburgh Local 5 Hosts VP, Labor Secretary for Roundtable on Organizing," IBEW Media Center, July 22, 2021, http://www.ibew.org/media-center/Articles/21Daily/2107/210722_Pittsburgh.

65. Ryan Deto, "Pittsburgh-Area Rep. Conor Lamb Announces 2022 Pennsylvania Senate Run," *Pittsburgh City Paper*, August 6, 2021, https://www.pghcitypaper.com/pittsburgh/pittsburgh-area-rep-conor-lamb-announces-2022-pennsylvania-senate-run/Content?oid=19966586.

66. Ana De Liz, "Steelworkers for Trump Billboards Changed After Complaint from Biden-Supporting Union," *Newsweek*, September 23, 2020, https://www.newsweek.com/steelworkers-trump-billboards-changed-complaint-biden-supporting-union-1533887.

67. Sung Eun Kim and Yotam Margalit, "Informed Preferences? The Impact of Unions on Workers' Policy Views," *American Journal of Political Science* 61, no. 3 (July 2017): 728–43, https://doi.org/10.1111/ajps.12280.

68. Sam Janesch, "Here Are All of Donald Trump's and Hillary Clinton's Campaign Stops in Pennsylvania Since June," *Lancaster Online*, November 6, 2016, https://lancasteronline.com/news/local/here-are-all-of-donald-trumps-and-hillary-clintons-campaign-stops-in-pennsylvania-since-june/article_17eda882-a367-11e6-8367-fb4571a4487f.html.

69. Colin Deppen, "Trump Promised to Bring Back Pennsylvania's Coal, Steel and Energy Jobs, but Can He?," *Penn-Live Patriot News*, November 17, 2016, https://www.pennlive.com/news/2016/11/trump_promised_to_make_pennsyl.html.

70. Bill Ruthhart and Jonathon Berlin, "Map of Trump and Biden Campaign Stops," *Chicago Tribune*, November 5, 2020, https://www.chicagotribune.com/politics/ct-viz-presidential-campaign-trail-tracker-20200917-edspdit2incbfnopchjaelp3uu-htmlstory.html.

71. Scott Horsley, "Trump Formally Orders Tariffs on Steel, Aluminum Imports," *NPR*, March 8, 2018, sec. Politics, https://www.npr.org/2018/03/08/591744195/trump-expected-to-formally-order-tariffs-on-steel-aluminum-imports.

282 • 5. FROM UNION BLUE TO TRUMP RED

72. Rachel Brewster, "Gender and International Trade Policy: Economic Nostalgia and the National Security Steel Tariffs," *Duke Journal of Gender Law & Policy* 27, no. 1 (March 10, 2020): 59, https://djglp.law.duke .edu/article/gender-and-international-trade-policy-brewster-vol27-iss1/.

73. Jacob Pramuk, "Trump's Tariff Plan Blows Up Party Divisions in Critical Pennsylvania Special Election," *CNBC*, March 7, 2018, https://www .cnbc.com/2018/03/07/pa-special-election-trump-tariffs-get-support -from-lamb-and-saccone.html.

74. Steve Liesman, "Trump's Tariffs Are Equivalent to One of the Largest Tax Increases in Decades," *CNBC*, May 16, 2019, https://www.cnbc .com/2019/05/16/trumps-tariffs-are-equivalent-to-one-of-the-largest -tax-increases-in-decades.html.

75. Andrew Van Dam, "Analysis: Trump Said He'd Rebuild Manufacturing. Now It's in Decline. What Happened?," *Washington Post*, September 5, 2019, https://www.washingtonpost.com/business/2019/09/05/trump-said -hed-rebuild-manufacturing-now-its-decline-what-happened/.

6. ON UNION DECLINE AND THE POTENTIAL FOR RESURGENCE

1. Leonie Huddy, "Group Identity and Political Cohesion," in *Emerging Trends in the Social and Behavioral Sciences*, ed. Robert A. Scott, Marlis C. Buchmann, and Stephen M. Kosslyn (New York: Wiley, 2015), https://doi.org/10.1002/9781118900772.etrds0155.

2. Theda Skocpol, *Diminished Democracy: From Membership to Management in American Civic Life* (Norman: University of Oklahoma Press, 2003).

3. Paul Frymer and Jacob M. Grumbach, "Labor Unions and White Racial Politics," *American Journal of Political Science* 65, no. 1 (January 2021): 225–40, https://doi.org/10.1111/ajps.12537.

4. Tore Bjørgo and Hanna Munden, "What Explains Why People Join and Leave Far-Right Groups?," University of Oslo, Center for Research on Extremism, September 7, 2020, https://www.sv.uio.no/c-rex/english /groups/compendium/what-explains-why-people-join-and-leave-far -right-groups.html.

5. Gallup Inc, "Approval of Labor Unions at Highest Point Since 1965," *Gallup.com*, September 2, 2021, https://news.gallup.com/poll/354455 /approval-labor-unions-highest-point-1965.aspx.

GLOSSARY

AA: Alcoholics Anonymous.

AFL: American Federation of Labor.

AFL-CIO: A federation of American labor organizations that resulted from the merging of the AFL and CIO in 1955. The AFL-CIO encompasses most but not all North American labor unions.

AFSCME: American Federation of State, County, and Municipal Employees.

BAC: Union of Bricklayers and Allied Craftworkers.

CIO: Congress of Industrial Organizations.

EMSC: East Monongahela Sportsmen's Club.

EPA: Environmental Protection Agency.

FAA: Federal Aviation Authority.

GOP: "Grand Old Party," another term for the Republican Party.

HFIAW: International Association of Heat and Frost Insulators and Allied Workers.

IAM: International Association of Machinists.

IBEW: International Brotherhood of Electrical Workers.

IBT: International Brotherhood of Teamsters.

Insulator: A member of the Heat and Frost Insulators and Allied Workers union.

NEA: National Education Association.

NRA: National Rifle Association.

OPEC: Organization of Petroleum Exporting Countries.

OSHA: Occupational Safety and Health Act.

PATCO: Professional Air Traffic Controllers Organization.

SEIU: Service Employees International Union.

Steelworker (with a capital "S"): A member of the United Steelworkers (USW) union. Being a Steelworker does not necessarily mean that one is employed in the steel industry. The USW now represents many workers in other industries, including nurses, rubber workers, and librarians, who are sometimes nominally referred to as "Steelworkers." Note that, in this book, most Steelworkers who we quote are indeed employed in the steel industry.

steelworker (with a lowercase "s"): An individual employed in the steelmaking industry, generally at a steel mill or plant. There are steelworkers who are not "Steelworkers" (i.e., non-union steelworkers), but that group is not a focus of this book.

SVA: Steel Valley Authority. The TCS organized the SVA in the early 1980s to support efforts by local leaders to create government-supported community corporations to prevent the closure of mills and plants in western Pennsylvania.

TCS: Tri-State Conference on Steel. One of the grassroots organizations that emerged during the steel industry collapse to attempt to save steel mills and industrial plants largely in Ohio and western Pennsylvania.

UAW: United Auto Workers.

UBC: United Brotherhood of Carpenters.

UE: United Electrical, Radio, and Machine Workers.

UFCW: United Food and Commercial Workers International Union.

UMWA: United Mine Workers of America.

UPMC: University of Pittsburgh Medical Center.

USA: Union Sportsmen's Alliance.

USW: United Steelworkers of America. Used to be abbreviated USA. Members of the USW are referred to as "Steelworkers."

WABCO: Westinghouse Air Brake Company.

INDEX

AA programs. *See* Alcoholics
    Anonymous programs
abandonment, feelings of, 175, 205,
    210, 230–31, 241
abortion, 187–88, 206, 209, 239;
    megachurches opposing, 148;
    Tea Party on, 195
access: abortion, 209; to Medicare, 50
affirmative action policies, 36–38, 95
Affordable Care Act, U.S., 195–96,
    206, 218
AFL. *See* American Federation
    of Labor
AFL-CIO. *See* American
    Federation of Labor and
    Congress of Industrial
    Organizations
African American/Black, 95;
    mid-century unionists, 35–44,
    53, 55, 72–73; Steelworkers, 36,
    38; women, 38–39, 41–43, 72–73,
    222, 252
African American Grand United
    Order of Odd Fellows, 53, 55

Alcoholics Anonymous (AA)
    programs, 64–65, 105
alienation, 231, 237, 241
Aliquippa (county), 17, 50–51, 66–67,
    71. *See also* Local 1211, USW
"Aliquippa Steelworker," (USW
    Local 1211 newsletter), 25, 50–52,
    62, 75–76, 76, 78, 79, 80, 81
Allegheny (county), 12, 13, 164, 165,
    246–47; unemployment in, 173.
    See also Homestead, Allegheny
    County; Pittsburgh
Amazon, 180–81
American Federation of Labor
    (AFL), 36, 211–13
American Federation of Labor
    and Congress of Industrial
    Organizations (AFL-CIO), 6,
    37, 145, 184
American Flint Glass Workers
    Union, 57, 58
American Legion, 52
American Legislative Exchange
    Council, 103

energy policies, 97, 206–7; clean/
green, 208
Environmental Protection Agency
(EPA), U.S., 200
Erickson, Robert, 174
Erie (county), *12*, 71, *71*, 222, *246–47*,
Democrat success in, 13, 164, *165*,
166, 225
erosion, bottom-up union, 228–33
estrangement, industrial worker, 203,
205–11, 225
ethnic clubs, 130, 135–36, 186, 199,
232; mid-century unionists and,
50–53, *54–56*, 56–57, *58*, 59
ethnography/ethnographic
observations, 9, 16, 18, 185, 193
European immigrants, 32, 52, 53,
56, 67
ex-industrial towns, 15, 20, 137, 141, 205
exodus, worker, 173, 181–82
expectations, 80; gendered, 35, 46;
mid-century union, 23, 25, 29, 65
extremist groups, right-wing, 196,
198, 236

FAA. *See* Federal Aviation Authority
Facebook: gun clubs on, 142–43, 189;
Tea Party on, 197; USW, 215, *216*
Fairness Doctrine, U.S., 77
families/family structures, union,
7–8, 167, 225; "good union man" in,
22–28, 31, 44–45; in international
union magazines, 256–57,
259–60; of mid-twentieth century
unionists, 3, 23, 35, 44–49, *45*, 65,
237–38; in newsletter photographs,
252, *253*; role of men in, 124–31,

188–89, 237–38; transformations in,
20, 124–31, 188–89; in union hiring,
37, 126, 264n20
fatality rate, 34
Fayette (county), *12*, *246–47*,
unemployment rate in, *173*
Federal Aviation Authority
(FAA), 98
federal government, U.S.,
105–6, 192–93
federation/federated structure,
73–74, 199, 234
Feigenbaum, James, 6
fidelity, union, 23–24, 198
Firearms Owners Against Crime, 189
Firepower (Lacombe), 11
fixed workplaces, 124, 153, 160, 205, 211
Florida, 142–43
food pantries/banks, 65, 108, 110, 133
Ford, Gerald, 94
foreign-made cars, 1–2, 80
Forest (county), *12*, *246–47*
Fox News, 192
Fraternal Order of Eagles, 52, 265n44
fraternal organizations, 135–36, 199;
mid-century organizations and,
50–53, *54–56*, 56–57, *58*, 59
Freemont News-Messenger
(newspaper), 63
Friends of Coal campaign, 120–21
Frymer, Paul, 40
Furko, Don, 203

Gallagher, Daniel, 9
gay rights/marriage, 97, 193
gender/gender relations, 7–8, *45*,
212–13, 222–23; in changing

Printed and bound by CPI Group (UK) Ltd, Croydon, CR0 4YY

09/06/2025

14685929-0002